Letters from Hollywood

THE SUNY SERIES

HORIZONS OF CINEMA

MURRAY POMERANCE | EDITOR

Letters from Hollywood

1977–2017

Bill Krohn

SUNY
PRESS

Published by State University of New York Press, Albany

For information, contact State University of New York Press, Albany, NY
www.sunypress.edu

Library of Congress Cataloging-in-Publication Data

Names: Krohn, Bill, author.
Title: Letters from Hollywood : 1977–2017 / Bill Krohn.
Description: Albany : State University of New York Press, [2020] | Series:
    SUNY series, horizons of cinema | Includes bibliographical references
    and index.
Identifiers: LCCN 2019016747 | ISBN 9781438477633 (hardcover : alk.
    paper) | ISBN 9781438477640 (pbk. : alk. paper) | ISBN 9781438477657
    (ebook)
Subjects: LCSH: Motion pictures—California—Los Angeles—Reviews.
Classification: LCC PN1993.5.U65 K76 2020 | DDC 791.43/75—dc23
LC record available at https://lccn.loc.gov/2019016747

10 9 8 7 6 5 4 3 2 1

For my best friend, Dr. Barry Lew

Contents

Acknowledgments

I am grateful for the generous help of these people, who in various ways made it possible for me to write my letters from Hollywood: Catherine Benamou, Harold Bloom, Serge Daney, Manny Farber, Barbara Frank, Danny Johnson, Adrian Martin, Andy Rector, Ouardia Teraha, Serge Toubiana, and all contributors past and present to *Cahiers du cinéma*. My special gratitude to the staff of the Margaret Herrick Library, Academy of Motion Picture Arts and Sciences, Beverly Hills, in particular, Barbara Hall and Val Armendarez.

Introduction

1

How I Became the Los Angeles Correspondent for *Cahiers du cinéma*

I GREW UP IN A SMALL TOWN in North Texas on the Oklahoma border. Living in a big house on the edge of town, I had access to the larger world through radio—still in its "Golden Age"—and television: *The Adventures of Ozzie and Harriet* (1952), which I still enjoy in reruns; *I Love Lucy* (1951); the many Warner Bros. television series; and countless westerns, a staple in theaters that filled the airwaves as well. Every week on *Alfred Hitchcock Presents* (1955), which began airing when I was ten, the maestro personally presented concentrated doses of his trademark cinema of suspense and black comedy, while Rod Serling did the same thing on *The Twilight Zone* (1959), a weekly series that began airing five years later, offering tales of fantasy and science fiction introduced and narrated by Serling. I first encountered Orson Welles in *The Fountain of Youth* (1958), an unsold pilot that aired on CBS in 1958 and won a Peabody Award. (I would later introduce it to French audiences via the *Cahiers du cinéma* when Welles was receiving an honor for his life's work in France, accompanied by an interview conducted over the telephone between Los Angeles and New York for a special issue of the *Cahiers*.) The fundamentals of auteurism, a theory promulgated by the *Cahiers*, were already being communicated to me and future friends in other parts of the country, some of whom grew up to be auteurs of cinema and television: Joe Dante, John Landis, and in a more modest way me, when editor Ed Marx and I finished a film for Welles in 1994, the *Four Men on a Raft* section of *It's All True* (1943), a three-part film he shot in Latin America in 1942 and was not permitted to finish.

The proximity to Oklahoma was important because the TV station in Lawton, just across the border, acquired the package of pre-1948 horror films (including James Whale's *Frankenstein* [1931] and Tod Browning's *Dracula* [1931]) released to television by Universal Studios and marketed by Screen Gems beginning in 1957 under the title *Shock Theater*. All over the country—and Lawton, which boasted a guy in an ape suit named Poor Pitiful Pearl, was no exception—"horror hosts," who might be the local weatherman or TV news reporter, dressed up as ghouls, vampires, and monsters to introduce the films, creating a counterpoint to official religious celebrations on Sunday: a horror movie on Friday or Saturday night, viewed by teens (often in secret) without their families, and church on Sunday. Years later *The Rocky Horror Picture Show* (1975), starring Tim Curry as Dr. Frank N. Stein, paid tribute to this subversive dynamic in midnight screenings in movie theaters all over the country, as did Edward D. Wood Jr.'s *Plan 9 from Outer Space* (1959), which is explicitly being broadcast on TV, with TV seer Criswell as host—a genuine auteur effort (written, produced, and directed by Wood) undertaken in utter seriousness, which unintentionally achieved the same results with audiences as the campy *Rocky Horror*. I had read about these films in magazines like *Famous Monsters of Filmland* and *The Magazine of Fantasy and Science Fiction*, where horror and fantasy writer Charles Beaumont reviewed current films and compared them to the classics in "The Science Screen," so the idea of writing seriously about films was instilled in me when I was entering my teens.

During the early days, the oil boom made my small town big. We had two movie theaters, the Grand, where I saw Hitchcock's *Vertigo* (1958) when I was thirteen, and the Liberty, the kiddie theater, where the trailers for *Frankenstein Meets the Wolf Man* (1943) and *The Scarlet Claw* (1944) (which I hallucinated in color) introduced me to the work of Roy William Neill. Two publishers, Ballantine Books and The Science Fiction Book Club, stocked the shelves of a closet intended for toys next to my room with science fiction paperbacks and inexpensive hardbacks that introduced me to the novels and stories of Alfred Bester, Theodore Sturgeon, and lesser lights like George O. Smith. Subscriptions to *Galaxy Science Fiction*, *Astounding Science Fiction*, and *F&SF* also played an important role in my unofficial education.

My time was spent within the narrow confines of Electra, Texas, and nearby Wichita Falls, where my mother parked me, while she did her shopping, at theaters looking into the wider world of low-budget science fiction and horror, including England's relatively sumptuous Hammer Films. But I spent a month every summer in Santa Fe, New Mexico, where I could buy my favorite science fiction magazines at newsstands, along with the early books about a phenomenon that was science fiction come to life: Unidentified Flying Objects or, as they were commonly known, flying saucers. That is where I first saw Hitchcock's *Psycho* (1960) and the greatest double bill in history, *The Revenge of Frankenstein* (Terence Fisher, 1958) and *Curse of the Demon* (Jacques Tourneur, 1957). And that is how the first part of my adolescence was lived, in oscillation between Texas and New Mexico, where the images that haunted me became real.

I would probably have spent the rest of my life in Electra, with side trips to Wichita Falls and Santa Fe, if my mother hadn't sent me away to a coeducational boarding school in Austin, St. Stephen's Episcopal School, where I was enrolled two years behind future filmmaker Terrence Malick. My new spartan lifestyle (students were called "Spartans") severely curtailed my consumption of films (I missed whole seasons of *The Outer Limits* [1963] and Boris Karloff's *Thriller* [1960]) but widened my perspective. It was there that I first saw Vincente Minnelli's *Lust for Life* (1956) projected in a sixteen-millimeter print in the school cafeteria and learned of the existence of other cinemas, notably the films of Federico Fellini and Satyajit Ray, from the St. Stephen's faculty, who were nothing if not arty. But that didn't stop me from sneaking away during a weekly town-trip to see Mario Bava's *Black Sunday* (1963), a black-and-white horror movie I had read about in *Time* magazine, and François Truffaut's *Shoot the Piano Player* (1960), a French film that was purported to contain a glimpse of a Michele Mercier's breast, which was my first contact with the New Wave and, through it, the *Cahiers*. The shot in question had unfortunately been cut from American prints. Much later I would travel all the way to France to see it—an adventure I subsequently recounted in the *Cahiers* special issue published on the occasion of Truffaut's untimely death.

The excellent preparation I received at St. Stephen's sent me away from Texas to Yale College in New Haven, Connecticut—narrowly avoiding a trip to Vietnam courtesy of fellow Texan Lyndon Baines Johnson—where my first act, after being deposited in my dorm at the freshman campus, was to see Fellini's *8½* (1963) at the Lincoln Theater, the local art house that would soon be rendered useless for my purposes by a record-breaking run of Vittorio de Sica's *Yesterday, Today and Tomorrow* (1963), featuring a striptease by Sophia Loren. (Stripteases were all the rage: Fellini's *La Dolce Vita* [1960] had featured one by Nadia Gray.) My Yale studies marked the beginning of my long discipleship with Harold Bloom, whose theories of influence are applied to film—a use Bloom never intended—throughout *Letters from Hollywood*. But they also introduced me to the *Cahiers*-influenced programming of the Yale Film Society, where I saw Sam Fuller's *Shock Corridor* (1963) introduced by Andrew Sarris, whose 1968 book *The American Cinema* became the bible of American auteurism. My cinephile friends at Yale bonded over a mutual love of *Shoot the Piano Player* (especially George Delerue's score) and mutual detestation of the *New York Times* critic Bosley Crowther, who had decreed that Jean-Luc Godard's films were silly japes on the level of TV's *Batman*. We were also privileged my freshman year to study art history with Robert Herbert, the Marxist expert on the Barbizon School. I learned visual analysis from Herbert, but when I returned to California it was Fuller I became friends with, and for the memorial issue on Truffaut I interviewed Delerue, a stocky peasant with a gift for writing breathtaking music, who revealed to me that throughout their relationship Truffaut never ate dinner with him until the very end, when he had the inoperable brain tumor that killed him. "When he asked me to dinner," Delerue said, "I knew he was going to die."

In the meantime I had become Los Angeles correspondent for the *Cahiers*, while writing for other publications both French (the magazine *Trafic*, which Serge Daney started when he left the *Cahiers*) and English (*The Economist*, the Australian blog *Rouge Cinema*, the American blog *Kino Slang*, and an array of others, many now lost to history). "Los Angeles correspondent for *Cahiers du cinéma*" is a title I still hold, although it has become purely honorific. Having transferred from Yale to the Graduate Center of the City University of New York to pursue my interest in the ideas of Georgian sage G. I. Gurdjieff—and to see more movies than I could see in New Haven—I became the American version of what French cinephiles would call "a rat of the Cinémathèque." During my immersion in the culture of New York City, I took as my guru Greg Ford, a student of the great critic Manny Farber, whom I knew through a Yale connection, his wife Ronnie Scheib. The epicenter of that culture was the screening program at the Museum of Modern Art, where Adrianne Mancia was programming complete retrospectives of filmmakers like Raoul Walsh. Apart from these cinephilic excursions, my immersion in the Bohemian culture of New York was complete: I was living in the D Block of the East Village, known as "Little Saigon."

One day, however, I noticed that the Bleecker Street Cinema in Greenwich Village was playing interesting double bills, like *Nathalie Granger* (1972) by Marguerite Duras and *Cops* (1922) by Buster Keaton, so I arranged an introduction to Jackie Raynal, the French woman who programmed the Bleecker. Jackie had left France after May '68, during which she had been gang-raped by gendarmes, and had become a construction worker in upstate New York, where she met and married Sid Geffen, a real estate broker with an interest in film who bought her the Bleecker to program. She showed me her film, a radical example of the underground cinema financed by the heiress Sylvina Boissonnas for her Zanzibar films—*Deux Fois* (*Twice Upon a Time* [1968]), which ended with a twenty-minute scream by Jackie—hoping that as a film critic I could suggest a way to sell it, although the extent of my film criticism at this point was a piece on Terence Fisher and a blurb on Walsh's despised remake of *The Strawberry Blonde* (1941), *One Sunday Afternoon* (1948), published in magazines that were mimeographed and distributed to cognoscenti in New York.

In the course of our discussions I discovered that Jackie had gone to high school in Paris with Daney, who had become the editor-in-chief of the *Cahiers* after Parisian intellectuals' disastrous fling with Sinophilia post–May '68. Now that the *Cahiers* was bouncing back from publishing only articles about vaccination programs in Red China, Serge wanted to let Americans know that it was back by staging the first Semaine des Cahiers at the Bleecker Street. He was coming to New York to present a selection of films by new directors ranging from Chantal Akerman to René Allio, and Jackie wanted to publish a little booklet to accompany the series. Accordingly I typed up a series of questions which Jackie delivered to Serge in Paris; my questions and his responses became the core of the booklet that was distributed at the Semaine.

I did eventually meet Serge at Sid and Jackie's apartment on Central Park South, and we became friends. To secure my position with the magazine I obtained an interview with Nicholas Ray, who was teaching at the Lee Strasberg School, and Serge named me the American correspondent for the magazine: the third in its history after Herman G. Weinberg and Axel Madsen. I flew to Paris, where I oversaw the layout of the interview in the *Cahiers*, meeting Serge's friend Jean-Claude Biette, who had recently joined the magazine, and other collaborators who had been only illustrious names to me before this. (Jean-Claude found what he described as "a sublime typo" in the article: "Nicholas *radis*," which is French for "radish.") On my return to the States, however, I flew to California and interviewed Roger Corman about his activities as a producer and "maker of filmmakers"—then unknown in France—and subsequently chose to live in Los Angeles, where I learned my way around the studios.

In fact, after settling in Westwood, I found the negative for *It's All True*, a film Welles had shot in Brazil but hadn't been allowed to finish, in a vault at Paramount. While waiting for that project to come to fruition, I got a job editing press kits at 20th Century Fox—a wait that lasted eleven years. During the day I was an employee of the marketing department at Fox, sitting in on meetings of the department and observing the workings of a major studio firsthand; at night I wrote my articles for the *Cahiers* and faxed them to the magazine's general secretary, Claudine Paquot, and her assistant Delphine Pineau, who faxed them back to me translated for my corrections the next day. This rhythm continued from 1982 to 1993, when I quit my job at Fox to go to Brazil and film the documentary portions of what became *It's All True: Based on an Unfinished Film by Orson Welles*, which premiered at Lincoln Center in 1994 and bombed. My subsequent trips to France were made for personal reasons that have nothing to do with the magazine, although its writers and editorial staff always supported me when I was in Paris en route to the South of France, where my new interests took me. Living at that time in the college town of Westwood, I was able to offer visiting writers for the *Cahiers* a place to sleep and a guide to California when the adventurous ones leapfrogged over New York, reputed to be the center of American culture, and made straight for California, where I have been living since that time—first in Hollywood and, for the last year, in the seaside town of Long Beach.

Sadly, I understand from a friend who recently visited Paris that young people there think the *Cahiers* isn't worth reading anymore, which is the death blow for a magazine that has never had more than five thousand paid subscribers but has exercised an influence out of proportion to its circulation.

I have a plan to repair the damage, but that's another story. Meanwhile, you hold in your hands an important part (newly edited for this volume) of my contribution to the magazine, which will always have a raison d'être as long as good films, and passionate writing about them, exist.

Notations

The eulogy for François Truffaut was "Detour" in *Le roman de François Truffaut*, supplement to *Cahiers du cinéma* 366 (December 1984): 121.

My interview with Nicholas Ray is in *Cahiers du cinéma* 288 (May 1978).

My interview with Roger Corman is in *Cahiers du cinéma* 296 (January 1979).

2

On Daney (1977)

The Tinkerers

IN 1951 ANDRÉ BAZIN FOUNDED the *Cahiers du cinéma* and gathered into it a group of writers—Eric Rohmer, Jacques Doniol-Valcroze, François Truffaut, Claude Chabrol, Jean-Luc Godard—who collectively rewrote the history of film, in more ways than one. This all happened a long time ago. The old *Cahiers* is no more, but you can still see it—being brandished, read, and blatantly peddled, sometimes just pinned to the wall (looking strangely at home amid the period decor of *Jules et Jim* [1962])—in the early films of the New Wave.

La nouvelle vague, la politique des auteurs: these catchphrases and what they represent are still with us. The auteur theory is solidly entrenched in the pages of our film magazines, and attempts at overthrowing it have usually paid it the compliment of imitation, with more filmographies, hierarchies, biographies, interviews, and retrospectives: the screenwriter, the cameraman, the editor, the producer as auteur, as hero, as sage. Nicholas Ray and Vincente Minnelli are taught in our universities. And whenever a handheld camera wobbles unsteadily toward its target and dialogue is overwhelmed by street noises, wherever improvisation (or its outward signs, which are easy enough to fake) suggests that what we are watching is not a movie but life caught in the raw, the influence of the New Wave on filmmakers is still in evidence. Perhaps too much.

When they finally came, the changes that occurred in the magazine in the late sixties were long overdue. These changes were a response to two events that profoundly affected the Parisian intellectual circles where the *Cahiers* is produced and read: the advent of structuralism and the thwarted revolt of students and workers which began in May of 1968. After 1968 the *Cahiers* became politicized (Marxist), and harder to read, because of the influx of structuralist and post-structuralist ideas.

But even though the magazine is less widely read today than it was in the early sixties, when I imbibed its influence through the intermediary of my college film society, the theories and values put forward by the new *Cahiers* (there have been at least three since 1968) have had an impact here. Today, structuralist and Marxist film magazines abound. Some of them have published articles from the *Cahiers*, and a few are completely written in a weird language that is also beginning to turn up in the pages of respectable academic journals: Frenchlish, a compound of structuralist jargon, high-mindedness, and English words used as if they meant the same thing as their French cognates. Most specialists have read the translation of the *Cahiers*' collective text on *Young Mr. Lincoln* (1939—written by Serge Daney and Jean-Pierre Oudart: an expansion by Daney of Oudart's short piece "The Mother and the Law"—published in *Screen* [Autumn 1972]), and even Robin Wood, who was once content to talk about Howard Hawks's "vision of the world" and adolescent moral code as F. R. Leavis before him had talked of Donne or Lawrence, has recently been writing sensibly about the ideology of free enterprise in Capra and Hitchcock and nervously about the respective virtues of "closed" and "open" form in films by Jean-Luc Godard and Jean-Louis Comolli.

It would be impossible to say how much of this is direct influence. Other French film magazines—*Cinéthique* and *CA*, for example—have developed along similar lines, and the influences that affected the *Cahiers* (political upheaval in the late sixties and structuralism) have been widely

felt in America as well during the last ten years. But between the old and
the new, it would be safe to say that most film criticism written in this
country bears the mark, conscious or unconscious, of some relationship
to what the *Cahiers* has been and is today.

So it seemed like a good idea, on the occasion of the upcoming
Semaine des Cahiers at the Bleecker Street Theater, to publish something
about what has been happening to the *Cahiers* in recent years, and the
simplest way to get the story was to interview one of the editors, Serge
Daney, who has been with the magazine since 1964 and is now, with Serge
Toubiana, *Redacteur en chef.* The interview was conducted—appropriately,
for reasons that will soon become apparent—in writing, and translated
from the French.

There is little I can add to it. Daney's thoughtful and forthright
replies to my questions are an insider's account of the stormy years
during which the *Cahiers* almost ceased, for a short time, to be a film
magazine, nearly extinguishing itself in the process, and then evolved to
the point it has reached today: more open, more eclectic, more readable,
but permanently marked by the commitments and struggles of the last
decade. The interview emphasizes continuities; particularly toward the
end, moral questions which can only be called Bazinian, coupled with
the word "auteur," insistently turn up. In retrospect it is easier to see
why this magazine, when its passion for films like *Baby Face Nelson* (1957)
and *Rancho Notorious* (1952) had finally played out, turned its attention
to films made in factories, ghettos, and armed camps all over the world.
And why today they are more obsessed than ever with the films of Jean-
Marie Straub and Danièle Huillet, and with Jean-Luc Godard.

I would just like to fill in at a couple of points where I think Daney
risks being misunderstood. First of all, the word *bricoleur.* Speaking of
the period when theory reigned supreme (1969–1972), Daney says that
what was happening then was a "savage application" of theories produced
elsewhere, in particular by the Marxist theoretician Louis Althusser and
the psychoanalyst Jacques Lacan; and he adds, "None of us was a high-
ranking academic—more like tinkerers (*bricoleurs*)." The word *bricoleur*
has its own history in structuralist thought, beginning with Claude
Lévi-Strauss's comparison, in *The Savage Mind*, of the tinkerer and the
engineer, by way of illustrating the difference between primitive mythmaking and modern science:

> The characteristic feature of mythical thought is that it
> expresses itself by means of a heterogeneous repertoire which,
> even if extensive, is nevertheless limited. It has to use this
> repertoire, however, whatever the task in hand, because it has

nothing else at its disposal. Mythical thought is therefore a kind of intellectual "bricolage." . . . Like "bricolage" on the technical plane, mythical reflection can reach brilliant unforeseen results on the intellectual plane.

Perhaps Daney did not have this passage in mind, but his colleague Jean-Pierre Oudart did, in 1969, when he described Luc Moullet's films as works of bricolage, which resemble the films of the other moderns (the New Wave, etc.) as "a bicycle assembled, from mismatched parts, by a savage who was ignorant of its function" might resemble a real bicycle. This is a peculiar compliment, but it is a compliment nonetheless. (When I brought up the bricoleur business recently during an abortive interview with Luc Moullet, he gave me a funny look and replied that his brother had made a musical instrument, called a "percophone," out of old bicycle brakes, which "gives a very interesting sound.") Elsewhere in the pages of the *Cahiers* Jean Rouch, one of the technical and spiritual fathers of the New Wave, has also been called a bricoleur; so has Godard, the mad scientist of the group.

And I can't think of a better word to describe the speculations published in the *Cahiers* during the period when wildly original thinkers like Lacan, Lévi-Strauss, Georges Bataille, and Jacques Derrida were being enlisted in the service of film theory. Working with what was at hand, the *Cahiers* writers knocked together eclectic assemblages out of the most heterogeneous elements imaginable: Lacan and Fritz Lang; Bataille and Jerry Lewis; Lévi-Strauss and Jacques Demy; Lacan, his student Serge Leclaire, Derrida (it took three of them), and Howard Hawks. The Hawks article, "*Rio Lobo*: Vieillesse du Même," was written by Daney in 1971 (*Cahiers* 230). It is a Bugs Bunny cartoon boinging onto the screen after one of Lacan's famous "seminars," and, like many of the Bugs Bunny cartoons, it is a work of concentrated brilliance.

What it does, among other things, is to propose a new definition of *auteur*: an auteur is an obsessional neurotic. "Who would ever want to write with images?" Daney had asked in an earlier article: "It is time to understand that such a wish, often formulated, was only formulated by those (from Eisenstein to Bresson) for whom it was uninteresting to have ideas, unless they were *idées fixes*, on the order of obsessions (sexual, no doubt) and phantasms, so that only a unique, terrorist discourse could take them in hand" (*Cahiers* 222). It is not a bad hypothesis. What other kind of personality would it take, after all, to collect everything it takes to put together six hundred pieces of film with any kind of consistent tone or purpose, particularly when the end product has to have the illusory qualities of "continuity and transparency" (as if the camera weren't there) that characterized classical cinema? And to do it time and again, despite scripts, budgets, producers, and changing fashions, so as to leave one's mark, even though it might be invisible to the naked eye?

So in the *Rio Lobo* piece Daney treated Hawks as he deserved to be treated at least once in his career: as a good subject for a case history, where all the "tics and obsessions" dear to the auteurist (the fascination with closed spaces, the boy-scout skills of the Hawks hero, the unnerving jokes about castration and gender confusion, the ritual exchanges of hostages, the urge to repeat, the refusal to grow old, or to look death in the face) come together in a new configuration and begin to make a lurid kind of sense. Perhaps he was inspired by reading Dr. Leclaire's account of one of his own patients, a former military man named "Jérome," whose favorite fantasy—that he was a mummy, incorruptible and beautiful in his sarcophagus, safe behind a maze of walls and armored doors—throws new light on *Land of the Pharaohs* (1955), the film Hawks *had* to make, and the great commercial bomb of his career. Unless, of course, "Jérome" was just someone who had seen *Land of the Pharaohs* one time too many.

Apparently he did see a sensational documentary called *L'Afrique vous parle* (1939), and it made quite an impression on him:

> Then he remembered a documentary film: in it one sees a crocodile that seems to be asleep, floating like a dead tree trunk, then suddenly he opens his mouth and gobbles a Negro in less time than it takes to tell it. . . . No, of course, he had not seen this scene of incorporation, it had been cut; but he knows that by an exceptional stroke of luck the filmmaker, cold-bloodedly confronting this scene, had devoured everything with his eye of glass without losing a crumb.

At any rate, this is the best clinical example I've seen of the obsessional pattern that Daney and Pascal Bonitzer discovered in the articles André Bazin wrote on the limits of montage, where the need to film this kind of thing in a single take is illustrated with fantasies of death and incorporation:

> Difference, rupture, discontinuity are not absent from Bazin's discourse, or from the cinema he defends; in fact they are always present, almost to the point of shattering the screen. The cinema of continuity is also a cinema which dreams of filming discontinuity, difference. . . . Not cutting up the screen, but representing cutting up on it.

For anyone who has immersed himself in film, the aptness of the examples that start turning up when you read through the literature of psychoanalysis is a little spooky, particularly when, in the recent literature, the patient is almost as likely to be talking about a film he saw as about a dream he had.

The application of structural psychoanalytic theory to the study of film was one of the most successful pieces of sustained tinkering produced by the *Cahiers* during this period, and Lacanian terms still turn up throughout Daney's interview. One that calls for a brief comment, because of the special way it is being used, is *imaginary*, which is one of the three orders of human experience described by Lacan: the real, the imaginary, and the symbolic. According to a French dictionary of psychoanalytic terms, imaginary relations include "(a) from the intrasubjective standpoint: the fundamental, narcissistic relationship of the subject to his ego; (b) from the intersubjective standpoint: the so-called dual relationship based on—and enthralled by—the image of a similar being (erotic attraction, aggressive tension). For Lacan, a fellow being—an other who is me—exists only because the ego is originally an other."

The face in the mirror, in other words, isn't you; it is your other self, your alter ego, and the model for all the "other selves" with whom you enter into imaginary relationships when you use other people as mirrors to see your own face. Archetypally, the origin of this enthrallment is the game a child plays ("Now I see me, now I don't") when learning to identify with the image in a mirror, a movement in which Oudart ("La suture," *Cahiers* 211–212) saw the underlying logic of the *champ-contrechamp* sequence ("Now I see me, now I see what me sees") in film. But when Daney speaks of an imaginary, he means something like a stock of images in which a particular social group recognizes itself and rejects what isn't it. Today most of these would be film images from the little "portable cinematheques" we all carry around in our heads.

Cf. *Fahrenheit 451* (1966), which can be read as a description of a presymbolic world (the world of infancy), or of a society enthralled by an imaginary perpetually reproduced on its wall screens (an imaginary "family" to which everyone belongs, except traitors) or simply of the phenomenology of a classic film by, say, Alfred Hitchcock. In the Fahrenheit world people are interchangeable; Doppelgängers abound; sexuality is narcissistic and obsessive; disembodied heads seem to address you from the wall (they are really addressing the Void); movements are parallel, fluid, and continuous. Beyond the city walls is a world of crisscrossing and divergent movements, autonomy, solitude, and aimless wandering: the order of the symbolic, in which the child is enrolled when he acquires the use of language. The land of the "book-people."

Which brings up the only thing in the interview that is actually a little confusing: Daney's use of the word "writing." When he says that the cinema defended by the *Cahiers* has always been a cinema haunted by "writing," Daney does not mean scripts. In fact, he means just the opposite. Here is a slice of polemic from an earlier period, when Fereydoun Hoveyda, who is now ambassador to the United Nations from Iran, was entrusted with a humbler task, in the service of a very different *politique*: the defense of Nicholas Ray's *Party Girl* (1957) against its detractors.

> The subject of *Party Girl* is idiotic. What does this prove? If the intricacies of the plot which unfolds on the screen constituted the essence of the cinematic work, the best thing to do would be to annex the Seventh Art to Literature, let the directors content themselves with illustrating novels and short stories (which is in fact the case with a number of directors whom we do not esteem) and abandon the pages of the *Cahiers* to the literary critics. I don't wish to open an old debate, but, with clock-like regularity, certain critics continue to insist on the importance of scripts, acting and the system of production. While we are at it, why not take into account the influence of the heavenly spheres? (*Cahiers* 107)

The interview should make it clear that the *Cahiers* critics are no longer contemptuous of subject matter, or indifferent to the influence of the production system on filmmaking. But the taste for films in which the "writing" is in excess of the ideology is a constant; it accounts for the fact that Daney still dismisses a director like John Huston for illustrating the script instead of "writing with images," like an auteur. This idea, too, has undergone some modifications.

All this would be clearer if he had been less modest in his account of the period of theoretical bricolage. He should have added, "And thanks to Daney (*Sur Salador*, etc.) there was a savage application of Derrida." Jacques Derrida is a philosopher who has been exploring the implications of Ferdinand de Saussure's famous assertion, in his *Course in General Linguistics*, that "in language there are only differences," by tracing the theme of writing in the history of Western thought. According to Derrida, writing, since Socrates condemned it as a deceitful and dangerous "ghost" of the spoken word, has been the object of a scapegoat ritual in which it is made to embody qualities in language that are alien to traditional religious and metaphysical conceptions of the *logos*. In this sense "writing" is the play of differences which constitutes the linguistic sign and perpetually defers access to the thing signified. To sum all this up, Derrida coined the word *différance* ("differment" would be a near equivalent in English), which can be used more or less interchangeably with "writing," in the special sense he has given it.

Crudely put, what Daney did was to graft this philosophical idea of writing onto the old idea of writing with images. In this sense, "writing with images," as he explains in the interview, would imply "spacing" (another Derridean term), and in film the space between images is the off-space. What the cinema of the *champ-contrechamp* shows us is "that images do not articulate first with one another—that instead the filmic field (*champ*) articulates with the absent field, the imaginary field of the film" (Oudart, *Cahiers* 211). So between the look (*champ*) and what is seen (*contrechamp*), between Gloria Grahame's last moment of happiness and Glenn Ford's realization that she is dead (*The Big Heat* [1953]), falls the off-space, the void on the other side of the screen. This is a problem that "each important filmmaker resolves" in a unique way.

Writing as *différance* also implies deferment, as opposed to a simple meshing of the sign and what it signifies, because something written in a phonetic alphabet is merely the sign of a sign. And in film, deferment means the effect of *déjà vu*. What falls between the image and whatever it is supposed to represent is another image, all the other images one has seen of the same thing. Especially if one has seen *all* those other images. "What is death," Daney asks in his article "Sur Salador" (*Cahiers* 222), "for this generation of film-freaks who have buried themselves in the cinematheques, if not the effect produced by bodies toppling over in films?" This presents special problems to filmmakers who started out as film-freaks—Godard, for example, at the point in his life when he finally realized his dream of doing a big-budget movie with real stars, Jack Palance and Brigitte Bardot:

> What happens in *Contempt*? Always the same story: one comes too late, one inherits a game that has already been played. . . . Homer writes *The Odyssey* and Moravia, *Ghost at Noon*; Prokosch wants to put it into images and Ponti, to bring it to the screen. They summon famous "artists" (Lang, Godard). . . . Each new player in this game of Capital and Culture must respect (but not reflect) in his work the traces left by whoever preceded him, which he must undo.

The conclusion: "Every film is a palimpsest," a text written over another text. And this is also a problem that each important filmmaker must now resolve.

Daney's Derridean speculations are in the background of the article that we are printing with his interview: "The T(h)errorized" (the *h* is silent in French). It is about Godard, the *enfant terrible* of the New Wave, who recently did a series of shows for French television during which he apparently would write messages from time to time on the inside of the TV screen, like Winky Dink in reverse. What Daney seems to be saying in this piece is that Godard has joined Truffaut's "book people" in that curious wintry landscape, and that his voice (his soundtrack) has taken on all the qualities that Socrates distrusted in writing. Orphaned, cut off from its father (its author), it wanders around talking to whoever will listen, not knowing whom to address and whom to avoid. And when you question it, it can't answer you; all it can do is repeat what has already been said. It encourages confusion between words and things and turns words into things—a petrified discourse, dangerously close to nonsense, like the orange electronic letters that appear and disappear on a black screen in *Numéro deux* (1975), making and unmaking sense.

The equivocal meditation on "Godardian pedagogy" is a good companion piece to Daney's interview because it concerns a filmmaker whose evolution since 1968 has closely paralleled that of the *Cahiers*, particularly during the period of Marxist-Leninist dogmatism (*Cahiers* 1973–1974), when the magazine began to read like the soundtrack of *La Chinoise* (1967) and speculation was temporarily suspended while anonymous voices posed soul-harrowing questions about the social function of educators: teachers (Daney, incidentally, is a schoolteacher), social workers, film club programmers, semioticians, editors, film critics. And perhaps one virtue of the films of the "Dziga Vertov Group" was to demonstrate, "as always, by the absurd," through a happy combination of morality and perversity, how the militant cinema that was a touchstone for the *Cahiers* during this period actually functioned. In psychoanalytic terms, the "t(h)errorized" is someone who terrorizes others by theorizing about them, because he is himself "theorized," and terrorized, by what Lacan calls the Discourse of the Other.

Anyway, it took a new kind of open-mindedness about the real complexities in the relationship of art to politics to acknowledge that Godard, indispensable as he is, has not exactly been making propaganda films. In this respect, "The T(h)errorized" also marks the beginning of a new phase in the magazine's development, during which the restrictions on play have gradually been lifted. In an article on Jean-Louis Comolli's film about a nineteenth-century anarchist commune, *La Cecilia*, Pascal Kané compares the anarchism portrayed in the film to the games of childhood and observes that "childhood can be . . . an age of intense activity: it is a time for exploring knowledge, experimenting with discourses. It is the age when the intellectual life is all-powerful, when ideas reign without opposition, and where desires find an appropriate scene for satisfaction. . . . A childhood which it is difficult to see that we can dispense with "revisiting," if we wish to question the origin of our own ideas, our own desires" (*Cahiers* 265).

"Art," he had noted earlier, is also "a game played in the margins of the Law, filming is also playing the child: following one's idea, letting one's speech rule, sheltered from the real." This was a valuable rediscovery, which has occasioned a certain number of revaluations. Jean Rouch, for example: dismissed, respectfully, in 1971 as a petit-bourgeois ideologue who had turned ethnographic cinema into a glass-bead game without serious political consequences (*Cahiers* 234–235, 236–237), he can be acknowledged today as a tinkerer of genius who was one of the first to explore the possibilities of *infra-cinéma*: "the new cinemas of the Third World, experimental cinema, militant cinema, amateur cinema, video groups, independent filmmakers . . ." (*Cahiers* 275). Play, in other words, can have serious consequences, and tinkerers may achieve "brilliant unforeseen results" beyond the reach of mere engineers.

"So the link to cinema, after the detour of militancy, was reaffirmed." The last few years have been a period of great activity, not all of it theoretical: besides Comolli, several of the *Cahiers* editors have been involved, in one capacity or another, in making films. Like the recent Godard films, recent issues of the *Cahiers* have made room in the ongoing meditation on film for investigations of other media: photography, painting, television, and radio. The *politique* governing all this does not seem to have changed fundamentally. Daney, at least, shows no sign of having forgotten those painfully acquired political ABCs. One constant has been the opposition to the French Communist Party, which is escalating now that "Eurocommunism" is getting a piece of power in France and Italy. Another is the preference for filmmakers who have chosen aesthetic options corresponding to the most marginal forms of political activity: terrorism and utopia building. There has also been, however, a rediscovery of "the liberty of eclecticism"; recent issues have embraced films as ideologically diverse as *People's War* (1969), *Le camion* (1977) ("Karl Marx, c'est fini"), *The Devil, Probably* (1977), and *King Kong* (1976). Phrases like "a cinema which militates as cinema" can stretch a long way, and where the *Cahiers* will go from here is anyone's guess. But an aesthetic that demands at least as much attention to "writing" as to ideology, coupled with a moral concern for one's human writing materials, has always been a good place to begin.

Interview with Serge Daney

This interview with Serge Daney was originally published in *The Thousand Eyes*, a magazine published by the Bleecker Street Cinema, in 1977.

Q: When did you join the *Cahiers du cinéma*? What was it like in those days? What have you been doing when you weren't editing the magazine? What was May '68 like for you (if you'd care to talk about it)?

A: In 1959 I bought, for the first time, the *Cahiers*. It was number 99. A Lang special. One used a lofty and complicated vocabulary to talk about Lang's American films, much despised at the time by "serious" criticism. This paradoxical artistocratism pleased me. After many years of assiduously frequenting the cinematheque (Rue d'Ulm; then, after 1964, Palais de Chaillot), one got to know certain critics from the *Cahiers* (especially Jean Douchet.) With two friends, in 1963, I put out a magazine that ran two issues: a Hawks special and a Preminger special. Which shows how much we defined ourselves at that time almost exclusively in relation to the American cinema, taking as its summit what was in fact its twilight. In 1964, with Louis Skorecki, I went to the US to meet filmmakers and do interviews (Hawks, Leo McCarey, Jacques Tourneur, Jerry Lewis, Sternberg, Keaton). That's how we "negotiated our entrée into the *Cahiers*." In 1964, a grave economic and ideological crisis shook the *Cahiers*. Eric Rohmer had to give up the chief editorship and was replaced by Jacques Rivette, then by Jean-Louis Comolli. At the same time the magazine was taken over by a publisher (Daniel Filipacchi) until 1969, a date when, principally for political reasons, the magazine become autonomous again.

At this time "being on the *Cahiers*" didn't have the same meaning as today. There was no editorial committee, and all the important decisions were made by one or two people. There were a lot of freelancers who wrote a piece from time to time that might or might not be accepted, without feeling themselves to be part of a global point of view. It was that way until 1968. The magazine evolved considerably, abandoned its blind Americanism, and adopted an increasingly intellectual, theoretical approach to problems. This was, in France, the breaking of the great wave of structuralism (and the first works by Christian Metz).

The year 1968 was experienced differently by the people on the *Cahiers*, insofar as I was concerned, as a profound shake-up and a wavering of all certainties. It seemed that one could never do films or a film magazine as one had before. The ideas developed by the Situationists on the "society of the spectacle" affected me greatly. Basically, our way of being "affected" by '68 consisted of putting in doubt and into play, in a slightly mystical way, what had been the source of our enjoyment: the position of spectator. During this period, I pulled away from the *Cahiers* and didn't rejoin them until 1971. In the meantime, I took long trips (to India and Africa). The magazine, it seemed, was becoming more and more politicized.

Q: There were great changes in the magazine at the end of the sixties—how did they come about?

A: I believe that the great event of those years was the introduction into the *Cahiers* of a very theoretical way of talking about film far removed, in appearance, from the old cinephilia. There's nothing very astonishing about it: for the first time authors like Michel Foucault, Louis Althusser, Jacques Lacan, and Claude Lévi-Strauss reached beyond their usual public and were read by a larger group who immediately attempted a kind of savage application of their ideas. Very simply, the *Cahiers* was the first magazine to plunge in this direction, with no precautions. This earned us, at the time, the sarcasms of "normal" criticism—impressionistic and hedonistic—which did not tolerate the use of a "jargon" to talk about films (this was the period of the polemic between Barthes and [Raymond] Picard).

So there was a savage application of Althusser and particularly of Lacan, thanks to Jean-Pierre Oudart ("La suture"), beginning in 1969. There was also the influence of the magazine *Tel Quel*. The *Cahiers* at the time played the role of the middleman: they introduced theory to cinema and cinema to the university. Which is somewhat paradoxical, since none of us was a high-ranking academic—more like tinkerers. I think that this period is over. There exists more and more a monopoly of academic discourse on cinema, and the new generation of "cinephiles" will be formed more in the universities than in the cinematheques. We played a part in this mutation. Today we believe it's important not to limit oneself to the university. The *Cahiers* has always been an uncomfortable and paradoxical place where it was possible to write about films and make films at the same time (see Godard).

Q: The "new" *Cahiers* was critical of its heritage: you reread Ford, dissected Bresson, psychoanalyzed Bazin. Why was this necessary?

A: This criticism was obviously a last homage, more or less avowed, that we rendered to what we have always loved. We wanted to reread Ford, not Huston, to dissect Bresson and not René Clair, to psychoanalyze Bazin and not Pauline Kael. Criticism is always that: an eternal return to a fundamental pleasure. As concerns me, why was my relationship to cinema bound up with *The Indian Tomb* (1959), *Rio Bravo* (1959), *Ugetsu Monogatari* (1953), *Pickpocket* (1959), *North by Northwest* (1959), *Paisan* (1946), *Gertrud* (1964)? There is a dimension to cinephilia that psychoanalysis knows well under the name of "mourning work": something is dead, something of which traces, shadows remain.

Incidentally, in the collective text on *Young Mr. Lincoln* (1939), we distinguished clearly between ideology and writing. We were very conscious then of the danger (which we subsequently did not always avoid) of confounding ideology and writing. Now—it's quite simple—the cinema loved by the *Cahiers*—from the beginning—is a *cinema haunted by writing*. This is the key that makes it possible to understand the successive tastes and choices. This is also explained by the fact that the best French film-makers have always been—at the same time—writers (Jean Renoir, Jean Cocteau, Marcel Pagnol, Sacha Guitry, Jean Epstein, et al.).

Q: "The cinema that interests us is the one which plays on off-spaces . . . The great filmmakers—Hitchcock, Lang, Mizoguchi, Tourneur, Dreyer, Duras, Straub, Godard—are those whose mise-en-scène, writing, montage are articulated by off-space effects . . ." Why? And what about Griffith, Walsh, Chaplin, Hawks, Allan Dwan, Renoir, Monte Hellman?

A: This phrase of Pascal Bonitzer's is a little provocative in that it risks giving the impression that we only love those filmmakers. There are others, of course, including the ones you cited. As a matter of fact, it's the same question as the previous one and the one that follows (on naturalism). The cinema that interests us is haunted by writing. Writing implies spacing, a void between two words, two letters, a void that permits the tracing of meaning. Writing implies, not immediacy, but an eternal movement of "boustrophedon." So how does all this happen in film? There, too, there is spacing, but it isn't the invisible bond between frames—it's the off-space. Each shot secretes its off-space. There are different off-spaces and different ways of playing on them. There are off-spaces directed by the eye (fetishistic framing) and off-spaces directed by the ear (fundamental voice, voice of the mother). There is a way for the voice to block or give access to the image. Each important filmmaker resolves this problem. So, when the *Cahiers* was politicized, they took their examples more and more from the Soviet cinema of the twenties, but again it was to distinguish between Eisenstein (who "wrote") and Pudovkin (who "didn't write"), and this was the same as the distinction between Hitchcock and Huston. Today it may well be that with people like Godard and Straub we have reached the extreme limit of writing. These are filmmakers for whom an image is closer to an inscription on a tombstone than to an advertising poster. And cinema may no longer have any choice but to be a poster or an epitaph. In writing, you know, there is a relation to death.

Q: Public enemy number one, still at large: naturalism. Why do you distrust it?

A: The hatred of naturalism is as deep as the taste for writing, because it is exactly the converse. In naturalism there is a kind of "special effect" or trickery that is fundamental: the frame is there by chance and transforms the spectators into voyeurs. Naturalism confuses the repressed with the invisible. One example: for years, in French films, one doesn't see immigrant laborers. Filmically, they don't exist. After 1968, the immigrants participated in numerous struggles and were politicized, so the French cinema is somewhat obliged to show them. Then we'll show them, but as if they had always been there and one had just forgotten to show them, when in fact one had repressed them, and for political reasons. This is ethnological voyeurism. On the *Cahiers* we think that the question is not just one of "correcting an omission" but of lifting a repression: why has their image been missing? Cinema usually shows us people, events, places that we don't know; there's no reason for it to give us the impression that they are there, next door. Naturalism (precision of description) is only one part of the task. If you don't go beyond it, you necessarily end up asking questions about cinema in terms of advertising (as if it were nothing). This is unfortunately what is happening more and more.

Q: What happened to the *Cahiers* in 1973?

A: I'll have to tell the story of post-'68 in intellectual circles. It's the story of a shift. The year 1970 marked the apogee of the "Maoist" movement in France (with groups like "La gauche proletarienne," then "La cause du peuple"), its greatest moment of political inventiveness. After this date there is a decline in the movement, first in its spontaneous form ("Maoist"), then in its dogmatic form ("Marxist-Leninist"). Intellectual circles were affected by leftist ideas after a kind of delay. Why? It was especially those who have never belonged to the French Communist Party (like the people on the *Cahiers*) who were affected by leftism. When the whole French cultural scene was politicized, it was natural to approach the French Communist Party in order to assess their positions on questions of art and culture. The FCP, on the other hand, after having been badly burned in the debates in the fifties on "socialist realism," had renounced any conspicuous interference in the domain of art and had, at the same time, renounced any theory, any investigation of the relation between art and politics and, more precisely, of propaganda literature. Now the *Cahiers* and *Tel Quel* were magazines that had fought to introduce new methods (derived from structuralism) into the study of literary and cinematic texts. So there was an exchange of procedures: the FCP would supply political ideas and the ideal militant, and we would supply specialized (avant-garde) work of which the FCP was cruelly in need. But it didn't work out. Because basically the cultural policy of the party was more cynical: on the one hand, to amuse a few researchers into "specific" questions (this was the period of Althusser and the famous duo "ideology/practice," the period of "theoretical practice"), and on the other hand, to infiltrate as many cultural institutions as possible—the "Maisons de la Culture"—and train cultural programmers, relays for diffusing exactly the same culture and the same relation to culture as the bourgeoisie.

Now the lack of political history on the part of the members of the *Cahiers* staff meant that they could not be satisfied with the position of a laboratory cut off from everything else, isolated researchers, academics. We had to have the experience (painful but inevitable for any French intellectual) of the real. And "real" here should be understood in the sense of "bad encounter, trauma" (Lacan). We had to emerge from cinephilia and go to the forefront of concrete tasks, new interlocutors, and so on. This kind of "old style" engagement was basically nothing but a sped-up repetition of what the engagements of French intellectuals close to the FCP have had to be since 1920. And this caricature-repetition was something we could only live out through the intermediary of little "Marxist-Leninist" groups who themselves, hysterically (like a son who reproaches his father for not being severe enough), were living out their mourning for Stalinist politics through a Chinese imagery. They supplied the group superego and taught us our political ABCs, and we supplied "specific work on the front of culture." Reference to the text of Mao (*Talks at the Yenan Forum on Art and Literature*) permitted us not to fall into the Trotskyist position, always lax and contemptuous toward art.

All this led to the "Cultural Front," composed of people like us who believed in politicizing culture and of leftist ex-militants who had understood perfectly their own political failure and had sought refuge on a "secondary front" where they could continue to intimidate others, while all they were really doing was negotiating their own survival (a few years later the most brilliant ones—like André Glucksmann—landed on their feet: journalism, literature, the pose of the "beautiful soul"). The result was: the artists were intimidated by the sheer weight of errors to be avoided and tasks to be undertaken, and the militants hid their lack of ideas and motivations behind an overly general discourse. This double block kept the Cultural Front from ever functioning. It evolved toward a growing interest in an area that had been long neglected: popular culture, the tradition of the carnivalesque, popular resistance, the popular memory, etc. The importance of Foucault can be seen here. A film like *Moi, Pierre Riviere . . .* (1976) would never have been made without the questions advanced by the Cultural Front. And so the link to cinema, after the detour of militancy, was reaffirmed.

Q: What did you learn in your study of militant films? Why all these imaginary voyages to liberated zones: territories, factories, prisons? Why is the sound so important in these films?

A: I would say that the interest in militant cinema is as much an effect of cinephilia as of the political superego. In *Cahiers*-cinephilia (the kind staked out by Bazin), there is a demand for risk, a certain "price" paid for the images. In militant cinema there is also this idea of risk. No longer a metaphysical risk, but a physical one: the risk of not being there at the right moment, the risk of not having sufficiently mastered the techniques (militant filmmakers are amateurs), legal risks (Belmont and *Histoires d'A*) and even the risk that the film, once it's been made and shown to the people it concerns (those who are fighting and who are not cinephiles), will not please them, will not help them, will not even be understood by them. Cinephilia is not just a special relationship to cinema; it is a relationship to the world through cinema. I remember what people like Luc Moullet and Godard said in the fifties: they had learned life from the cinema. And *Cahiers*-cinephilia, the cinephilia of the "Hitchcocko-Hawksian," is special in that it is a relationship—a perverse one—to the people, because the films of Hawks and Hitchcock at the time they were made were seen by the people and looked down on by cultivated persons. It's a relationship to the people through the forms which the people were subjected to and that they loved for a period of fifty years. When I started going to films, I was quite conscious in that this choice was bound up with my hatred for the theater. I hated, in theater, the social ritual, the assigning of seats in advance, the need to dress up, the parade of the bourgeoisie. In cinema—the permanent cinema—there is a black space that is fundamental, infinitely more mysterious. The sexual aspect—more specifically, the prostitutional aspect—is very bound up with this kind of cinephilia: look at Godard, Truffaut, Straub—it's all they talk about.

To get back to militant cinema, if we have moved away from it, it's because it failed to furnish this imaginary encounter with the people. Because these were nothing but sectarian films, made hastily by people who didn't care about cinema. (But there are exceptions: *Attica, Kafr kasem, The Promised Land.*) Today I think that militant films have the same defect as militant groups—they have the "mania of the All": each film is total, all-inclusive. A true militant cinema would be a cinema which militated as cinema, where one film would make you want to see a hundred others on the same subject. That kind of militant cinema would have to break with the ponderous models of commercial cinema. I've had friends who spent a year editing a 16-mm film about a strike at a printing plant, at the cost of unheard-of efforts and sacrifices, and the film had become totally incomprehensible by the time of its "release." The old militant cinema is bad because it includes no reflection on its economy. It's a big mess that doesn't think of itself as a big mess. It's too expensive, too long, too general, it takes up too much time in the lives of people who do it, and etc.

In our frequenting of militant films what we learned was, precisely, morality. That is, the way that the power which the camera represents (its capacity to intervene, interfere, extort, and provoke, to modify the situation which it grafts itself onto) is or is not thought about by the people who make the films. Paradoxically, films denouncing bourgeois power, injustice, and oppression are themselves totalitarian, nondialectical, laid on like veneer. And it is of course by means of the voice (the voiceover which is the principal resource of any edifying cinema) that this operation of the forcing of the image is effected. There comes a time when you realize that what's important is not agreeing or disagreeing with the explicit ideology of the film, but seeing how far someone is able to hold on to his ideas while at the same time respecting the audiovisual material he has produced. It's a dialectical movement: at first the filmmaker—guided by ideas, tastes, convictions—produces a certain material, but then the material teaches him things by resisting him (minimal materialism). Straub is the most coherent about this. There has to be a confirmation of what you already thought and an affirmation of something new to think.

Q: Has your attitude toward the Chinese films changed? You seem more inclined to criticize them now.

A: The Chinese films have never really interested us. And we've never vaunted them or even found them good. The only one I liked was *Rupture*. I had a strange feeling watching it: that in this dance film full of movement there was a mise-en-scène of the official ideology as naive, consistent, and total as in certain American films with, say, Debbie Reynolds. Europe, since its misadventures with fascism, no longer has the capacity to embody—in the form of puerile images—a moral consensus (good conscience). I think it's only imperialist countries that have the capacity to represent, in the imaginary, the moral consensus (the norm) and what menaces it (the blot, the scapegoat). It's only imperialist countries that can afford disaster films. And the Chinese films I've seen follow this model (like, on the other hand, Soviet films in the style of *Le prime*, coming twenty years after *Twelve Angry Men*).

Q: Why do you object to films like *Z* and *1900*? Are there any examples of good left-wing films being made for large audiences—in Italy, for example?

A: This has to do with the ideological and moral consensus in Europe today. *Z* and *1900* (and *Solemn Communion, The Question, The Red Poster, Exquisite Cadavers*, etc.) try to unify the biggest possible audience around a moderate imaginary of the Left. In order to not offend anyone, the unification is accomplished with metaphysical themes devoid of concrete history: in *1900* the revolts of the anarchist peasants of Emilia-Romagne at the beginning of the twentieth century become a kind of peasant upheaval that anticipates the "historical compromise" of today; in *The Red Poster* the actions of the francs-tireurs becomes an episode in the history of the FCP; in *The Question* the courageous attitude of a Communist militant (in disagreement with his party) becomes a kind of abstract courage to resist in general, etc.

So the unification always happens on the basis of a kind of amnesia and the desire to nourish this amnesia with beautiful images (the red flags of *1900*). This amnesia is a paradoxical but important phenomenon in the lives of Franco-Italian intellectuals: these cultures imbued with Marxism are cultures where the history of the workers' movement is not well known, because it is the parties who write history.

On the other hand, for people haunted by writing like the *Cahiers*, it's clear that writing divides, while images unify (through common fear or recognition). Today, in France, in cinema, you have to divide. And it can only be done by making contemporary films (and not moving evocations). For example, it's quite possible to make a Communist trade unionist a fictional character; it's what Godard does in *Comment ça va*. It's quite possible to film the suicide of a young person; it's what Bresson does in *The Devil, Probably*. But these are contemporary films, which do not surrender to the simulacrum of memory.

Why divide? The reason, I think, is sociological. The cinema is less and less a popular form of expression and more and more recognized as "art" by the middle class. Its instructional function has terminated (television has perhaps replaced it). It is seen more and more by an increasingly enlightened petit-bourgeois audience and tends to play the role that theater used to play: a place of prestige, debates, parades. It's not at all clear that this new audience is better than the old. It is, at any

rate, more adrift, less spontaneous. And around the films a whole apparatus of language has been established (critics, publicists, press attachés,
the university), which means that there is no longer any freshness in the
way they are received.

As for the question of whether there are any good left-wing films
"for large audiences," it seems to me that this question divides into two
parts: (1) I think that films with "burning political themes" never go very
far, are superficial because they are too general. They aren't political films
at all, but films expressing the politics of the union of the Left in France
(and in Italy), vague and reformist, imprecise and unifying, right-thinking.
These are films that could be called "operational," which is to say that
they are immediately taken and digested as films illustrating the politics
of the united Left. Their mode of functioning is closer to an advertising
poster than to any work with the signifying material. (2) Conversely, in
all these films you can see a veritable fascination with power conceived
as manipulation (one of the big problems of the European cinema is to
create a successful stereotype of the "leftist cop"—cf., Francesco Rosi,
Yves Boisset). There does exist a tradition of comic films, mainly in Italy,
where questions of class and power are not ennobled and mystified but
on the contrary rendered trivial and laughable, common. For me, the
only good "left-wing films" have a carnivalesque dimension (cf., Mikhail
Bakhtin) that is completely missing in French films, but still present in
films by Dino Risi (*A Difficult Life* [1961]) or Luigi Comencini (*Lo Scopone
Scientifico* [1972], *The Adventures of Pinocchio* [1972]).

Q: The magazine has been changing again—a casual observer might
say, "returning to normal": more stills, articles about all kinds of films,
references to old American films . . . What is happening now? What
hasn't changed?

A: What hasn't changed? There are bits and pieces of an answer in
everything I've said. There is a moment when you are led to renounce
the "passion of the All" and when you want to elucidate (theoretically as
well) on the basis of what fundamental experience you feel authorized
to write about the cinema, and also to write in the direction of other
people who come out of other experiences in the cinema.

Q: Why are you getting interested in "underground" films?

A: When the French film industry has gone under, there will be a place
for an underground cinema in France. As has already happened in England. Up until now the big difference between France and the US was

this: there is no bridge between underground films and the industry in the US, while there has always been one in France. In France there has always been the possibility of making a difficult film and commercializing it, even if only a little bit. The crisis (the end) of the film industry has very curious consequences: there is an acceleration of all the processes. For example, twenty years ago there were French filmmakers *de série* with no talent, but a lot of know-how, who made one film a year. This was *la qualité française*. These people no longer exist. The big companies are perfectly ready to offer enormous possibilities to young talents who come from the avant-garde. The example of Chantal Akerman is proof of this. So in France there is, for the moment, a big mix, rather than segregation. It seems to me that segregation has existed for a long time in the US because of patronage and the recognition of the function of art as unproductive expenditure. We're interested in the underground as something that will one day become a reality in France, a "domestic" cinema. Occasionally it happens that we see magnificent films—the films of Stephen Dwoskin and Jackie Raynal. There are no doubt many others. What's much less interesting is the critical discussion of these films. Probably the position of the critic is no longer justified at all in the case of these films, because these films don't need mediation, since most of them play directly on primary processes. It's one big difference between them and the European avant-garde (the one that interests us most: Godard, Straub), where any play on primary processes (on perception) has real impact only if it's also brought to bear on elements of thought, of the signified.

Q: Women's films: by women, or simply about women, about female sexuality . . . What are these films showing us? Why are they so violent?

A: Since this has to do with cinema, and therefore with the eye and ear, it would be better to talk about how cinema *au féminin* (made by men eventually) makes us rediscover what the imperialism of the eye (it's men who are voyeurs) had repressed: other modes of montage of impulses where what is seen and what is heard change perspective. For example, I said that militant cinema foundered on the question of the voiceover (the protected voice)—well, just as we saw feminism develop from the decomposition of the Marxist-Leninist militant political groups, so from the failure of the voiceover we have seen a whole adventure of the voice develop, an adventure that has been conducted *au féminin* (Duras, of course, Akerman, Godard, Marco Ferreri). This is also one of the limits of cinephilia: rediscovering the voice of the mother heard from the interior of the body, before vision. The feminine limit of cinephilia.

Suddenly I think the visual element is totally changed: in the three films by women that have impressed me the most—*Deux fois* (1968), *Je Tu Il Elle* (1974), *Le camion* (1977)—there is something extraordinary: the way the actress-auteurs are on both sides of the camera, without this having any consequences. There is a calm violence that points up the difference with the male actor-auteur. Look at Lewis or Chaplin: for them, passing from one side of the camera to the other means risking travesty, feminization, and playing with this risk. Nothing of the sort with women.

Q: You've been talking openly about "cinephilia" again—the hardcore variety: loving Tourneur, De Mille, the late films of Fritz Lang . . . Do you see a virtue in it?

A: That is a very special kind of cinephilia. It isn't the whole of American cinema that is in play; it's a part, often the most despised: Lang, De Mille, Tourneur, Ray . . . I remember in 1964 we saw George Cukor and confided to him that *Wind Across the Everglades* (1958) was one of the most beautiful American films. He broke out in a peal of laughter where all the contempt he had for this little film could be read. We were very wounded, but we have never changed our minds. In American cinema I think that it is easier to see, as it recedes, what interested us: always the excess of writing over ideology, and not the reverse (Huston, Delmer Daves, William Wyler, today Altman). It's clearly a paradox: because this led us to take an interest in filmmakers who were not exactly left-wing. This excess of writing over ideology is only possible in the framework of a prosperous industry and a real consensus. This occurred in Hollywood until sometime in the fifties; a little in France before the war; in Italy; in Egypt and India, no doubt; in Germany and England before the war. Outside this industrial framework (industry + craftsmanship), it's the reverse that happens: excess of ideology over writing. Look at the countries of the Third World, including China. This cinephilia is historically dated: the terrain from which it sprang is this mixture of industry and craftsmanship. It's not possible to revive it. But in the precision of the writing of Tourneur, Lang, or De Mille, there is an exigency that continues with Godard, Straub, Robert Kramer, Wim Wenders, Akerman, Jean-Claude Biette, Benoit Jacquot.

Q: You said recently that the filmmakers who interest you now are all moralists. It's strange to hear words like "morality" and "tragedy" again. Why have they become so necessary now?

A: What is a filmmaker if not someone who, at one point or another, says: I don't have the right to film that, or to film that like that? And who believes that it's up to him to make that decision, that nobody else can make it. One of the texts that particularly marked me when I was a young reader of the *Cahiers* was a piece by Rivette on Gillo Pontecorvo's *Kapò* (1960). He described a scene in the film, the death of Emmanuelle Riva near the barbed wire. Pontecorvo—at the moment of his character's death—did a camera movement in order to reframe the face in the corner of the screen and make a prettier shot. Rivette wrote: the man who did this traveling shot is worthy of the most profound contempt. More and more, there are two kinds of filmmakers: those who have the feeling that "everything has been filmed" and consider it their mission to work with images that are already there, like a painter adding an extra coat of paint. And then there are those who are always aware that what they are filming also exists outside the film, is not just filmic raw material. Morality begins there. Always the idea of risk.

More generally, morality becomes a living question again because everyone has experienced the fact that there exists no morality for someone who thinks in terms of power (to be seized, held on to, or dreamed of), and therefore no morality on the Left or in Marxism. Morality is something individual; it's natural that returning to a certain *politique des auteurs* should reintroduce morality.

Q: What is television doing to our minds? What has Godard been doing to television?

A: It's a great mystery. I think that television is not taken seriously by anyone. Neither by those who make it (and who are all haunted by the cinema they can't make, which means that the possibilities of video have been explored ridiculously little and that one continues to produce in France horrible "dramas," very expensive, neither cinema, nor theater, nor television). Nor by those who are subjected to it. TV is a cool medium from which people do not expect any truth. Its principal impact resides in the fact that it becomes a background noise that keeps you from hearing other sounds. The catastrophic conceptions which would have us believe in television's power of stupefaction are very complacently exaggerated. What Godard has done to television is indeed considerable. He has demonstrated how it functions, as always, by the absurd, by doing it too much. He has shown that the simple fact of letting someone talk for one hour at a stretch is already enough to break the hum, whatever is being said. He has shown that television, far from making people passive, demands from them on the contrary to produce a kind of work that the journalists don't produce.

Q: What about Jacques Rivette? You haven't spoken of him in a long time.

A: We have been very unfair to Rivette.

Q: What do you see now in American film that interests you? Why don't you like Robert Altman? Have you seen *Star Wars* (1977), etc.?

A: Robert Kramer, John Cassavetes, Paul Newman, Stephen Dwoskin, Monte Hellman, among others. As for Altman, I have the disagreeable feeling that he is a little master, very at ease in the notation of naturalistic detail, who has taken it into his head to rival Bergman or Antonioni. What is very unpleasant in his cinema is that the only thing he asks us to believe in is the intelligence of the auteur. The auteur is always more intelligent than his guinea pigs, he always knows more than they do, but his knowledge is always protected. You don't find this contempt—I purposely cite very lofty auteurs—in Bresson or Antonioni, because these are people who could care less about what one has to look like one is thinking in order to appear intelligent (that is to say, "non-dupe," in Lacanian jargon). The films of Jerry Schatzberg, Scorsese, Coppola, among others, do represent a respectable and somewhat academic tradition. But I still have the impression that there has been no real innovation, for almost twenty years now, in this cinema.

Notations to "The Tinkerers"

Robin Wood's writing on Godard and Comolli is to be found in two issues of *Film Comment*, January–February and May–June 1977. He died in 2009.

The quotation by Claude Lévi-Strauss is from *The Savage Mind (La pensée sauvage)* (London: Weidenfeld & Nicolson, 1996).

The crocodile story is from Serge Leclaire's *Démasquer le reel: un essai sur l'objet en psychanalyse* (Paris: Éditions du Seuil, 1971), 124.

According to Bazin, "in *L'Afrique vous parle* a Negro is eaten by a crocodile." André Bazin, *What Is Cinema? I*, trans. Hugh Gray (Berkeley: University of California Press, 1967), 155.

For qualities Socrates distrusted in writing, see Plato, *Phaedrus*, trans. James H. Nichols Jr. (Ithaca: Cornell University Press, 1998).

Fereydoun Hoveyda (1924–2006) was a diplomat and thinker; from 1971 to 1979 he was Iranian ambassador to the United Nations.

Salador was a salad oil, and Daney's article was a semiotic analysis of a TV ad for Salador like the semiotic analyses in Roland Barthes's *Mythologies* (Paris: Éditions du Seuil, 1957).

For the application of Althusser's argument, see the translation of a manifesto by Jean-Louis Comolli and Jean Narboni, "Cinema/Ideology/Criticism," *Screen* 12, no. 1 (Spring 1971): 27–38.

Oudart's seminal Lacanian article, "La suture," had not been translated when this piece was written in 1977, but it appeared as "Cinema and Screen," trans. Kari Hanet, *Screen* 18, no. 4 (1977): 35–47.

On imaginary relations, see "French Freud," *Yale French Studies*, no. 48 (1972): 191, and the dictionary translated from Jean Laplanche and J.-B. Pontalis's *Vocabulaire de la Psychanalyse* (Paris: Presses universitaires de France, 1967). This issue of *Yale French Studies* contains a translation of Lacan's seminar on Poe's "The Purloined Letter." Other Lacan essays have been translated in Jacques Ehrmann, ed., *Structuralism* (Garden City, NY: Anchor, 1970), and in Anthony Wilden's *The Language of the Self* (Baltimore: Johns Hopkins University Press, 1974).

On portable cinematheques, see *Cahiers du cinéma* 257 (1975): 6–21; *Cahiers du cinéma* 262–263 (1976): 60–61; and *Cahiers du cinéma* 265 (1976): 267.

The book that introduced me to Jacques Derrida's writings ("cited" by Godard in *Le gai savoir* [1968]) was *De la grammatologie* (On grammatology) (Paris: Éditions de Minuit, 1967).

Notations to the Interview

Serge Daney programmed a five-day film series at the Bleecker Street Cinema—Godard's *Ice et ailleurs* (1976), *Numéro deux* (1975), and *Comment ça va* (1976); Wenders's *Kings of the Road* (1976); Chantal Akerman's *News from Home* (1977); Benoit Jacquot's *L'Assassin musicien* (1976), Jean-Marie Straub and Danièle Huillet's *Fortini/Cani* (1976); and Rene Allio's *I, Pierre Rivière . . .* (1976)—and the theater published a special issue to promote the event. I've deleted a few questions that relate only to this series. The issue also included an introduction by me, which detailed the changes the *Cahiers* went through in the late 1960s and early 1970s, and a translation of Daney's essay on 1970s Godard.

Charles Belmont and Marielle Issartel's *Histoires d'A* (1974) was a film championing women's right to an abortion.

Boustrophedon is line-by-line notation where the writing direction alternates.

3

Serge Daney (1944–1992)

I MET SERGE IN 1977, WHEN Jackie Raynal and I organized the first
Semaine des Cahiers in New York. I interviewed him by letter for a
booklet Jackie and Sid Geffen had commissioned me to write on the
recent history of the *Cahiers* (see chapter 2 in this volume) and met him
for the first time when he arrived with the films for the Semaine (such
as *Numéro deux* [1975], *Ici et ailleurs* [1976], and *Fortini/Cani* [1976]), which
I ended up boycotting, for personal and political reasons.

Serge was the first *Cahiers* editor to set foot on American soil since
the start of the Vietnam War, as far as I know, and certainly the first I
had met in person, so we did a lot of talking while he was in New York,
mostly in English, which he spoke perfectly. "I like to talk to a man who

likes to talk," I said to him at one point, quoting Sidney Greenstreet's compliment to Humphrey Bogart in one of my favorite films, and it was a compliment that suited Serge to a T. After he left, Jackie and I showed her film *Deux fois* (1968) at a nearby university he had spent a few days at and found the faculty member who had organized the local Semaine in the middle of a nervous breakdown brought on by all the questions Serge had raised in his mind during his visit.

Often our conversations in New York took a confrontational turn, because I had been reading the *Cahiers* since 1965 and had a few questions of my own. I particularly remember one long conversation in a cab rocketing through the night along Broadway, during which I thrust a still from *Frenzy* (1972) under his nose: a close-up of a strangled woman, her tongue protruding from the side of her mouth. "Why didn't you talk about *this*?" I demanded, and Serge replied, with unflappable good humor, "It's *hard* to talk about that!" Later in the same conversation he asked me to define the real or possible link between the American independent cinema and Hollywood, and I answered fiercely, "Me!" Before going back to Paris he invited me to write for the *Cahiers*, emphasizing the absolute importance of having something coming in from America once a month, "like a machine." It was a dream that was never to be realized, and I'm sure he was aware of the irony of the situation, and relished it, even as he said the words. I won't rehearse the story of my turbulent early years as the magazine's correspondent in LA, except to say that they presented Serge, back in Paris, with many more opportunities to demonstrate his generosity, sangfroid, and gallows humor, which he had already given ample proof of by picking for the job someone with no journalistic, cinematic, or academic connections, who looked as if he had been living in the subway. But social pretense was never Serge's long suit, even years later, when he had become a great man.

To me he was a great man before I ever met him. I had cut my cinematic teeth on Hawks's late period, and the greatest joy I ever experienced as a reader of the *Cahiers* was picking up the July 1971 issue in Rizzoli's Bookstore on Fifth Avenue and discovering Serge's essay on *Rio Lobo* (1970), "*Rio Lobo*: Vieillesse du Même." At the time I had to spend a year reading Lacan and Derrida to be able to understand it; I reread it again yesterday, and I still consider it the best thing Serge ever wrote. Describing as neurotic symptoms the "tics and obsessions" by which the most perverse and self-effacing auteur never failed to signal his presence to his hierophants, "Vieillesse du Même" answered all the questions that had come crowding into my mind the afternoon I discovered Hawks, and cinema, in a suburban movie theater where *Red Line 7000* (1965) was making a brief appearance. I also believe that it was with that essay, less well known than the famous collective texts on Ford and Sternberg that preceded it, that a page of intellectual history was turned, and an era came lucidly and unsentimentally to a close.

Someone who first read Serge in the pages of *Libé* would have a different view of him, but for me he was an older intellectual brother who became a cinephile during the same period I did, when the great directors were making their last films and the classical cinema was dying. (His first essay, he told me when I visited him in Paris last fall, was a defense of *Rio Bravo* [1959] written in the pages of an exam book he despaired of filling with answers to questions about geography, a subject on which he was later to become quite an expert. It was published in the first issue of *Visages du cinéma*, a short-lived magazine he edited with Louis Skorecki.) After championing the dying gasps of that cinema, he and his comrades, with well-concealed mixed emotions, deconstructed it, and then during the most beautiful phase of that generation of *Cahiers* writers, from 1977 to 1983, they buried it.

Having accomplished that, Serge very sensibly left the magazine to begin his new life at *Libé*, writing about film and, increasingly, about other things. Because I wasn't a subscriber to *Libé* I had to read him in book form when volumes of his collected essays (*La rampe*, etc.), which he faithfully sent me in America, began to appear. For me those writings, less systematic as a rule than his major *Cahiers* essays, are conversational riffs set down on paper, recording one out of every fifty space probes he was able to send off in all directions on any subject chance or a friend might propose. They consoled me then, and they console me now, for all the conversations distance kept us from having. *Trafic* gave us a chance to work together again and was the occasion for my last visit with him in October, which I prolonged by several ruinous phone calls after my return to Los Angeles, also on the pretext of business.

I was asked to write about my friendship with Serge and his intellectual influence on me, and I see I have not really done either. It never occurred to me that I had been under his influence, much less that I should examine the extent of it; that means it must have been immense, and I'm the worst person to write about it. As for friendship, that is something that "lives in the details," particularly when both people are taciturn about expressing their affection, so that the friendship becomes a series of little symbolic acts that would not mean anything to a third party. Serge was very private about some things, and I wouldn't feel right talking about the funny inscription he wrote in my copy of *La rampe*; or the very funny thing he invariably said, in English, when we were saying goodbye after one of our rare encounters; or the touching proof of his generosity, which he gave me the last time he said it. I can only repeat the message I sent to the memorial service on June 16th: Serge changed my life when he invited me to write for the *Cahiers*, but the greatest gift he gave me was his friendship. It was a gift he gave freely to all kinds of people all over the world, demanding nothing in return but what was easiest for us to give—our love, and our fascinated attention.

Notation

This obituary appeared in the *Cahiers du cinéma* 456 (July–August 1992): 15–16 at the time of Daney's death.

Directors Who Started in Silents

4

Allan Dwan

The Cliff and the Flume

Dedicated to the memory of Sol Wurtzel, Edward Small, Herbert J. Yates, and Benedict Bogeaus, who supplied the frame.

IN HIS EULOGY FOR ALLAN DWAN, Jean-Claude Biette called him "a great storyteller" and "a great poet of space." An anecdote Dwan told Peter Bogdanovich about his early days shows how these compliments are linked: scouting for ideas with his cast and crew near Lakeside, California,

---

This chapter originally appeared in the online journal *Senses of Cinema* 28 (October 2003).

the young director saw a cliff and filmed a fight that ended with the hero throwing the villain over it. Still in search of a story, he then saw a flume "like a great bridge," which carried water from one ranch to another. Result: a two-reel melodrama in which the villain poisons the flume to kill his neighbor's cattle and is punished by being thrown off the cliff at the end of the film.

The story has an archetypal quality. On the one hand, the setting (the cliff) inspires the action that takes place in it (without determining it: other actions could easily have been envisioned); on the other hand, a division of space (the two ranches) and the passageway that links them (the flume) generate a story to justify the action (*The Poisoned Flume* [1911]). These narrative paradigms could also be used separately, as we can see from the plots of two other Dwans: *The Love Route* (1914): "A new railroad line disrupts a girl's ranch"; *Cheating Cheaters* (1919): "Living side by side, two groups of crooks impersonate rich people, each planning to rob the other."

Adjoining spaces are the most common spatial paradigm for Dwan's plots: a bank and a barber shop (*Man to Man* [1930]), two airfields (*Look Who's Laughing* [1941]), two hotels (*Here We Go Again* [1942]), neighboring farms (*Rebecca of Sunnybrook Farm* [1938]), buildings that look out onto the same courtyard (*Calendar Girl* [1947]), a house and a stable (*I Dream of Jeannie* [1952]), two silver mines (*Belle Le Grande* [1951]), two ranches (*Cattle Queen of Montana* [1954]), two savage tribes (*Enchanted Island* [1958]), competing saloons that face each other on a rowdy street in Tombstone (*Frontier Marshal* [1939]). Less frequently, the story can arise from a connection between two places, notably in *Rendezvous with Annie* (1946), where a soldier on an army base in England secretly goes AWOL and impregnates his wife in New Jersey, then has to convince the world that he is the father of her child.

Dwan the engineer was naturally attracted to stories about building bridges between places separated by geography: the Holland Tunnel in *High Air* (1955), the B-29 long-range bomber in *The Wild Blue Yonder* (1951), and the Suez Canal in *Suez* (1938), whose hero is told by a fortune teller that his destiny is to "dig ditches." Those words turn out to be both an ironic prophecy of the hero's role as architect of the canal and a metaphor for the often dubious political machinations that will make it possible. At first Louis Napoleon refuses to finance the project for fear that it will cause the Red Sea to flood the Mediterranean, inundating the port cities of the Mediterranean basin, and that is just what happens—metaphorically speaking—when the misguided hero seeks to make peace between the National Assembly and Louis, who seizes the opportunity to arrest his opponents and proclaim himself Emperor, after which he agrees to finance the canal.

On the other hand, Dwan was not particularly inspired by the paradigm of the voyage (*Around the World* [1943], *Escape to Burma* [1955]), unless it was joined to a second paradigm: the border that has to be crossed in *The River's Edge* (1957) or the two-pronged retreat in *Hold Back the Night* (1956), which looks on a map like the high-angle shot of a pursuit along forking trails in *Tennessee's Partner* (1955). In *Black Sheep* (1935), a story he concocted to restart his directing career in the early 1930s, the characters travel from Cherbourg to New York on a ship with separate levels for first- and second-class passengers, two paradigms that combine with a third—a stolen necklace whose possessor can leave the ship only by passing through Customs—to produce a delightful comedy-drama of crisscrossing destinies that come together and resolve themselves on the docks of New York. (It's too bad Dwan wasn't able to make his film of Thornton Wilder's *Bridge of San Luis Rey*.)

Not all of Dwan's films grow out of spatial paradigms, but it could be argued that the best ones do. Someone was trying to sketch in a spatial situation at the beginning of *Northwest Outpost* (1947), for example, but not much came of it. Perhaps that is why the mad stew of elements failed to cohere, whereas the equally outré *Woman They Almost Lynched* (1953) is one of Dwan's best films, in part because of its spatial premise: during the Civil War, a town bisected by the border between North and South is kept neutral by a wealthy matron whose control of the region's lead mines give her power over the warring sides and the town, where she imposes an iron law of nonviolence, enforced by frequent lynchings.

What starts off as a parody of Ford becomes increasingly perverse: the repression of violence creates a second division, perpendicular to the first, between the domain of men (a saloon) and the domain of women (the mining company, where the matron holds sway). Then this bizarre variation on the standard Hollywood displacement from politics to sex is given an even more perverse twist when the saloon is inherited by a woman, leading to the famous showdown between female gunslingers and the heroine's near-lynching.

Dwan's spatial imagination sometimes took him to strange places: in *Sailor's Lady* (1940) an enlisted man comes home to get married, only to discover that his wife has adopted a baby and bought a house in a neighborhood inhabited solely by the families of naval officers. When her fiancé's rowdy friends sabotage a party with the brass in attendance, the young woman retaliates by planting the baby on their battleship as it sails off to engage in maritime war games.

More dizzying variations are played on the disjunction between "container" and "contained" during the first ten minutes of *One Mile from Heaven* (1937). Sent on a wild goose chase by her competitors, a blond girl reporter finds herself in an all-black neighborhood, where her attention is attracted by the dazzling skills of a tap dancer who is playing Pied Piper to the neighborhood children. One of the children is white and very blond, too, even though her mother is black. (This enigma supplies the basis for the plot.) She happens to be carrying a birdcage with a cat in it. (Nothing is ever said about this.) A final surprise: when the tap dancer puts on his coat, he turns out to be a very impressive-looking policeman.

Chinese box construction, a more traditional use of the container/contained paradigm, sets the stage for *The Inside Story* (1948), which is told in flashback inside a bank vault inside a small town that was almost destroyed by the Great Depression, inside a devastated country that we see in nightmarish visions superimposed over a close-up of the story-teller. During those dark days, we learn, a thousand dollars came to town and was placed in a safe, only to escape and circulate from character to character, after which it left as it had come, like the hero of a western, having put the town on the road to recovery.

Turning to the "cliff" part of Dwan's method, his use of settings: Biette's description of him as a poet of space harks back, I believe, to Eric Rohmer's 1948 article "Le cinema, un art de l'espace," which distinguishes Chaplin's use of cinema to express psychological states from Keaton's use of it for, literally, the beauty of the gesture, inscribed within "a completely-filled rectangular space occupying a relatively restricted portion of the visual field." Among the examples of films containing "a sense of space that many avant-garde films might envy," Rohmer cites "the films of Douglas Fairbanks," with whom Dwan collaborated five times during the silent era.

But the fact that Dwan and Fairbanks were making a different kind of film than Chaplin (cf., the anecdote about Chaplin's joke on the set of *Robin Hood* [1922]) doesn't mean that they, like the decadent sculptor in *Manhandled* (1924), sought an art of "pure plasticity." During the first half of *Robin Hood*, where gestures are stripped of psychological significance by immense spaces that dwarf the human figure, Fairbanks is weighed down by armor and ritual. In the second half, when he takes refuge in the forest with his outlaws, he liberates the castle from its usurping master with the kind of extravagant acrobatics that made *The Mark of Zorro* (Fred Niblo, 1920) a joy from start to finish. But in *The Iron Mask* (1929), Fairbanks's swan song, Nature is absent, and the shadowy maze of lavish sets in which D'Artagnan and his comrades battle a usurper impart a hollow ring to the title card announcing that one character after another has died "for the glory of France."

Dwan remade *Robin Hood* in the sound era with Shirley Temple: the heroine of *Heidi* (1937) is taken from the mountaintop where she lives with her grandfather and imprisoned in a great house in the midst of a great city, where she heals a crippled child despite the intrigues of yet another evil usurper, Fraulein Rottenmeier. (Outside the walls of the "castle," three blasts on a coachman's horn, which Heidi mistakes for the horn of Peter the Goat Boy, recall the signal Alan-a-Dale blows before Fairbanks is rescued at the end of *Robin Hood*.) An organ-grinder's monkey performs Fairbanks's acrobatics, and Heidi herself repeats his famous slide down an immense tapestry when she slides down the banister of the great house to make her getaway.

The poles of this story were reversed in Temple's swan song at Fox, the delightful *Young People* (1940), where a family of vaudevillians from the big city who have retired to a Maine village are treated badly by the villagers, until they finally succeed in imposing their optimistic perspective on these rural reactionaries. Besides giving Temple the only chance she ever had to play herself, *Young People* prepared the way for *Driftwood* (1947), the beautiful film Dwan made at Republic with Natalie Wood as a saintly orphan named Jenny. After the death of her preacher grandfather, Jenny leaves Bullfrog Springs, the ghost town where she grew up, for Panbucket, a conservative village she calls "Sodom and Gomorrah" until her uncompromising truthfulness transforms it into "Heaven."

It seems that Dwan was not the Rousseauist he is sometimes mistaken for—it would certainly be hard to hang that label on *Pearl of the South Pacific* (1955), where the script's paean to Man in the state of Nature is constantly undercut by the garish artifice of John Alton's colors and Van Nest Polglase's sets. Just before the end Dwan turned that turkey on its head in *Enchanted Island*, which comes as close as anyone dared in 1958 to retelling Herman Melville's *Typee*: a refugee from civilization living among Tahitian savages discovers that the savages have killed his best friend, that he is their prisoner, and that they are cannibals (only hinted at in the film). Made on location in Mexico—like his last film, *The Most Dangerous Man Alive* (1962), for which there was no money to build sets—*Enchanted Island* returned Dwan to the conditions in which he made his first two-reelers, which spawned an art where themes like Nature and Civilization were less important than the plastic invention that playing variations on them made possible.

Given Dwan's formal concerns, it is at first surprising to see how often maps in his films—scale models of the narrative terrain—play the role of the "bad object" in the Lacanian sense (Gertie's garter, Mabel's slip,

the Queen's necklace in *The Three Musketeers* [1939], the pearl necklace
in *Black Sheep*), one whose mere possession stigmatizes the possessor:
the woman with the map in *Woman They Almost Lynched*, for example,
is presumed to be a traitor, while the man with the map in *Tennessee's
Partner* is a murderer.

Moreover, maps don't always clarify the action—the one used to
plan the first holdup in *Montana Belle* (1952) is noticeably inaccurate.
We never see the aerial map consulted by Edgar Bergen in *Look Who's
Laughing*—only a view of the terrain below that is as unintelligible as
the aerial views in *The Wild Blue Yonder*. (Those extreme high angles turn
out to be as useless to the B-29 crews as they are to us—bombing from
twenty-five thousand feet up, our heroes are missing more targets than
they hit.) *Escape to Burma* opens with a map, but before we can read it
the camera moves in on a drawing of the palace of Sakar, then dissolves
to show us the throne room, in the same way that the perplexing aerial
view of Wistful Vista in *Look Who's Laughing* dissolves to give us our first
look at the inside of Fibber McGee's house.

Instead of a map, *Belle Le Grande* opens with an extreme wide-angle
shot of a courtroom seen from the jury box that turns out on close
inspection to be a painting. Seconds later, a long, gorgeously composed
dolly shot follows the devastated heroine, just out of jail, as she slowly
makes her way along a street that leads to a friend's home. Transitions
like these that endow a flat image with depth enact the struggle at the
very heart of Dwan's cinema, which is filled with settings whose topography we know intimately (the house in *The Gorilla* [1939], the tennis
court in *Suez* [1938]), where windows and doors always open on a busy
world beyond. The town in *Frontier Marshal* (1939) is all one set, and at
the end of the film, when Dwan dollies in on Doc Halliday's tombstone,
he takes care to put a tiny wagon train heading west in the background
of the shot.

Maps are "bad objects" because they threaten the illusion of depth,
as in *Hold Back the Night*, one of the few films where a map actually
works—the whole first part is played against undisguised back projections,
so that the long march of the retreating marines is also a difficult journey
back to three-dimensional space. Similarly, in *Getting Gertie's Garter* (1945),
the actors are grouped in two-dimensional compositions until night falls,
when modeling with light and shadow (Dwan's preferred palette) begins
to create dramatic perspectives symbolizing the growing complexity of
the action. The shift is marked by one of those 180-degree cuts Dwan
frequently uses to show the image's backside, like the photograph in *Look
Who's Laughing* that shows its subjects' backs when you turn it around.

Dwan nonetheless flirted with the temptation to transform the image into a map in *Friendly Enemies* (1942), a jingoistic World War I drama he was offered while waiting to make *Brewster's Millions* (1945). When he filmed (in nine days!) this story of two German immigrants, one of whom sides with America, the other with Germany, he replicated the form of their quarrels, always shown in two-shots, by grouping all his characters in symmetrical compositions until the third act, when the loyal German learns that his son has joined the American army. After that the groupings become unbalanced, until an explosion of war images restores the harmony that reigned initially despite conflicting loyalties in the last shot.

Dwan subsequently adapted this formal invention in *Brewster's Millions* to portray the ironic fate of a man who has two months to spend a million dollars. Here the balance between asymmetrical compositions (the desired state) and symmetrical ones (the state to be avoided) is ever shifting, as the hero's attempts to practice what Georges Bataille calls the general economy (unproductive expenditure) are repeatedly brought into line with the restrained economy (a return on one's investment) which his fiancée and friends consider normal. *Brewster's Millions* is a film that aspires to the void. Its first shot (a black servant visually erased by the soap he has applied to a window) gives way to a film that gradually fills up with proliferating bodies, until they are all eliminated in the last shot: another empty frame.

Watching a minimalist experiment like *Friendly Enemies* sensitizes us to the spatial art Dwan puts to subtler uses in films like *Brewster's Millions* or the anti-McCarthy western *Silver Lode* (1954), where an image that moves in and out of two-dimensionality is used to graph shifting allegiances and lines of flight in a small town whose leading citizen has been accused of murder by a self-styled marshal from a town two hundred miles away. (The townspeople have no way of knowing the truth because the telegraph line connecting the towns has been cut.)

Dwan had fifty years of unequaled productivity to explore the properties of an art where the rectangle of the screen can create the illusion of a world that exists and continues beyond the edges of the frame. In *Heidi* a cut takes us from the household singing "Silent Night" to the bustling street outside, where everyone seems to be singing the same song—a lovely example of the kind of sidelong glance that earned Dwan his reputation as a contemplative filmmaker. But violence can also be disclosed by a pan—through the wall of a house, for example, where a woman is singing to her baby, and into the crowded street outside, which is suddenly thrown into tumult by an eruption of gunfire (*Frontier Marshal*).

Even more disconcerting, a sudden pan in *Abroad with Two Yanks* (1944) reveals a mirror in the off-space that reflects our two heroes (already in drag) as grotesquely distorted anamorphic images (a device Dwan first exploited in *Stage Struck* [1925] with Gloria Swanson).

The dangers lurking just beyond the frame that menace the magic rectangle (which Louis Seguin has explored in *L'espace du cinéma*) are summed up in a very late and very weird western, *The Restless Breed* (1957). It begins with an exposition scene that makes considerable use of the most useless map in all of Dwan's cinema. "Our investigators' report has given us a very graphic picture," says the character who is handling the exposition, pointing emphatically at three spots on the map that have nothing to do with anything. His confident assertion is then undermined by a series of flashbacks which introduce us to the setting of the film, a little town consisting mostly of windows, gates, and doors, that is held together only by the gazes of the characters. They spend an inordinate amount of time spying on one another, but to no avail—the town never escapes from the quagmire of spatial incoherence into which it has been plunged by that first "graphic" account. *The Restless Breed* is the cinematic equivalent of Mallarmé's *Un coup de dés* (A throw of the dice), where the text is dismembered by the spaces between the words, and yet Dwan, like Mallarmé—having finished the work of fifty years with this astonishing film—might also say, looking back, that "nothing will have taken place except [the] place."

Notations

Marie Anne Guerin's eulogy for Jean-Claude Biette, "L'arrêt sur mémoire," appeared in *Trafic* 47 (Autumn 2003): 16–24.

Eric Rohmer's *Le cinema, un art de l'espace* is reprinted in his book *Le gout de la beauté*, translated into English by Carol Volk as *The Taste for Beauty* (Cambridge: Cambridge University Press, 1989). Rohmer's observation about the "completely-filled rectangular space" is found on page 21 and the comment on examples of films containing "a sense of space" is found on page 27.

Charlie Chaplin's joke on the set of *Robin Hood* was to emerge from Dwan's mammoth castle set and put down a cat and a bowl of milk.

Readers can find the Mallarmé poem at https://en.wikipedia.org/wiki/Un_coup_de_d%C3%A9s_jamais_n%27abolira_le_hasard_(Mallarm%C3%A9). Jean-Marie Straub and Danièle Huillet filmed *Toute révolution est un coup de dés* (1977) in the Père Lachaise Cemetery in Paris. Various people stationed around the cemetery spoke lines from the poem, and they filmed them and cut them together in the order of the poem on the page.

5

Raoul Walsh

Objective, Burma!

O<small>BJECTIVE, *B*URMA!</small> (1945) was the last of four war films Raoul Walsh made with Errol Flynn during World War II. Although it is by far the most realistic of the Walsh-Flynn wartime collaborations, the British press was outraged that it portrayed a band of American commandos carrying out the raid that set the stage for the Allied invasion of Burma, a predominantly British campaign that was still fresh in their

---

This chapter originally appeared in the online journal *Senses of Cinema* 28 (October 2003).

memory when the film was released in the UK after the close of the war—so much so that Warner Bros. withdrew it from UK distribution shortly after it opened. *Objective, Burma!* was not the first American film to indulge in this kind of propaganda—one Gallup poll showed that many Americans believed the US had won the war single-handedly, and movies were the single largest source of misinformation about world affairs in 1945, as television is today.

That being said, the film's distortions seem less important now than its accurate portrayal of combat. The War Department, in vetting the script, did everything they could to make the film realistic, and while the filmmakers ignored their larger strictures (for example, warnings that there were relatively few Americans in Burma, and no paratroopers at all), the physical details were done right for once—so much so that Israel's Haganah used *Objective, Burma!* as a training film for its own commandos after the war. American critics praised the uncompromising realism of Walsh's direction, and the screenplay, written by Ranald MacDougall and two future members of the Hollywood Ten, Alvah Bessie (original story) and MacDougall's cowriter, Lester Cole. However, the numerous points where the film diverges from the script are instructive.

As one would expect from the presence of Cole and Bessie, the shooting script Walsh was handed was toting a fair amount of ideological baggage. For example, the savage indictment of Japanese torturers by the reporter Williams (Henry Hull), when he cries out at the film's darkest moment that the Japanese enemy should be "wiped off the face of the earth," may originally have been intended to evoke the Allied discovery of the death camps in Europe as well. But while Lieutenant Sidney Jacob (William Prince), the victim whose suffering provokes Williams's outcry, was written as Jewish, he was cast as a blue-eyed blonde kid from Sche- nectady. On the other hand, to Walsh's credit, he cuts immediately from Williams's diatribe to a closeup that wasn't in the script of the markedly Oriental features of Captain Li (Frank Tang), a member of the Chinese army who has been fighting side by side with the American commandos. Perhaps it is not entirely a coincidence that Walsh's cameraman was born in Canton. A legendary perfectionist who also shot *The Strawberry Blonde* (1941) and *Pursued* (1947), James Wong Howe seems to have been given all the time he needed to bring the jungle landscape of the film to luminous, three-dimensional life—principal photography for *Objective, Burma!* lasted six months.

Adding the closeup of Li to undercut the racism of Williams's indictment was not the only change Walsh made to the script. It has been said that Walsh's heroes are motivated only by the spirit of adven- ture, but that is certainly not the case with Captain Nelson (Flynn) and his commandos. It would be more accurate to say that they never talk about what they are doing—they just do it. Several brief speeches that would have glorified or explained the characters were jettisoned during filming, much to the dismay of the star, who went on strike at one point because all his dialogue consisted of giving orders. He didn't realize how that elimination of all discussion would ultimately serve the film's style, which is a remarkable distillation of Walsh's cinematic art. Nonetheless, Flynn's underplaying of Nelson is in perfect harmony with the whole.

6

Haunted Hollywood

1979

N OT FAR FROM HERE, IN THE amusement park that bears his name, the heirs of Walt Disney have built a haunted house populated by solid-looking but transparent holographic specters, which, like the famous Lincoln robot, realize far better than anything he created in his lifetime Disney's obsession with the uncanny, the animation of dead matter. The sense of tradition is very strong today at the Disney studios, who lost their audience to George Lucas and Ralph Bakshi in the seventies and are trying to get it back. The "nine old men" who drew the great cartoons are retiring, to be replaced by nine young men steeped in

Disneythink and determined to revive the glories of the past by a return to the dangerous source of Disney's art, melodrama. Their first feature cartoon, a sword-and-sorcery epic called *The Black Cauldron*, is due in 1980. In the meantime, the Disney theatrical division has successfully launched their blockbuster for Christmas, *The Black Hole* (1979), a science fiction epic that will be the last hurrah of Disney production designer Peter Ellenshaw. All this is encouraging, but there is no need to believe the wild tales told by Kenneth Anger in *Oui* a few years ago—that "he" is still running the studio, while his body lies preserved on ice atop the Sleeping Beauty Castle—to sense the tug of darker forces: one look at the titles of the films is sufficient to measure what is really at stake in these shadowy engagements.

Serge Toubiana once described Hollywood as "a factory without reserve stocks": I used to think so, too, but as the tone of my sporadic reports from here should have indicated, I don't anymore. This is a haunted city if there ever was one. So it is only appropriate that I should add my note to the chorus of spooky vibrations that have made 1979 seem like one long Halloween (one of the events of the year was the runaway success of an exploitation film by John Carpenter called *Halloween*) by looking backward myself to some of the topics that have come up in the *Cahiers* in the course of the year for an "update."

First some production information:

Fresh from the success of *Escape from Alcatraz* (1979), Don Siegel is in London shooting a thriller with Burt Reynolds, *Rough Cut* (1980); John Cassavetes is in New York shooting his first studio picture since *A Child Is Waiting* (1963), an intimate thriller called *One Summer Night*, for Columbia; and Joseph Mankiewicz is getting set to direct his first picture in five years, an adaptation of a Frederick Forsyth thriller with a mythical African background, *The Dogs of War* (1980), to be produced by Norman Jewison. Among the younger directors: Bob Rafelson is shooting a remake of *The Postman Always Rings Twice* (1981), starring Jack Nicholson, in period costume near Santa Barbara; Brian De Palma, who has been teaching film while waiting to start his new thriller for Filmways, made a low-budget comedy called *Home Movies* in 16 mm, with a student crew, starring Kirk Douglas; Paul Schrader moved to New York after he wrapped *American Gigolo* (1980), to teach film at Columbia University and take a course in ethical philosophy; and John Milius will soon be off to the steppes of Russia to shoot a film about Robert Howard's sword and sorcery hero, *Conan the Barbarian* (1982), starring Arnold Schwarzenegger. Joining Milius in his pursuit of the bubblegum brigade will be Robert Altman, who is preparing an epic version of *Popeye* (1980) with TV star Robin Williams, to be produced by the Disney studios in association with Paramount, and Gene Kelly is slated to direct *Santa Claus*, a $20 million epic that will be produced by David Niven Jr. for worldwide release during the 1980 Christmas season.

All this is very encouraging, but it seems to be getting harder than ever to make a movie. Michael Cimino ran way over budget during location shooting of his epic western, *Heaven's Gate* (1980), and there were rumors of stuntmen nearly losing their lives as Cimino retook dangerous scenes for the twentieth time. William Friedkin, who never seems to get the easy assignments, caught hell from New York's gay militants all through the shooting of *Cruising* (1980), a horror film loosely based on a series of grisly murders a few years back whose victims were denizens of Greenwich Village's S&M "leather bars." And Steven Spielberg, responding to audience boredom during a preview of his epic slapstick war film *1941* (1979), recut the film and shot a new ending on a closed set at Universal: a close-up of TV star John Belushi saying a single word. It had better be funny. "Making a film," Spielberg was quoted as saying shortly afterward, "is the hardest thing I can imagine anyone doing." His next will be *Raiders of the Lost Ark* (1981), with a script by George Lucas, for Paramount.

Problems of another kind have plagued Jerry Lewis, in the form of Joseph Proctor. Two weeks into the shooting of *That's Life*, and one week after he had changed his name to "Joseph Ford Proctor," Lewis's new producer turned out to have less access to cash than he was letting on and disappeared into the wilds of Canada, the last refuge of tax shelters and desperate men. But *Hardly Working* (1980) was finished before his departure, and Lewis has taken over as producer of *That's Life*, which may yet see the light of day. He can take courage from the example of Otto Preminger, when the producers of *The Human Factor* (1979), his adaptation of Graham Greene's best-selling thriller with an apartheid background, ran out of money in the middle of shooting, leaving the director to come up with $7,500,000 of completion money on his own. Preminger is a brilliant producer: in my imagination, I always see him surrounded by an army of tax lawyers and followed by swarms of film students, who reportedly work on his crews for low wages, just for the experience. Who wouldn't? He found new investors and brought the film in under budget in time for an Oscar-qualifying run in Los Angeles in December. It has been picked up for distribution here by MGM, and according to a friend who saw it, it is lovely.

Follow-up on the interview with Roger Corman: Louis Skorecki didn't care much for *Rock 'n' Roll High School* (1979), but the film has a certain historical interest—it may be the last low-budget film from Corman's company, New World, according to an article by Michael Goodwin in the October issue of *Penthouse*. The reasons for this were spelled out in the interview: New World is being squeezed by the studios, who are making exploitation films with multimillion-dollar budgets and using their power with exhibitors to block independents from getting "playdates," according to statements made by Corman during the widely publicized battle over LA playdates for *Saint Jack* (1979). The picture of Corman that emerges from Goodwin's article is of a man in crisis, "deeply troubled" by something, according to his closest associates, and lacerated by the perennial conflict raging within him between the demands of art and commerce. But the rumors of a shutdown of all production seem to be premature: New World is producing a full slate of science fiction and horror films for 1980, budgeted at between one and two million dollars each, a New World special effects studio is being constructed in Venice, and a remake is in the works of *Knute Rockne, All American*, with TV star Ed Asner in the role created by Pat O'Brien.

In the meantime, *Rock 'n' Roll High School* may be the last of its breed. It seems to have been made against Corman's will, and solely because of the conviction of director Alan Arkush, a low-budget cinephile and rock fanatic who was delighted to learn, near the end of shooting, that the high school he was using as a set, which is blown up at the end of the picture, was originally used for *Rock Around the Clock* (1956), the film that launched the big cycle of teenage exploitation films in the fifties. Sparked by the energy of P. J. Soles and rock group, the Ramones, the film got made in spite of a $200,000 budget, a four-week shooting schedule, and the inedible fast food supplied by Corman for the cast and crew, but it almost cost Arkush his life. Halfway through the fourth week he succumbed to shooting pains and a fit of uncontrollable shaking. "I'm dying," he cried, recognizing the symptoms of a heart attack, "Get me a doctor!" "They got him paramedics instead," writes Goodwin, "and sent him off in an ambulance." But as Arkush lay unconscious in intensive care, his friend Joe Dante, with whom he collaborated on *Hollywood Boulevard* (1976), stepped in and finished the picture; producer Jon Davison also lent a hand, and New World stalwart Paul Bartel (*Death Race 2000* [1975]) directed the beautiful sequence starring a paper airplane. It may not be the remake of *The Girl Can't Help It* that Arkush was dreaming of, but *Rock 'n' Roll High School* is a fitting memorial to a highly personal system of production whose passing Hollywood can only mourn, as it mourned a few months ago the death of the "Queen of the B's," Claudia Jennings, a former Playmate of the Month who starred in countless New World quickies, in a car accident in Malibu at the age of twenty-nine.

Follow-up on the interview with Tom Luddy: Luddy left the Pacific Film Archives in 1980 to start a new cinematheque in San Francisco, under the auspices of Francis Ford Coppola's American Zoetrope; the new facility will probably be housed in the old Fox Theater, adjacent to Zoetrope's San Francisco offices. Luddy hopes that a cinematheque in San Francisco, outside the confines of the University of California at Berkeley, will better enable him to realize his plan for a regional film center in Northern California, the region where American film culture was born.

In the meantime, a visit to the Archives is always an opportunity for unexpected discoveries. In November Berkeley audiences had a chance to see the work of a forgotten American independent, John McDermott, a former Marine and Disney artist who was also a *bricoleur* of genius: between 1938 and 1964 McDermott made five war films in the vicinity of his home in Weston, Connecticut, working with primitive equipment and a cast and crew composed of his family and neighbors. Only one of them, *Pickett's Charge*, which recounts one of the bloodiest episodes of the Civil War, was ever shown publicly, when CBS broadcast it in 1958 as an *Omnibus* special. *Pickett's Charge* had its second public screening at the Archives in a program with *Belleau Wood*, a recreation of the famous battle of World War I which McDermott made in 1964 on a Ford Foundation grant of $10,000. Only a few months after McDermott's death, the films were unearthed by Luddy and two filmmakers, Irvin Kershner and Dennis Jakob, the author of the short that opened the McDermott program: *The Invaders* (1972), a tale of revenge set against the backdrop of the Civil War, in which can already be discerned the lineaments of the most enigmatic talent of the School of San Francisco.

In his program notes on McDermott Jakob quotes Orson Welles on the problem of verisimilitude in historical films ("A real man is to be photographed next to a real tree in real—present—time"), and asserts that in the case of McDermott, "The amateur succeeded where the professional failed." He attributes McDermott's success to his graphic sense and the use he makes of audiovisual counterpoint, in the style of the Russians, for purposes of realism; to that I would add the decentering effect of a shooting style in which shots are not conceived as rungs in a hierarchy scaled to the human body, an effect that is accentuated by the perverse variations in focal length, which were possible in 1958, according to Jakob, only with the home-movie equipment McDermott was obliged to use. As Pascal Bonitzer would say, everything in *Pickett's Charge* is "in close-up," and the voices of Pickett's troops have the ghostly effect of direct sound used as voiceover in a documentary. There are also enough fake beards in every shot to remind us that what we are watching is a reenactment, like the reenactments that are still staged in New England towns to commemorate famous battles of the Revolutionary War, and this palpable dimension of memory only enhances the dreamlike suspension of disbelief which the film produces.

Later in November, Douglas Sirk paid a visit to the Archives. It was the first time Sirk had returned to the States since his departure in 1959, and when he arrived in Berkeley he found himself surrounded by Germans. Werner Schroeter was at all the Sirk screenings, and somewhere in the vicinity were Werner Herzog, who is making a documentary about American TV evangelists while preparing his new film for Zoetrope, and Wim Wenders, who had enough time to spare while waiting for the start of production on *Hammet* (1982) to marry country music star Ronee Blakley (*Nashville* [1975], *Renaldo and Clara* [1978]) and put the finishing touches on his Nick Ray film, *Lightning Over Water* (1980). During Sirk's visit there were screenings of the three new films he made at the Munich Film School and a selection of his American films of the fifties, which included studio vault prints of *The Tarnished Angels* (1957) and *All That Heaven Allows* (1955). (Seeing these films again, you feel like a tourist gawking at the pyramids. How did they do it? *Why* did they do it?) The three new films have already been described in the *Cahiers*, but I would like to add one observation of my own. These little experiments, which Sirk calls "film-poems," should be seen together and in sequence, as I was able to see them in Berkeley. Together they compose one poem whose structure is like an ode by Shelley: three movements, each with its own characteristic rhythm of loss and restitution, played out in a series of rooms that represent successive states of a single mind. Seen in context I feel sure that the last film of the trilogy, *Bourbon Street Blues*, would not have disappointed Skorecki, as it did when he saw it in isolation at Deauville.

To me it is the best of the new films, in large part because of a surprising performance by Rainer Werner Fassbinder as a failed writer: "Suppose I wanted to be a great artist but lacked the force and power! Suppose my books fell short of their final chapter, and even my verses languished incomplete! Suppose the curtains of my exalted fancy rose on magnificent dramas—but the house lights darkened before the curtain fell!" Sirk has always been preoccupied with failure, but to my knowledge this is the first time in any of his films that the specter of artistic failure is directly evoked, only to be exorcised by an affirmation *in extremis* of the power of the imagination that concludes the trilogy.

How should we interpret this affirmation? Ironically, no doubt. Theorists of influence have taught us to read in the precarious rhythm of the Romantic ode the dialectic by which poets defend themselves against the poems of their precursors, whom they can hope to equal only by an acceptance of equality in defeat, and it is impossible not to think of this melancholy pattern when one is confronted by the concatenation of allusions at the end of *Bourbon Street Blues*: arms outstretched over the reclining figure of a prostitute, a failed ephebe invented by a Chekhovian playwright and acted by a Sirkian filmmaker announces that his name is Chekhov, in a film by Sirk that consciously recalls, in the way it is staged and lit, the last scene of *Ordet* (1955). These intimations of resurrection can be interpreted only ironically, for if Dreyer returns in the films of the trilogy—and his influence is visible in every frame—it is in order to be corrected by a return to Sirk's theatrical sources: Arthur Schnitzler for the German period, and for the American period Chekhov, evoked here by his American disciple, Tennessee Williams. The resurrection partakes of the ambiguity of the state Harold Bloom calls *apophrades*, which is the last stage in the evolution of the Romantic ego, and its most powerful defense against its precursors: "The mighty dead return, but they return in our colors, and speaking in our voices, at least in part, at least at moments, moments that testify to our persistence, and not to their own."

In January the American Film Institute began its series of New American Filmmakers with, appropriately enough, a new film by King Vidor, a short called *Metaphor*, and it turned out to be a film about influence. In the opening scene Vidor, on his ranch in Southern California, receives a letter from the painter Andrew Wyeth, which informs him that his film *The Big Parade* (1925) has exerted a profound influence on Wyeth's work. Two shots and a transcontinental plane trip later, he is knocking on the door of Wyeth's house in Chadds Ford, Pennsylvania. Wyeth, unexpectedly elfin and every bit as eccentric as Vidor himself, begins the conversation by announcing that he has seen *The Big Parade* a hundred and eighty times. The first time was when he was eight years old, and the powerful unconscious shock produced in him by that screening has left traces throughout his work. The influence was at first a general one, "a strong courageous mood" that got into his blood, but there are more visible traces: *Winter 1946*, for example, the painting of a boy in a cap running down a barren hillside, is really an unconscious memory of the hill down which John Gilbert hobbles at the end of *The Big Parade*. Vidor is flattered, and later in the conversation he will return the compliment: on reflection, he is certain that one particular scene of a muddy road with wagons in *War and Peace* (1956) was influenced in turn by Wyeth's *Public Sale*—a painting of a muddy road with a pickup truck, in which the shape of the hill from *The Big Parade* is already visible.

Another example: the sharpshooter's medal in *The Patriot*, a portrait of Wyeth's neighbor Robert Kline in his World War I tunic, was added after the sitting was over, and only recently did Wyeth realize that the detail was suggested by a closeup of a sharpshooter's medal in *The Big Parade* (we see the closeup), which is awarded by his comrades to a doughboy who got a French girl pregnant. The medal, for Wyeth, has always been the center of the painting, more important than the subject's face—it is a metaphor, filled with all sorts of meanings. Mrs. Wyeth contributes a definition of "poetic realism" cribbed from a dissertation on her husband that someone sent her to read, and Vidor gratefully accepts it as a description of his own style, which evolved from a desire to show things "so that they would look real, but not be real." Of course, says Wyeth, the medal in the painting is only metaphorical because the medal in the film was already a metaphor in its own right. Vidor: "You've seen the film many times—would you say as many as fifteen or twenty?" Wyeth (firmly): "One hundred and eighty." Mrs. Wyeth: "He's not kidding." In fact, after repeated viewings, Wyeth is convinced that every image in *The Big Parade* is a metaphor, even the most banal ones—like the scene at the beginning when Gilbert introduces Claire McDowell to Hobart Bosworth. The scene flashes before us as Wyeth speaks: the father, seeing his son embrace his fiancée, goes over and stands behind the young couple, smiling paternally, but slightly out of focus . . .

Change of scene: a battered car plows through the snowdrifts; Wyeth is taking his guest to see Kuerner's Hill, whose topography is well known to art historians. Although it isn't said in the film, it was behind this hill that Wyeth's father died—N. C. Wyeth, a historical painter whose paintings, more than his son's, resemble Vidor's films in both their form and iconography. But when Wyeth painted Kuerner's Hill in *Winter 1946*, *Snow Flurries* and scores of other works, what he was really painting, he now realizes, was the equally famous hill at the end of *The Big Parade*. We see the scene again—Gilbert stumping crazily down the hill, Renée Adorée in hysterics, the final embrace—so familiar, even to cinephiles less fanatical than Wyeth, that one would have thought that it would have lost its power to move us. Vidor explains that the hill he used is today part of the UCLA campus, and promises to take a picture of it for Wyeth when he gets home. Wyeth remarks that in the film Renée Adorée still looks contemporary, while Claire McDowell looks old-fashioned because of her hair. Some things, like hairstyles and automobiles, date quickly in paintings as well as films; other things, like military uniforms, never seem to go out of style. Even this image of the two of them sitting in Wyeth's car at the foot of Kuerner's Hill, its elementary contour almost dissolved by the falling snow and darkening sky, which only serve to multiply its ghostly associations—even this image of the two of them at this very moment is already dated, because of the car. But what meanings does Wyeth's old black car convey? It isn't clear.

Before leaving Vidor quotes from another friend, the psychiatrist John Darcy: "Art constantly reminds us of the benefits of recognizing and evaluating relationships." Alone, he muses on the strange vocation of the artist and the pleasures it brings: foremost among them, the pleasure of meeting friends one has made at a distance, friends like Andrew Wyeth, and all the others one has yet to meet. This is the properly American response to the anxiety of influence, as it was set down once and for all by Ralph Waldo Emerson in his essay on "Self-Reliance": at once social and solipsistic like Whitman; radiantly optimistic, yet shot through with sly ironies, like Thoreau. Encountering it again upon my return to LA (and in a new film by King Vidor, sharp as a tack at eighty-five!) warmed my blood and almost made me forget the chilly scenes I had witnessed in the North.

Notations

Louis Skorecki was at the time a *Cahiers* editor, and he is currently the custodian of Jean-Pierre Oudart, a great theorist, who's alive and well, although Loulou tells everyone he's dead.

Arctic Rampage became *Death Hunt* (1981), directed by Peter Hunt. Joseph Mankiewicz lost *The Dogs of War* to John Irvin. *Knute Rockne* was never produced. Jerry Lewis's *That's Life* remains a rumor (his home movies are on DVD). Films are very typically floated in *Variety* and *The Hollywood Reporter* by publicists who are trying to make them happen; it's amazing looking back on this essay in 2018 to note how many of the projects mentioned here panned out. *Santa Claus* was eventually released in 1985, directed by Jeannot Szwarc. *Pickett's Charge* is a film I saw on a flatbed, so it exists; but it is not commercially available and cannot be found on the IMDb. Maybe someone will read about it here and unearth it. I'd love to see it again.

Douglas Sirk's *Bourbon Street Blues* can be seen on YouTube at https://www.youtube.com/watch?v=lrjdaZTQTOk. It has been there for years and doesn't seem likely to vanish.

Francis Ford Coppola and George Lucas, who lived in San Francisco, wanted to plow their fortunes into creating a studio in Hollywood that would not be beholden to the sharks who run the Hollywood studios. They bought Hollywood General Studios (now Sunset Las Palmas Studios) and equipped them to be state-of-the-art—notably including the digital technology that was then new and untested and is now the way almost all movies are made, although some diehards like Christopher Nolan champion 35-mm and 70-mm film as the best medium. The first film made at the new studio was *One from the Heart* (1982), which bombed because, whereas *Apocalypse Now* (1979) was an event in reference to the Vietnam War, which journalists could promote by spilling gallons of ink, you can't create an event by deploying new technology because there's nothing serious and important the press can write about. So Coppola declared bankruptcy and the studios were bought by some financier. Coppola's dream of a truly independent studio in Hollywood was shattered, and the center of his operations was transferred to San Francisco, where it was on top of a building that had interminable stairs you had to climb when the elevator wasn't working.

Tom Luddy, who lived in San Francisco and hated Los Angeles, was Francis Ford Coppola's right-hand man when he was making the *Godfather* films—hence the character "Tom" played by Robert Duvall in the first and second films—and when Coppola moved operations to San Francisco, he continued to be his capo. The new company was baptized American Zoetrope. Luddy founded the Pacific Film Archives, still operating under other leadership in San Francisco. The interview to which I refer was published in the April 1982 special issue of the *Cahiers*, "Made in USA."

In the spring of 1980, interviews would appear in *Cahiers* with four American television directors, in order to shed some light on a vast and important area of production that is just beginning to receive serious attention from students of film. For a new film by Samuel Fuller readers had to wait for the American premiere of *The Big Red One* July 18, 1980, or its French premier May 28. But *Cahiers* readers would get an advance peek via an extensive interview with Fuller about the making of the film, which was published shortly after this letter.

I smuggled Joan Didion's essay "Having Fun" into *Trafic* 6 (Spring 1994), with editor Serge Daney's permission; finally he found it "very queer"—I think that's why he liked it. This is the most influential—and widely misinterpreted—text that has appeared on the "New Hollywood." In my own essay in the same issue I treated Didion's piece as a lyric poem and read it according to Harold Bloom's theory of the anxiety of influence as her completion of F. Scott Fitzgerald's unfinished novel *The Last Tycoon* (1941). In the time-honored Bloomian way, I had Didion trumping (completing) Fitzgerald by identifying with his narrator, Cecilia Brady, the daughter of a studio head modeled on Louis B. Mayer, the fictitious nemesis of the brilliant producer Monroe Starr (*sic*). Starr was modeled on Irving Thalberg, whose star is doomed to be eclipsed (in the case of Thalberg because of his heart condition). I argued that Didion had thereby produced a strong poem, the work that will outlive all her novels, influencing many subsequent writers on Hollywood. (I had learned from Bloom when I was at Yale that immortality was the true goal of poets—and all artists—from Pindar to the present.) Applying Bloom's "map of misreading" to Didion's essay, I was able to break it down into a series of six "revisionary ratios" and read it as a sequence comprising *clinamen, tessera, kenosis, daemonization, askesis,* and *apophrades.* I was also able to dissect *2001: A Space Odyssey* (1968) this way in *Vertigo.* See Harold Bloom, *The Anxiety of Influence: A Theory of Poetry*, 2nd ed. (New York: Oxford University Press, 1997), and his *A Map of Misreading*, 2nd ed. (New York: Oxford University Press, 2003).

The tribute "The Films of John R. McDermott and Dennis Jakob" was at the University of California, Berkeley Art Museum—Pacific Film Archive on November 2, 1979. The Orson Welles quotation about filming the "real" is in Jakob's "Problems of the Historical Film," on pages 1 and 11 of the Art Museum's November 1979 Calendar.

Bloom's *apophrades* is found in *The Anxiety of Influence*, page 141.

As to the rumors about stuntmen on *Heaven's Gate*, they were false. I talked to people who worked on the film. Michael is dead, and I hate to slander his memory.

7

John Ford

December 7th: The Movie

In memory of John Hollander

THREE VERSIONS OF *December 7th* exist: the government-ordered cut-down of thirty-four minutes of fake footage of the bombing released in 1943; the eighty-two-minute version that Kit Parker restored and released in 1991, where real footage of the December 7, 1941, attack was cut in with the fake; and the twenty-minute cut-down that won the Oscar in 1943. Program notes for a 1980 screening of that version in Austin say that it was seventeen minutes long (roughly the same length as *Battle of Midway*, an Oscar winner in 1942) and was credited as "directed and photographed by John Ford," although the film was shot by Ford's uncredited collaborator, cinematographer Gregg Toland. One question we will try to answer, inevitably, is, "Whose film is this?" There are lots of layers in this palimpsest.

It's an axiom that the meaning of a film changes with time because it is in the eye of the beholder, so Fordians who saw this film for the first time during and after the Vietnamese War of Liberation saw the "other" being demonized. I can imagine how the scene before the attack, where the base's Catholic priest, who is also in the navy, orders his parishioners to their battle stations with a hasty sign of the cross for a blessing, played to the audience who saw the film at the National Archives during the second Nixon administration. That piece of Ford humor was bound to hit a sour note despite the disclaimer in the program about *December 7th* not reflecting current government practices, which notoriously included New York's Cardinal Spellman blessing planes taking off to incinerate Vietnamese freedom fighters.

The same priest oversees the placing of leis on American flags flying over white markers for lives lost at sea while the new young base commander and his wife watch at attention, and all vanish, leaving the cross to guard the shore as the now-heavenly choir sings, "Amen," even though this is the climax of the film's most beautiful sequence, which wouldn't have provoked a whisper of dissent in 1943.

Framing scenes featured Mr. C for Conscience (Harry Davenport), who appears and disappears with the suddenness of Jiminy Cricket, to burst the bubble of Mr. U.S. (Walter Huston)'s Hawaiian boosterism, accompanied by little films being shown to Mr. U.S., and to us (one of several meanings of his name), to burst that bubble.

A scene of the Japanese consul being *seig-heiled* by a German spymaster is obviously staged, but so are most of the scenes filmed in Hawaii, which afforded the filmmakers a cast of 157,000 Japanese. Before that, in a set that seems to have been constructed in a broom closet, the consul is briefed by the German about a scene we've just seen: ANGLED SHOT—CASINO neon sign; an ultramodern dance hall turns out to be a Japanese dime-a-dance joint; a soldier buys a string of tickets from a Japanese ticket seller, and his partner's image can be seen in reflection on the glass of the ticket booth, along with the dancers; cut back to the dance floor, which is now part of a little fiction; cut to the sailor whose voice we've heard saying, "Come on, cutie-pie," to his date, as now he politely serves her tea; cut in closer to a low angle on the dancers so we see that some impolite sailors park their hats on their partners' shoulders; cut to a shot of Our Couple talking (he had the decency to check *his* . . .) that returns us to documentary-style realism, illuminated by the girl's face as she listens to him; cut to the grinning Japanese spymaster making his report: [subtitles] "That poor soldier was so lonesome and the girl was so sympathetic." The consul smiles, listening. "Her report contained many new details of Hickam Field."

But the buzzer has announced the arrival of Herr Hanneman, the spymaster (played by Lionel Royce, an actor typecast as the evil German in B-movies), who introduces a new scene of idyllic life on the island with a blonde Nazi spy eavesdropping on two Southern navy brides whose conversation about romance includes a nugget of information that sank an American ship. These scenes are a part of a film-within-the-film conjured up by Mr. C warning U.S. (Uncle Sam) about Japanese spying in Honolulu.

Hanneman's little flashback is a film-within-the-film during C's spy movie, an invisible version of the nested flashback structure employed so visibly in *Citizen Kane* (1941). But the camera is still not being used in *December 7th* as it would be in a real documentary like *The Battle of Midway*. For example, the trick with the reflections—the foreground figure tapping his finger at frame left during the first shot of the dance floor and the framing of the spy cutie's face at its most sympathetically luminous over the shoulder of the backlit sap she's leading on—are part of a little sequence composed of Langian camera angles (the "CASINO" sign is half cut-off to conceal "DANCE HALL"), an all-around mise-en-scène that has plunged us into a low-budget version of the spy dramas made by Lang and Hitchcock during the War, except that in C's little movie the other is doubly other: spy and Japanese.

Mothers

Make that a triple, to use the baseball metaphor that Dana Andrews tortures during the film's epilogue in a veterans' cemetery in the longest version of the film, eliminated in the cut-down. It would not have added to the female presence if it had been kept, because that is fleeting after the atrocity. Women appear briefly being remembered by their dead in posed portraits of families back home who lost sons in Pearl Harbor, then viewed respectfully from a distance by Toland's camera in a Hawaiian cemetery where they are identified by a wreath that says GOLD STAR MOTHER(S), where the "S" is slightly truncated by a sunbeam. This reminds the spectator that Hawaiians perished in the atrocity, too, and leads into the most moving sequence in all versions of the film.

Kept at a distance in the funeral shots, the Gold Star Mothers of Hawaii are an unheard choir in opposition to the men's choir singing

"America, of Thee I Sing" All wear white, mourners and choir alike, because this is the tropics, the upside-down land under our feet. The mourners are unheard, but the tropical breezes in the palm trees sing the choral accompaniment to "Taps" for them: sympathetic magic woven by the most musical of the film's long tracking shots.

Mata Haris and Hula Girls

Before and after the attack, women wear every hat in the book to represent Hawaii: hula dancers, taxi dancers, servants, card-playing rich women, barbers, shoe clerks, spies. They predominate in the spying section, taking over entirely when the spymaster boasts of using his female agents, another B-movie trope, to spread disinformation. The power of gossip embodied in women is also a trope in Hollywood cinema, which cannot therefore be treated as a signature of John Ford. In any event, after two films with the master, Toland would be as adept at forging that signature as anyone.

Much of the time the women of *December 7th* take a back seat to buildings and businesses, and for the most part they get equal time with the male population, but the camera loves them (they are all young and beautiful in myriad ways) even in the wide shots, and they get their own catalogs of close-ups: the seven beauties, descending below the age of consent, who represent the races on the island, played against the unconcealed sexiness of the "Aloha" shots that illustrate U.S.'s peroration about diverse cultures blending with the American Way of Life (beauty contests and hula dancing), just before the film becomes a Chamber of Commerce pitch for tourism: white people sunbathing, kayaking, body surfing, and horseback riding while a middle-aged native woman—no longer good for anything else, we have to assume, helped by a little girl who's not "ripe" yet—makes leis for the tourists and darts an unreadable glance at the camera.

So it would not be stretching a point to say that women are the film's third other, a three-bagger that invites this faithful disciple of Jean-Pierre Oudart to attempt a perilous slide into home plate: The Other (the Unconscious) embodied in the triple mystery of female sexuality, foreignness, and treachery is a familiar trope of nineteenth-century painting and literature. (See for example Oudart on Syberberg's *Karl May* [1974].) But like baseball metaphors that run into extra innings, that awe-inspiring legend is scarcely a signature trope of John Ford or of any other director. Baseball phrases like "foul ball" and "home run" are part of the American language and its many colonial outposts (including postwar Japan). In the epilogue of the long version of *December 7th*, Andrews uses the baseball metaphor to map, in a graveyard, a postwar world where all creeds and systems will have a place "if they call a fair ball fair and a foul ball foul."

But a film that speaks in words universally understood to make its point can scarcely be cherished as idiosyncratic for the same reason. The themes and tropes of auteurist film criticism are powerless to establish authorship of a contested film when the signature, in the interest of ideological impact, is this all-American.

Mirrorland Mirror for the Future

The Gold Star Mothers of Hawaii are multiracial, like the home-front families (Mexican, Jewish, Black) seen in the Walker Evans–style filmed portraits when the dead begin to speak with the voice of George O'Brien. Reflected in the funhouse mirror of Hawaii (the graves that speak are marked by a cross and a lei), the concept of multiracialism embraces no less than seven races, represented by seven young women who recite their ethnicities and their numbers among the population in heavily accented English. Even the "Caucasian" speaks with a slight accent that signals she's an islander. The bereaved stateside families presumably have regional or European accents, but we never hear them, any more than we hear the Gold Star Mothers of Hawaii speaking pidgin English.

At the end of U.S.'s climactic paean to Hawaii, that "unripe" Japanese girl-child states her identity and gives a whole new meaning to the familiar figure of 157,000, saying it with just a touch of Walter Huston's sass, because his U.S. has taken over the narration again at this point. A funhouse mirror like the shot of the ultramodern dance floor where all the jive kittens are Japanese, Hawaii will be held up at the end of the film to the future United Nations as a model of multicultural tolerance and cooperation—like baseball, which would finally be integrated two years after the creation of the United Nations.

In fact the makers of *December 7th* go pretty far down the rabbit hole by which many filmmakers exited the funhouse when President Harry Truman launched the postwar anti-Communist witch hunts. Dana Andrews says in the film's ghostly coda that he's betting on "Roosevelt, Churchill, 'Stalyin,' and Chiang Kai Shek" to keep the peace, and the montage of flags that is the film's final image of community includes "Russia." But the USSR was still our ally in 1942, and the Nationalists were in charge in China, so that isn't what got the filmmakers in trouble.

A Word from Our Sponsor

U.S.'s hyperbolic dream of a multicultural Hawaii with no traces of colonialism is eventually sabotaged by his own images when the hula cuties go on parade. This interpretation isn't being imposed on the film—it is being produced by it: by the way U.S.'s little movies are shot and edited and by Huston's performance, because while the name "U.S." has meaning, or rather meanings (Uncle Sam, U.S., US . . .), as played by Huston he is not simply a recycling of the man on the recruiting poster but a reimagining of an icon like Lincoln in Ford's *Young Mr. Lincoln* in 1939. U.S. represents 130 million Americans (the ones the film has to convince) and not "Washington," C's synecdoche for the seat of power, which is very well informed about fifth columnists in Hawaii and way ahead of public opinion represented by out-of-the-loop U.S.

There are things about which U.S. is knowledgeable (pineapples and hula dancers) and things about which he's blissfully ignorant, summed up by the dissolve from the bleached statue of King Kalakaua to the American flag flying over the Capitol in Washington: an ellipsis as breathtaking as the transformation of Young Mr. Lincoln into the statue in the Lincoln Memorial. In each case whole chapters are being skipped over when History ineluctably turns the page, and while the history of Hawaii and Washington shed less blood than the Civil War, it's an understatement to say that many incidents worthy of note are deliberately elided by U.S.'s brief, cartoonish description of it.

Much the same thing happens to U.S.'s earlier "Song of the Pineapple," in which he compares the industrial farming of Hawaiian sugar cane and pineapples to the opening of the West, thereby positing Hawaii as the West of the West, a new frontier for American business, and caps his peroration by calling out the names of business's Big Five in the islands, while one of those visual catalogs shows the names, engraved in stone, of five Anglo-American businesses that turned "a village of grass huts" (!) into a metropolis: "the backbone, the nerve center, the brain of the territory." But these stony inscriptions brood like gargoyles over images of industrialization and urbanization in Paradise.

U.S. came to Hawaii looking for the paradise in the travel posters, but the images he and C call up will finally plunge him into a nightmare of enemies encircling him on the west and the east.

U.S. is certainly being disingenuous when he ends his comparison with the Old West by referring to Hawaii as a "territory," which has Wild West connotations. While many territories conquered and organized during the march westward were unofficial pieces of the United States with their own local governments before becoming states, Hawaii is a territory far from our shores with brown-skinned inhabitants. More visibly than in the towns of the Old West in westerns with "Territory" in their titles, whose historical counterparts were built on the bones of the Native American genocide, Hawaii is a colony with American businesses at the top and natives on the bottom, where many dusky races had found themselves since the nineteenth century.

A Mirror for the Past

This inequity between natives and colonizers is never shown or talked about by *December 7th*, being displaced, for reasons that gradually become clearer, to the colonized who are planted like pineapples in the worst soil of the island: immigrant laborers from Japan, not unlike the Irish when they first came to America (Ford's ancestors). Because these Japanese with no other name are exiles who have come to paradise to make a life, I'm sure there were many in Hollywood besides John Ford who could identify with them, even though the pineapples in Hollywood's fields were gold-plated. Slavery in the American South is another image that swims into the mirror, if only because of the studious avoidance by U.S. and C alike of the word "plantation" in their examination of the Hawaiian economy.

   The natives, while not invisible, are not given much of a voice or a history and the film seems to be complicit in this: the one Hawaiian-English street sign seen during U.S.'s hymn to acculturation (the tree-shaded corner of Punahou and Bingham) is a souvenir of the successful pacification and integration of the Hawaiian islands into the American empire. But replace phonetically spelled Hawaiian with Japanese ideograms displayed next to their English translations, and the mutated signs, embodying a contemporary contradiction (Japan and America would very soon be at war), go viral. There were indeed security problems on the island that Ford, wearing his OSS hat, had been tasked with spotting before Washington had him making documentaries after December 7. His superiors cannot have been unaware of this.

Shadowland

The film as a whole is broken into three movements, like the movements in the score by Fox musical director Alfred Newman, who also scored *The Battle of Midway*.

1. Shadow Play

Three hieroglyphic images of ruin and bloodshed are followed by written orders from the secretaries of the navy and the army to make a film about the attack on Pearl Harbor. *December 7th* proposes a little play with two characters who discuss the vulnerability of Hawaii to attack in a single set with Paradise just outside the window on a balmy day, December 6, 1941, when the bombs haven't fallen yet. The little play unfolds at an easy pace with blocking and performances that never distract us from the actors and the allegorical figures they depict.

U.S's much-needed Hawaiian vacation from the disastrous situation in Europe is ruined by C, his conscience, who also represents Yankee Common Sense (and perhaps Connecticut) as opposed to U.S., part-Irish and given to flights of poetry about the scent of flowers in the air—an illustrated Platonic dialogue between two principles that can certainly be seen at work in many Ford films: for example, Brandon and Marsh in *The Iron Horse* (1924). Like them, U.S. and C change camps more than once in the course of their dialogue, and so do the images illustrating their respective visions. Hegel's *Phenomenology of Spirit*, Walter Kaufmann says, taking *Geist* seriously like Heidegger and Derrida, is a spook show, a shadow play where spirits are called up to battle and vanquish one another, and that is what happens in the scenes between U.S. and C in *December 7th*.

Anamnesis: In reply to C's "lawyerly" (Socratic) question—"What do you know about sugar cane?"—U.S. launches into the peroration about what Big Business has done for Hawaii that turns into a Dole commercial. With Socratic irony C ripostes that his interlocutor is "as usual very well informed" but has forgotten one thing: Labor. Asked whose hands do all the hard work, U.S. says, "The natives. And they do a very good job!" C counters that U.S. is "playing ostrich" because he *"knows perfectly well"* (italics mine) that the majority of field hands are Japanese migrant laborers.

Like Socrates, C is asking questions to teach U.S. *what he already knows*. U.S.'s paean to Honolulu, we've seen, included one picturesque bilingual street sign (English and Hawaiian), but C's Japanese/English signs march across the screen in seemingly endless array, segueing into an avant-garde sequence of superimposed signs and faces that becomes progressively "dissonant," then "martial"—connotations supplied by the film's complex score.

C pointedly recalls a phrase in U.S.'s "Sugar Cane Rhapsody": like the white businessmen who preceded them, the Japanese have formed their own network of family and business alliances, and their numbers keep growing. This is the second time we hear the number 157,000, which has metamorphosed from a statistic into a threat: the Japanese are an ethnic minority in Hawaii, but they are the largest one. C will now oppose to U.S.'s capitalist dithyramb the dark threnody of fascism, which is even less than "3,400 miles away." Its agents are right here in Hawaii.

The Japanese are immigrant workers only partly assimilated, producing a semiological perversion of familiar signs shown in the marching catalog of literal signs for Japanese-American small businesses. Their mimetic abilities would make the Japanese in Hawaii a hell of a fifth column, even though when the smoke has cleared their role in *December 7th* will turn out to have been more cinematic than military. But first U.S. had to "remember" that they exist.

Signs of loyalty: One hundred and twenty thousand of those Japanese immigrants have become American citizens by choice, U.S. ripostes, suddenly an expert on people he had forgotten before C's question. Visibly on the defensive, he lets the Japanese chairman of the Oahu Committee for Home Defense speak for him in a long-held low-angle shot with spidery *Kane*-like shadows behind him. What I have loosely been calling Hawaii is in fact Oahu, the island of Honolulu and Pearl Harbor, but this is the only time we clearly hear the name of the part that stands in for whole, the Hawaiian islands. A "very hyphenated" territory, as C might say, in more ways than one, even if the name is never hyphenated with any race that populates it. Instead the OCHD chairman's powerful declaration of Japanese loyalty to the territorial government is supported by scenes of Japanese children pledging allegiance to the American flag, singing "God Bless America," and being Boy Scouts and Girl Scouts, *en masse* and all in English.

This brief montage is not terribly convincing because of its Reifenstahlish mise-en-scène, and like the "Song of the Pineapple" it contains the seeds of its own destruction. The chairman is eloquent, but he is one man; the children are puppets putting on a show that U.S. believes makes Hawaii "as American a state as any New England community." Too few and too many, U.S.'s "witnesses" form a territory that is not yet a state (or even a land mass) and a funhouse mirror subliminally reminding us that New England schoolchildren do these things in their sleep too, while their elders make speeches.

The propaganda purpose of *December 7th*, after all, was to turn those 130 million tired patriots who are U.S.'s cells, not yet recovered from World War I, into a war machine again, and this is also something U.S. has to be reminded of, so his boasting could not be better designed to trigger ricocheting doubts and derision in our heads, the affective underpinning of the film's dialectic even when the dry beauty of Toland's images threatens to turn it into an abstraction. What about the rest of the country? You couldn't fit that many kids into a New England town square! If you tried to do that in my town you'd have to line the kids up with a gun! Great *speech*! And even: I don't need a bunch of Japs to show me how to be an American! These inner voices speak during any film, but it took Ford to conjure them up for us in *The Battle of Midway* by having Hollywood stars speak them.

The colonial palimpsest: After U.S.'s little history of Japanese acculturation, C ripostes that the Japanese immigrants have divided loyalties, as seen in a montage of schoolchildren and Shinto worshipers going about their daily business speaking Japanese with no subtitles. A one-take declaration by a Shinto priest establishes that this "so-called religion" (still the most provocative phrase in the film) comes down to worship of the Emperor Hirohito. Unlike the OCHD chairman, the priest (Philip Ahn, a Korean actor who usually played in Charlie Chan movies) does not deliver a monologue; engaging in a lopsided dialogue with C, who asks him questions offscreen, he is played as the sneaky, silk-smooth antithesis of the chairman's ringing declaration, which acquires considerable democratic "cred" by contrast, even though the chairman is probably an actor, too.

Employing *reductio ad absurdum* to undercut U.S.'s protests about freedom of religion, C compares Japanese-Hawaiian Shintoism to inhabitants of Japan worshiping George Washington as a god, and the surreal image resonates with a bizarre discord in one of C's examples of the otherness of the Japanese in Hawaii: in the scene of Japanese schoolchildren singing a ceremonial song from the homeland, it is "Auld Lang Syne" in Japanese. Japanese culture had itself been colonized—as the colonies once were—by Commodore Perry, so making "Auld Lang Syne" a schoolroom standard is a *detournement* of one of those traces.

Spies: Offhandedly citing "Washington" scuttlebutt that U.S. hasn't heard, C makes the case for not cracking down on disloyal Japanese too soon: the army and navy have a "little black book" with all the suspicious characters in it, to be rounded up when trouble starts. Why not round them up before? asks U.S., suddenly advocating a policy he has been opposing. C replies with an ironic jab—"That's what I was going to ask *you*"—before explaining to U.S. that playing dumb in Hawaii gives "Washington" (FDR) time to fight the isolationists and build a war machine.

The word "war" provokes a Pavlovian reaction that sends U.S. into reverse, denouncing C as a "warmonger," and the dialogue is suddenly sprinkled with quotes, reminding us that our onscreen avatars are speaking with borrowed words: C puts the German spymaster's disinformation mantra in ironic quotation marks—the "stupid, incompetent children of the Orient" are going to blow up Fortress Honolulu someday, C says, and U.S. replies by unwittingly quoting Sinclair Lewis to the effect that "it can't happen here" as C grimaces in recognition. "Maybe not," he says rhetorically, then proceeds to describe how the Japanese consul's diplomatic pouch is being used to carry espionage reports to Tokyo. The consul is C's Dr. Mabuse, who will be called into question by another actor playing a reporter (Ralph Byrd, Republic's Dick Tracy), visible onscreen even as the bombs are falling.

If C *se fait des films*, they're definitely B-movies. But like many B-movies, this one, made a year after the bombs fell, is couched in the language of counterespionage and nourished by accurate information about how intelligence was collected and transmitted before the attack, which makes it all the more impressive when John Ford, the former OSS operative (and B-movie maker) making this film, ends up denouncing his own report as disinformation. (Most of the information the attackers needed was published in local newspapers anyway.)

2. The Radar Operator

We'll never see C again, as Fox's resident Jewish antifascist director, Irving Pichel, forcefully takes the narrative reins and the stunning reenactment of the infamous day begins with the missed warning from a radar operator, whose radio is "CENSORED." "Private Joseph Lockhard" becomes a Cassandra, like C, but a historic one justifying the narrator's lament that if they'd only had a few minutes warning, it might have been a different story.

Ford or one of his researchers probably talked to Lockhard. Despite that, Robert Lowrey ended up being photographed against a "CENSORED" radar machine that looks less like Lockhard's primitive equipment than like a discarded prop found in Fox's unused soundstage on Western Avenue, several miles closer to Skid Row than the main lot, where Ford and Toland shot the soundstage portions of the film.

A third "CENSORED" swatch is applied to a highway protected with barbed wire during the falling action, a black blob that seems to blot out one of the film's "watchers." The inkblot suggests a figure like a man in a hat, possibly a baseball cap, watching an indecipherable troop movement for some classified reason.

Moral of a shadow play: The magnificent thirty-four-minute film in which Lockhard is just one of a tiny "cast of thousands" seems at first to confirm C-for-Cassandra's dire prophecies, but it ends up showing in the "aftermath" portion that the Japanese population all pitched in (blood donations, militia drills) when their new homeland was decimated, and no acts of sabotage were committed. Thus U.S. was right after all, and so was "Washington" (FDR) when (as C explains) he didn't let the FBI come down on the Japanese locals, putting the president on the side of the angels in Hawaii, at least, where the head of the territorial government did not put American-Japanese in internment camps as FDR had done in the US immediately after Pearl Harbor. To be precise, 1 percent of Hawaii's Japanese American population was interned during the war, in Honouliuli Internment Camp on Sand Island.

December 7th reaches its emotional peak with bereaved families in the US and the Gold Star Mothers of Hawaii, where Hawaii's immigrants and America's are joined by death. The second movement ends with Paradise turned into a camouflage-colored twilight world (with even the all-white cruise ship *Lurline* metamorphosing into a completely different black battle cruiser by a flagrant artifice of montage), where even children become hobgoblins during gas attack drills and mothers form a long line to get scary "bunny masks" for their infants (one of whom is shown in children's high heels and the equally oversized mask, like a figure out of Bosch), ending with the call to arms that C wanted to hear: "All they that take the sword shall perish with the sword."

3. Dialogue of Shades

The film ends with a quiet coda filmed in two long shots, dappled with light and shadow, at a veterans' cemetery in Los Angeles that stands in for Arlington National Cemetery. The dialogue of the dead spoken by two contradictory ghost voices, without musical accompaniment, prophesies the coming of the United Nations in the image of Hawaii, a place that will no longer be spoken of in the film. Andrews takes control of the narrative again and utters the climactic prophecy that war will be replaced by the new World Series Pennant Race, where cultures, economic systems, and forms of government still contend bloodlessly, because without contraries there is no progression.

Framed as a rhetorical wager (a baseball bet), the third act of *December 7th*, like Andrew Marvell's "Ode to Cromwell," is a wager with Time—a wager that Marvell and Ford both lost (Cromwell became a tyrant, Truman and his right-wing advisers welshed on money for postwar recovery promised to Stalin and started the Cold War as soon as FDR died), thereby adding a layer of irony to both works.

During the tracking shots of the two ghost speakers' backs, their faces are turned away from us because their eyes are on the rows upon rows of identical tombstones the camera sees over their shoulders, first on their left, then on their right, while the World War I veteran shows the recent arrival from Pearl Harbor the sights, and their voices, which we overhear, tell us what they see. We never really see the Young Ghost's eyes or the Old Ghost's face. Their voices replace their eyes, which are turned away from us toward Death.

As Toland's camera follows the two ghosts through light and shadow from the trees, a visual chorus like the palms on Oahu, but silent like trees on an autumn day in Los Angeles, accompanies the voices of Andrews and Paul Hurst (the veteran actor-director of two-reel westerns who played the last role of his 237-film career for Ford as an army sergeant in Ford's favorite of all his films, *The Sun Shines Bright* [1953]), writing over their seemingly solid forms with light and shadow while their voices write over the landscape they're seeing the topography of Arlington, which is also, tropologically, Heaven—a more constricted Heaven than Hawaii, although dressed like Hawaii in white, filled with the dead of all our wars. A scene that could have been imagined only by John Ford.

Notations

John Hollander, to whose memory this chapter is dedicated, was a poet and film historian with whom I studied at the Graduate Center of the City University of New York.

Besides the film history that's in print about December 7th, see "Collective Text on Young Mr. Lincoln," *Cahiers du cinéma* 223 (August–September 1970): 29–47; James M. Skinner, "December 7: Filmic Myth Masquerading as Historical Fact," *Journal of Military History* 55, no. 4 (October 1991): 507–516; A. J. P. Taylor, *The Second World War: An Illustrated History* (New York: Putnam, 1975); Harold Bloom, *A Map of Misreading* (New York: Oxford University Press, 1975); Maureen O'Hara, *'Tis Herself: An Autobiography* (New York: Simon & Schuster, 2004); IMDb; Wikipedia (a Hawaiian word); and the internet archive for the Los Angeles National Cemetery.

The Jean-Pierre Oudart piece on Syberberg's Karl May is in *Cahiers du cinéma* 266–267 (May 1967): 78–82, under the title "Diffamations [Fragments]."

Regarding Walter Kaufmann on Hegel's *Phenomenology of Spirit*, see *Hegel, a Reinterpretation* (Notre Dame: Notre Dame University Press, 1977).

My thanks to Karl Thiede and Andy Rector.

8

Hawks at Work

The Making of *Land of the Pharaohs*

*L*AND OF THE PHARAOHS, Howard Hawks's only attempt at an epic
of ancient civilizations, figures in Hawks's filmography as a *film
maudit*. Defended at the time of its release by *Cahiers du cinéma*
(Rivette, Chabrol), it continues to intrigue Hawks's admirers, who have
always suspected that this bizarre deviation from our hero's habitual concerns (a story extending over thirty years instead of the usual fastidious

"Hawks at Work" originally appeared in the now-defunct Los Angeles "newspaper
on film" *Modern Times* no. 4 (April 1990), as a review article about Noël Howard's
"making-of" book, *Hollywood sur Nil*, which I had at the time in manuscript form. It
was subsequently reprinted as "Hawks à l'ouvrage: La genèse de *Land of the Pharaohs*,"
Trafic, no. 63 (Autumn 2007), and it is posted online at Andy Rector's blog *Kino Slang*.

"unities," focusing on a single powerful figure at the expense of the professional group, even more than in the anomalous *Red River* [1948]; flatly colloquial dialogue free of the pomposities of Hollywood epic speech-making, but also of any trace of humor; a tragic ending) must paradoxically contain the key to the art of this mysterious filmmaker. (See Jean-Claude Biette in his eulogy for Hawks: "The greatness he achieved in filming the Relative kept him from occasionally running the risk of confronting the Absolute. Nevertheless, he ran that risk once, in *Land of the Pharaohs*, an extraordinary film where the Relative admits its limits: the work leads, this time, to a gigantic apparatus of tombs"). Or what amounts to the same thing, the key to his unconscious mind (see Serge Daney's psychoanalytic overview of the oeuvre, "*Rio Lobo*: Vieillesse du Même," where pharaonic imagery abounds). So the existence of a book on the making of *Land of the Pharaohs* by Hawks's second-unit director Noel Howard (*Hollywood sur Nil*) raises hopes too high not to be dashed on a breathless first reading. Dashed first of all because Howard's book is written in the style of an old campaigner's memoirs by a craftsman for whom *Land of the Pharaohs* was a lark and an adventure (a view that happens to echo Hawks's own recorded sentiments about filmmaking), in a style that emphasizes the well-told anecdote over the telling detail, so that lots of time is spent on the spectacular physical problems of making a film about the building of a pyramid on location in Egypt, most of which seem to have fallen on the shoulders of Howard and the film's production designer, Alexandre Trauner.

Another reason for my initial disappointment is a limitation inherent in the genre: not only are such accounts usually a little boring—few things are less interesting than the making of a film—but they are also never very revealing. Certainly Howard has interesting things to tell us. We learn that he and Trauner excavated and dressed the foundations of an actual unfinished pyramid near Zaouiet al Atryanm, and that for the pan encompassing a huge quarry filled with thousands of extras they stitched two shots together by sticking a plastic boulder in front of the camera to conceal the cut, thus magnifying the number of extras. Hawks had already used that trick to magnify the number of cattle in the long pan that prefaces the cattle drive in *Red River*, quoted onscreen by Peter Bogdanovich in *The Last Picture Show* (1971), but homages to the analogous shot from *Land of the Pharaohs*—or any other shot from *Land of the Pharaohs*—are unsurprisingly few and far between.

But no book like this will ever tell us much about the director's creative processes—although Howard, a director in his own right, is in a better position than most chroniclers to understand—because directors on film sets are usually too busy to reflect on what they're doing. Add to that the enigmatic personality of Hawks, seen here at the height of the last great era of unselfconscious filmmaking in Hollywood, and the paucity of psychological material in *Hollywood sur Nil* is hardly surprising. Hawks appears in Howard's narrative as an ironic phantom, glimpsed in brief, laconic conferences with trusted lieutenants who have staggered back from the front to find their general playing golf (in Switzerland!), or tinkering with a new car, or thumbing through a copy of *Popular Mechanics*. We see him "direct" only a couple of scenes, which he seems to have had little to do with, and there isn't a word in the book about his direction of actors. (Not that there is anything implausible about this portrait. In fact, it corresponds trait for trait to what we see of Hawks in *Shoot-Out at Rio Lobo* [1970], George Plimpton's television documentary about the making of Hawks's last film.)

To know what Hawks was trying to do in *Land of the Pharaohs*, we need to hear him conversing at his leisure with Rivette, Truffaut, and Jacques Becker in an interview done for the *Cahiers* at the time of the film's release, where he talks about his intentions and the problems he encountered in realizing them. Conceived to take advantage of the recently perfected CinemaScope process (Hawks's only experiment with the format, which he never liked), *Land of the Pharaohs* began as a film about the construction of an aerodrome in China during World War II, which turned out to be unfeasible for political reasons. He gives considerable credit to William Faulkner, one of the film's three screenwriters, for his part in the elaboration of the story. He also pays tribute to Trauner and says essentially the same thing as Howard about the question of historical authenticity: a great deal of research was done, but it was not allowed to stand in the way of the filmmakers' imaginations. ("We're not making a documentary," Hawks gently reminds Howard at one point when the latter proposes an interesting solution to the problem of illuminating the stonecutters' tunnels during the quarry scene.) "I very much like this kind of work," he says in the *Cahiers* interview. "Enterprises like building an aerodrome or a pyramid show man's power, what it's possible to do with stone, sand and one's hands."

Little trace of these ideas appears in *Hollywood sur Nil*. Yet there is much in the book that repays a second reading, confirming once again that there is nothing harder for a critical eye to see than *l'évidence* (Rivette's term for the quality that pleased him most in Hawks's work).

The first point, so obvious that I hesitate to mention it, is that *Land of the Pharaohs* is a film about the making of a film. As such it would not necessarily have any special claim on our attention—all of Hawks's studies of mostly male professional groups in action can be seen as metaphors for the daily life of a film crew. But in *Land of the Pharaohs* for the first time the activities of Hawks's heroes directly mirror what used to be called "the process of production" of the film itself.

With respect to the dramatis personae, first of all. In this film about the building of a pyramid, the three main heroes are Khufu, the Pharaoh (Jack Hawkins), who orders and oversees the building of his own tomb (Hawks, the powerful producer-director); Vashtar (James Robertson Justice), the foreign architect who builds it for him (Trauner, the French production designer, charged with the construction of the pyramid for the film); and the high priest Hamar (Alexis Minotis), the Pharaoh's indispensable right hand (Noel Howard himself, whose own right hand we see in the film's second shot, tracing in hieroglyphics an account of the Pharaoh's deeds: the previous shot has shown the hand to be that of Hamar).

Second of all, with respect to the story, Hawks told the *Cahiers*, "We based our script on a single idea: the building of a pyramid." And in fact, more than for any other Hawks film, it was through the activities of Trauner, Howard, and their associates that the director's vision expressed itself in *Land of the Pharaohs*. Trauner actually designed the sets before he ever saw a page of script, commenting to Howard when he showed him the plans, "With all this, they can write what they like. We're ready."

As for the script that eventually did get written, all its main points grew out of the construction of the pyramid, the design for housing the Pharaoh's treasure, and the device used to seal the pyramid once the body and the treasure are inside. It was not until Hawks and Trauner hit on a way of accomplishing this last task, after most of the scenes of the pyramid's construction had been filmed, that Harry Kurnitz was able to write the final act. (According to what Kurnitz told Howard, Faulkner only wrote one line of the script, part of a scene where the Pharaoh, after work has been going on for several years, pays a visit to his chief architect: PHARAOH: "So . . . how is the job getting along?")

Considering the source, I'm skeptical about this piece of information, but it is emblematic of the subordination of writing to architecture in the making of *Land of the Pharaohs*—a subordinate role that Kurnitz freely admitted: "He thinks in images," he told Howard when asked about Hawks's contribution to script conferences. "I bet you no matter what I write, he already knows what he wants to shoot." A whole drama of palace intrigue unfolds around the scenes of construction, but it is those scenes—the only ones Howard writes about in his book—that are the real film. The film is the pyramid, and it ends logically with the image of the pyramid's completed form.

If we concern ourselves only with what I have called "the real film," *Land of the Pharaohs* is something very modern. What we see on the screen mirrors the process of production, which immediately generates what we see. For example, at the start of filming, Howard hits on the device of having a singer chant through a microphone to set the rhythm for the scene of the Pharaoh's workers dragging blocks of stone from the quarry, but as the crowds grow bigger and more unruly, the singer is replaced with a drum and a cymbal. This shift becomes thematic in the film. At first the builders of the pyramid sing, rejoicing in their task, but as they grow bitter and rebellious they fall silent, and a drum is used to direct their movements. The Pharaoh's goal is to build the biggest pyramid in history; Hawks's, according to Howard, is to film crowd scenes with more extras than had ever appeared in any film by De Mille—an obsession that finally provokes a mutiny by three members of the Egyptian army who have been dragooned into playing slaves. Hawks and his lieutenants have to beat them back by physical force.

Howard never underlines these parallels, but he can't have been unaware of them. After the revolt was quelled, he tells us, he experienced "a mixture of frustration and guilt" at the part he had played in the episode. One evening in the hotel bar, Faulkner makes a speech to Howard and Kurnitz about how a film company is "a state within the state," and the three men fall to imagining a *coup d'état* to topple Nasser with an army of extras flying flags emblazoned with hawk heads. A few days later Kurnitz comments to Howard that if Hitler's father had given him a movie camera for his eighteenth birthday, World War II might never have happened. And in the film, when the inhabitants of Egypt hear Pharaoh's challenge to build the pyramid, which fantastically takes the form of a voiceover proclamation that can be heard in every corner of the kingdom, like a voice on the radio, they respond with a version of the fascist salute. Like Edgar G. Ulmer in *L'Atlantide* (1932) and Jacques Tourneur in *War Gods of the Deep* (*City Under the Sea* [1965]), Hawks in *Land of the Pharaohs* holds up a mirror to his own creation. What the mirror shows him is the image of a tyrant—complex, all too human, courageous, and even sympathetic, but a tyrant nonetheless—who rules over a universe of death.

Two remarks before concluding: (1) Howard is not totally incurious about the effect of Hawks's psychological quirks on the film. For example, he records only two story ideas proposed by the director during the production, and the first of these—"That our Pharaoh will have the greatest gold treasure ever assembled"—Howard portrays as being rooted in a personal obsession. (It is certainly not a given in stories about pyramids. Hawks builds his film around the Pharaoh's fear of grave robbers and his stratagems for defeating them but never even alludes to the most famous aspect of Egyptian burial practices: mummification.) "Hawks certainly had an eye for handsome women," Howard remarks later in the book, "but what he loved more than anything was wealth, riches, gold, money. He was always ill at ease when, during a casual conversation, someone would mention the very rich men on Earth: Paul Getty, Howard Hughes, etc." And he follows this surprising observation with an illuminating anecdote.

> One day Hawks disappears. After a long search Howard finds him on the set of the Pharaoh's treasure chamber, lost in contemplation of the dazzling array of fake gold ornaments created by Trauner and his collaborators.
>
> "I sat down silently, stopped a few steps above him and waited. Hawks didn't turn around. His head moved slowly from side to side like a camera panning on its tripod. He seemed to be in a trance. We stood there for quite a while, as I didn't dare interrupt his deep contemplation. How many times had he gone down alone, switching on the lights to illuminate this "temple" where he came to worship his treasure? Suddenly a great noise broke the silence behind us: clicking his sandals, singing a preposterous song with his booming voice, Sydney Chaplin was coming down the steps, dressed in his treasure guardian's costume. Hawks spun around. His mouth open, he threw him such an outraged look that Syd stopped dead in his tracks. Hawks quickly regained his habitual poise. Indicating the set with a grand sweep of his hand he said with deep conviction, "Sydney, look at all this . . . isn't it . . . BEAUTI-FUL?" Sydney gave the wondrous sight a quick glance. "Not bad," he said, walking up the steps. "You should see my old man's cellars!"

This anecdote also serves to point up the naked honesty of Hawks's self-portrait in the character played by Jack Hawkins, who has a similar moment when he shows his young son the treasure room. After the boy's mother has taken him away to eat his supper, the Pharaoh lingers to caress one of the ornaments, first wiping his hand on his tunic with a little convulsive movement—a gesture that Hawkins acts with the finesse of Fernando Rey revealing an unsuspected perversion in a film by Buñuel.

(2) Sometimes the connections to be made are too abstruse to be evident to an eyewitness, and it is the critic's turn to help the historian. Hawks's second recorded contribution to the story is made when Trauner and Howard show him a sarcophagus dating from 800 BC that was sealed with a great rock dropped into place by a hydraulic system that ran on sand—a device that immediately suggests to Hawks a method of killing off the Pharaoh's scheming second wife, Nellifer (Joan Collins), who has

murdered both the Pharaoh and his faithful first wife in order to seize the throne, and the treasure, for herself:

> When Trauner, pencil in hand, explained the idea to Hawks, he listened intensely. Then he got up and looked at [the sarcophagus] for a long time. Finally he turned around. He was smiling. "The whole inside of the pyramid will function on this principle," he said. "One single gesture will start the whole thing going. Large stones sliding down galleries will break hundreds of potteries, releasing tons of sand, setting huge blocks of granite in motion, locking Joan Collins in forever next to the man she wanted to rob!" He shook our hands and went to see the writers.

In the climactic scene, Nellifer stands in the burial chamber next to the Pharaoh's sarcophagus, and Hamar instructs her to pull the cord setting the infernal machine in motion, while twenty-four faithful monks whose tongues have been cut out—can a grimmer reduction be imagined of the "little Hawksian group"?—impassively watch her seal her fate.

Hawks had already used this scene at the end of *Twentieth Century* (1934), when Oscar Jaffe (John Barrymore), a tyrannical theater producer down on his luck, feigns death to trick the star he "created," Lily Garland (Carole Lombard), into signing a contract that will save his career and bind her to him for eternity. The mise-en-scène is identical. Jaffe, stretched out like the Pharaoh in his sarcophagus, seems to be breathing his last as he extends the contract with a trembling hand to his sobbing protégée, begging her to put her name on it "so that it can be buried with my body." His two faithful stooges watch impassively, one of them indicating to the victim the place where she should sign . . .

Was it just a typical piece of "Hawksian humor" (the only one in the film) to end his only tragedy with a scene from his most raucous comedy? I think the connection is a more meaningful one. Oscar Jaffe is Hawks's first artist-hero and Khufu the Pharaoh is his second. For that reason the economic and psychological reading of *Land of the Pharaohs* suggested by Howard's account is not the only one possible. Hawks made *Land of the Pharaohs* to produce a blockbuster and thereby augment his personal fortune, but the film begins when the Pharaoh has already amassed the greatest treasure in history, just as *Red River* (1948) begins when Matt Dunson (John Wayne) has already built up the biggest herd of cattle ever owned by one man. Dunson needs a son to leave his empire to, and at one point he offers Tess Millay (Joanne Dru) half his fortune if she will bear one for him, before finally accepting Matthew

Garth (Montgomery Clift) as his heir; the Pharaoh, returning from his last campaign with all his goals of plunder satisfied, demands the same of his wife, who gratifies him by producing the desired heir, but even that is not enough—he must be assured of possessing the treasure in his second life, and that is why he undertakes the building of the pyramid.

Immortality—a subject that crops up more than once in Hawks's films—is the concern of artists, and in the Pharaoh's speech to his son he equates the gold he has amassed with power, another concern that artists share with tyrants. (At the end of the first day's shooting, Howard tells us, Hawks pointed to the can of undeveloped negative that was to be shipped back to Warner Bros. and said, "It's worth its weight in gold.") I think Hawks, who always denied that he was an artist (that would have meant admitting his kinship with Oscar Jaffe), made *Land of the Pharaohs* for an obvious reason. He was trying to create a masterpiece that would live forever. "The pyramid will keep his name alive," says Vashtar to his son. "In that, he built better than he knew."

I also happen to think that Hawks succeeded, but it's no secret that in the process he created the biggest flop of his career. Coming after a series of films that carried his form of classicism to its apogee (*Red River, I Was a Male War Bride* [1949], *The Big Sky, Monkey Business* [both 1952]), but which Hawks himself told Peter Bogdanovich he considered failures, the disaster of *Land of the Pharaohs* was the last straw. There followed four years of reflection before he returned to filmmaking in 1959 with *Rio Bravo*. The profound transformation that occurred in his work at this point comes down to one decision: get rid of the story (they've all been told countless times on television anyway) and make the film out of the interaction of the characters. Insofar as *Land of the Pharaohs* does have a complicated melodramatic plot—one of the most beautiful of any film epic—it represents the past, but what I have called "the real film," the self-reflecting narrative of the pyramid, already sets up a system that will culminate in *Hatari!* (1962): a plotless film about a hunting season in Africa, in which Hawks claimed, at least, that he filmed the actors actually capturing a series of wild animals and devised a plot to fit as he went along, although screenwriter Leigh Brackett, with whom Hawks regularly collaborated, and the stuntmen might tell a different story. From a formal standpoint, in any event, what we see in *Land of the Pharaohs* is both the final form of a certain classicism—that was the business of Faulkner and his collaborators—and the birth of a certain modernism, one whose progeny extends from Miklós Jancsó to Jean-Marie Straub and Danièle Huillet, and that is the story that Noel Howard tells in his invaluable book.

But *Hollywood sur Nil* would not be the document it is were it not also a personal narrative, one that at its best often concerns Noel Howard himself—his reaction to his friend Robert Capa's death in Indochina, or his many reactions to the landscape of the real Egypt surrounding this tale of tombs and palace intrigue: the terrible poverty of the inhabitants, which continually preys on his mind; a moonlit ride on the Nile with a drunken boatman; the spectacle of a burial chamber suddenly illuminated by hundreds of ancient lamps; or the unexpected discovery, which Howard was the first Westerner to share, of a solar boat buried in the wall of Cheops's pyramid. Howard wanted to make a documentary about that boat, and Hawks supported him in his project. Warner Bros., however, preferred to have a documentary about a newly discovered tomb that promised to be "as big as King Tut," so they dropped the boat project and went to film the ceremony of the unsealing, in the presence of Nasser and the American ambassador. The tomb, of course, was empty.

Notations

Serge Daney's "*Rio Lobo*: Vieillesse du Même" [The one grows old], *Cahiers du cinéma* 230 (July 1971).

The Howard Hawks interview with Jacques Rivette, François Truffaut, and Jacques Becker is in *Cahiers du cinéma* 56 (February 1956): 4–17.

I translated the quotes from *Hollywood sur Nil* (Paris: Ramsay, 2001) and Jean-Claude Biette's critical anthology *Poétique des auteurs* (*Cahiers du cinéma*, 1988), and even though the *Cahiers du cinéma* interview with Hawks has been published in *Howard Hawks: Interviews* (Jackson: University Press of Mississippi, 2006), I have revised the translation for this essay.

George Plimpton's first-person documentary *Shoot-Out at Rio Lobo* (1970), which fleshed out my ideas about Hawks's working methods, can be seen on YouTube at https://www.youtube.com/watch?v=UUVM_DVpyGA. The film in question is on YouTube at https://www.youtube.com/watch?v=HH9CzTNGAeo. Like *Bourbon Street Blues*, both the Hawks film and the Plimpton documentary have been there for years and show no sign of vanishing, so it would be helpful if the reader knew where to see them.

Hawks orchestrated the tricky circular pan of the pyramid builders in *Land of the Pharaohs* nineteen years after the circular pan showing the murder of Batala in Jean Renoir's *Le crime de Monsieur Lange* (1936), which the Francophile Hawks and his camera team, Lee Garmes and Russell Harlan, could have seen only in a private screening (it was first screened in the United States in 1964 at the Lincoln Center Film Festival), and twenty years before the circular pan of a Roman auditorium that is the *point d'orgue* of *Moses und Aron*, the film of Arnold Schoenberg's unfinished opera by Jean-Marie Straub and Danièle Huillet, which had its US premiere at the same festival in 1975. When I asked Straub about this in 1975, he copped to the Renoir homage and denied the homage to *Land of the Pharaohs* . . . but he had to think about *Land of the Pharaohs* for a few seconds. To my suspicious ear, that suggested that the Straubs had overcome the influence of Hawks—they didn't even try to deny the relationship between *Geschichtsunterricht* (their 1973 adaptation of Bertolt Brecht's *The Business Affairs of Herr Julius Caesar*) and *The Big Sleep* (1946)—by identifying with Renoir. This textbook example of transumption, one of the six "ratios of revision" Harold Bloom enumerates in *A Map of Misreading* (New York: Oxford University Press, 2003), would never have occurred to my revered teacher in his most fevered nightmares, but I'm happy to say that since my interview with the Straubs appeared in the 1975 *Cahiers du cinéma Hors-serie* on *Moses und Aron*, the Hawks-Straub relationship has been acknowledged in *Cahiers* circles, at least (see Serge Daney, *La rampe*, 1982). In fact *Land of the Pharaohs* supplied Daney with a key theoretical concept in "Vieillesse du Même": Khufu's gold vault suggested "the place of gold," a psychoanalytic metaphor for the image (the vagina), which has to be occupied by the hero (the phallus), come hell or high water, if he wishes to exist, cinematically, at all.

Apart from all that, one key theoretical concept I allude to in "Hawks at Work" is "the process of production," an idea elaborated collectively in *Cahiers du cinéma* by analogy with the pseudo-materialist literary theories of the *Tel Quel* group in the tumultuous 1970s. The "film text," we were told, should reflect its production, which was a lot easier to understand than the recondite arguments of Julia Kristeva and Philippe Sollers in *Tel Quel*, which were ultimately derived from Ferdinand de Saussure's *Course in General Linguistics*, trans. Wade Baskin (New York: Columbia University Press, 2011).

The "little Hawksian group" (aviators, hunters, race car drivers) was first theorized by the *Cahiers* critics in France and in English-speaking territories by Robin Wood.

Jacques Rivette's theory of *l'évidence* in Hawks is available to English speakers in Joseph McBride, ed., *Focus on Howard Hawks* (Englewood Cliffs: Prentice-Hall, 1972).

9

Alfred Hitchcock

Shelling the *Lifeboat*

THE NEW RESTORATION OF *Lifeboat* (1944) should spur the rediscovery of the film as one of Hitchcock's best. It has been a long
journey.

According Patrick McGilligan's *Alfred Hitchcock: A Life in Darkness and Light*, the project began much earlier than has been previously
thought. Robert Boyle, the production designer on Hitchcock's previous
film, *Shadow of a Doubt*, recalled Hitchcock showing him during that
production a clipping about a lifeboat with the cryptic comment, "It's a
small space, like a closet, isn't it?" The technical challenge of setting a

picture in a lifeboat was in his thoughts even before *Shadow*—he proposed it to that film's producer and to his employer David O. Selznick at the time—much as, while he was shooting *Dial M for Murder* (1953), he was already planning the details of *Rear Window* (1954). *Lifeboat* was as ambitious as that later "single set" film, and on its own terms was just as successful.

Unfortunately, *Lifeboat* was buried by the studio after opening in New York because Bosley Crowther, the newly installed *New York Times* film critic, had written: "The Nazis, with some cutting here and there, could turn *Lifeboat* into a whiplash against the 'decadent democracies.'" (People who suffered through the end of Crowther's twenty-five-year reign at the Gray Lady still remember his 1964 review of *Dr. Strangelove*, where he wrote: "I am troubled by the feeling, which runs all through the film, of discredit and even contempt for our whole defense establishment, up to and even including the hypothetical Commander in Chief.")

Lifeboat proposed a political analysis of the Allies' situation in 1944 and still worked as drama, like many films of the foreign masters whom Crowther would champion over Hollywood after the war, like Roberto Rossellini, Jean Renoir, Luis Buñuel, and Satyajit Ray. But Crowther's objection to Hitchcock was political, like the violent attack by the respected liberal political columnist Dorothy Thompson, who no doubt had noticed that the character of the mink-clad journalist in the lifeboat (Tallulah Bankhead) was based on her.

Crowther's review and an even harsher follow-up op-ed piece produced an effect reminiscent of the scenes in the film where the characters, despite being literally in the same boat, fall out and quarrel with each other to the delight of the German captain (Walter Slezak) whose submarine sank their ship: stung by the charges, John Steinbeck had his agent send Crowther his treatment, a short novel that had been substantially altered by Hitchcock and screenwriter Jo Swerling when they turned it into a movie. Crowther then wrote a third piece putting the blame on Hitchcock for the supposed defeatism and other purported failings, like racial stereotyping, that he could blame on Hollywood, rounding it off with a blast at the director for trampling on the creative rights of a great man of letters.

Because of the hysterical misreadings it provoked from Thompson, Crowther, the Office of War Information, and a nameless array of pressure groups, *Lifeboat*'s hermeneutic voyage now took a detour—a long one—through France. The film was held back from overseas distribution at the suggestion of the OWI, with the result that Hitchcock's French champions, so important in shaping his critical reputation, were late in discovering it. André Bazin, the founder of *Cahiers du cinéma*, and his

chief disciple, Eric Rohmer, saw it when it was commercially distributed
in France for the first time in 1956, with the dazzling example of *Rear
Window* fresh in their minds.

They knew a masterpiece when they finally saw it—Bazin called
Lifeboat "one of Hitchcock's most brilliant films." But so long after the
war, the film's "ideological" aims—the need for "righteous anger [to]
sweep away Anglo-Saxon pragmatic liberalism, that is to say the need
for war"—had become a problem. In addition, the rhetoric of those aims
(a message movie) had become suspect. For Bazin, reality in cinema, his
aesthetic touchstone, could not be made to serve a cause or ideology.
Because the residue of political meaning bothered him, he suggested the
thought experiment of imagining *Lifeboat* without its soundtrack: "We
would attribute to characters and events motives stripped bare of any
ideology. I believe that way the film is almost perfect."

In his own review Rohmer defended the film's dialogue and concluded that it was an unembellished apologue for Hitchcock's dark view
of humanity, which decrees that the passengers, even though they are
right, become "ignoble" when they murder the Nazi. Rohmer was turning
the volume down when Connie Porter (Tallulah Bankhead) says loud and
clear: "We weren't a mob when we killed him. We were a mob when we
sat around and let ourselves become prisoners of the man we'd saved,
kowtowing to him, obeying him, practically heiling him because he was
kind enough and strong enough to take us to a concentration camp."

Six years later when François Truffaut interviewed Hitchcock,
the interviewer made a show of rejecting the party line—"everyone is
guilty"—and the director rewarded him with his famous description of
the murderous passengers looking "like a pack of dogs," which has stuck.
The ambiguity of reality and the ambiguity of the human soul—both
Bazinian articles of faith—had carried the day over the outdated political message. This way of defending *Lifeboat* against its own ideological
baggage became canonical: it is still the standard interpretation, and such
a strong one that it would be foolish to try to read it out of the film.

Instead I would like to try starting from the assumption that *Lifeboat*
is a great political film, along with *Aventure Malgache* (on the same DVD),
one of two shorts Hitchcock made after wrapping *Lifeboat* to promote the
cause of the French Resistance. *Aventure Malgache* focused its bare-bones
Brechtian dramaturgy on divisions within the Free French, and appears to
have been withheld from distribution, like *Lifeboat*, for being too incisive.

The word "Brechtian" may seem out of place in the same sentence
with the Master of Suspense, but Brecht's plays were by this time part
of American theater and film culture. Steinbeck certainly knew Brecht's
work, and we can assume that inveterate theatergoers Alfred and Alma

Hitchcock did, too. (In England Hitchcock had twice filmed dramas of ideas with political import: Sean O'Casey's *Juno and the Paycock* [1930] and John Galsworthy's *The Skin Game* [1931].) And the testimony of Barbara Harris, an expert on theater and film acting who appeared in *Mother Courage* on Broadway (from March to May 1963), about being directed by Hitchcock in his last film, *Family Plot* (1976), is pertinent to *Lifeboat*:

> I call it Brechtian-type directing. Because he sees a scene, not so much for the subjective emotional intent that he's interested in, but what the scene is about. In the cab scene [of *Plot*], I didn't know if I was supposed to be a sex-starved girl with my boyfriend, or what. He said it was a business scene. So then I became a businesswoman. Which is a Brechtian idea. Brecht would say, "Well, what would Hamlet be like in the kitchen with the servants?"

Following Harris's hint, the catchphrase that identifies the businessman Rittenhouse (Henry Hull) the moment he climbs into the lifeboat—hands rubbing together: "We're back in business now"—is a Brechtian *gestus*: facial and gestural expression indicating social relations at a historical juncture. Virtually everything Rittenhouse does and says is a *gestus*, and the same is true, to differing degrees, of the other passengers: Joe the black porter (Canada Lee, fresh from playing Bigger Thomas in Orson Welles's production of *Native Son* [March–June 1941]); Connie with her mink; John Hodiak as Kovac the engineer (almost a Communist, Hitchcock told Truffaut); Gus, a patriotic working man (William Bendix); a pacifist nurse (Mary Anderson); a Cockney radio operator (Hume Cronyn) who represents America's British allies; and a British woman with her dead baby who recall their sacrifices before America entered the war.

Willie, the German submarine captain, is a Brechtian character for a different reason: we are immediately shown what he is and what he is up to, the better to watch him manipulate his captors. That's how Hitchcock had started off *Shadow of a Doubt* (1943), with serial strangler Uncle Charlie (Joseph Cotten) lying in bed surrounded by loose cash, as he learns from his landlady that two men are looking for him whom he's been expecting, even though he has never seen them. The rhyming scene in *Lifeboat* would be Willie yawning and stretching out to sleep while the suicidal mother is being tied to her chair after physically attacking him for killing her baby.

After that, like Uncle Charlie, we are given many glimpses of him not vouchsafed to the other characters, even as we watch them (like

Uncle Charlie's innocent niece, Young Charlie [Teresa Wright]) gradually figure him out. Hitchcock would call this suspense, not surprise, both of which are supposed to be the antithesis of Brechtian stagecraft, but Hitchcockian suspense makes the spectator an active participant in the drama. This is accompanied by a certain de-dramatization. For example, two big acting opportunities for Bankhead—raging about losing her camera and offering the mother with the dead baby her mink—are elided, the first by flat delivery ("as if she were quoting," Brecht would say) and the second by occurring offscreen. One can understand her supposedly irrational hatred of Walter Slezak, a sly underactor who steals the film from her as soon as he appears. The use of backs, which isn't limited to the killing of Willie (cf. Anderson's confession to Cronyn), is a highly stylized form of de-dramatization.

Hitchcock's approach is the opposite of realism, as has been noted by critics of *Lifeboat* ranging from Rohmer, who regretted the studio-bound setting (and later did it himself in *Perceval* [1978]); to the generally favorable 1944 *Time* review, which cites impossibilities like the absence in close-ups of swollen, chapped lips; to the great skeptic Manny Farber, who wrote in 1944: "You will come out of this movie knowing no more of what it is like in a lifeboat with a few people in mid-ocean than you did when you went in." Absurdities range from the impossibility of one man, even hopped up on Nazi bennies, rowing a lifeboat that size, to the appearance of a comical carp (a freshwater fish) in underwater shots that scream "Fish tank!"

Farber forged his own version of a realistic aesthetic during the war years, comparing British and Hollywood war films and finding the former better in exemplary ways. (His favorite film of 1942 had been Noel Coward's *In Which We Serve*.) Made according to that aesthetic, *Lifeboat* might have followed Steinbeck's heavily researched short novel by having the bearded men put on Connie's lipstick to protect their lips, which would have been an interesting image if the film had been made, as was briefly planned, in color. But Hitchcock had other fish to fry.

In his own follow-up article on *Lifeboat*, Farber formulated a theory of film space that is also a theory of *Lifeboat*, starting from a metaphor coined in that first review: "The lifeboat gives less the illusion of a lifeboat . . . than of an expansive, well-protected stage." Extending the metaphor he posits that "the use of 'theatrical' as a movie description depends essentially on the way the events of the film are related to the camera eye. . . . If the events are not treated as spontaneous, unaltered happenings witnessed by an impersonal camera, but are arranged before it as though it were the eye of an audience and the events developed in order that they might be seen by the camera in the role of an audience, the process is essentially a theatrical one." Presented by Farber as a destructive trend in Hitchcock's work, this is nonetheless the best description I've seen of *Lifeboat*'s visual style: those magnificent frescoes that enable Hitchcock to sell "solid talk in rather close quarters" by creating "a certain realism on a theatrical level."

As Hitchcock explained to Truffaut, cinema began with the theatrical proscenium, and for him there was always a theater lurking inside any film image, which is metaphorically evoked by the train in *The Lady Vanishes* (1938) (a political allegory about Munich), the courtyard in *Rear Window* (a film that begins with a curtain rising), and the cafe where humans taking shelter from a bird attack hold their war council in *The Birds* (1963). In fact Hitchcock was already working out the blocking of *Lifeboat* in *Saboteur* (1942) during the debate inside a cramped circus-car full of freaks, which he restaged in *Torn Curtain* (1964) with a bus full of East German freedom fighters.

Hitchcock's little theater is less a microcosm—although Hitchcock himself called it that in *Lifeboat*—than a constant collision of perspectives. This description is better suited to the dynamism of a film that constructs its hypnotic flow and symphony of blacks and grays from shots of which few are repeated. Quick fades to black (or an occasional gorgeous dissolve, like the one from Slezak to Cronyn and Anderson against an abstractly rendered night sky) take the place of cards between scenes of the play ("Capital accuses Labor of Marking the Cards"): little blackouts in the film's synapses that suggest that the lifeboat is a brain malfunctioning as we watch, until the primitive part takes over and older patterns of behavior appear.

Hitchcock's little theaters are populated by characters from all of society, a capacity the Russian theorist Mikhail Bakhtin attributes to the scene of carnival, the equivalent of the public square where ancient carnival rites were enacted on the steps of the town cathedral in medieval Europe. Carnival festivities, in which all levels and conditions of society can collide and converse, producing a babble of perspectives, are a period of ritual disorder when the world is turned upside down and a criminal rules in place of the king. At the end of the carnival period, depending on the local custom, the king might actually be killed and ritually dismembered (*sparagmos*).

This is what we see enacted on the "stage" of *Lifeboat*, whose properties as described by Farber are designed to display just such an action. The inversion that occurs when Willie, a prisoner, becomes the captain of the lifeboat (the king) and the passengers become his prisoners, can only be resolved with the last great fresco of figures who conceal their deed from our sight, as it would have been concealed in Euripides. One indelible image shows Slezak's face bobbing up, disfigured by the savage beating so that it is no longer really a face, before being swallowed again by all the passengers, whose backs are to us except for two glimpses of the gentlest characters, the nurse and the radio operator, who seem to be doing the bulk of the killing. This is the final act of the collectivity formed when the world is upside down and society's values are replaced by the gut and "The Divine Bottle" (Rabelais)—distantly evoked, perhaps, by Gus's bottle of brandy, in which the level never changes.

Carnival patterns are one way Brecht's theater produces catharsis as well as understanding (the clash of perspectives). His *Threepenny Opera* (opening August 1928) inverts the social hierarchy, casting cutpurses as capitalists, and sacrifices its mock king, Macheath, on the gallows (a mock execution interrupted by a royal pardon). In fact it has been suggested that "the carnivalesque . . . is more fundamental to Brecht's art and peculiar outlook than his espoused loyalty to left-wing politics" (Hans-Peter Breuer, "The Non-Political Brecht," in the 1992 Symposium *Brecht Unbound*). Of course this assumes that the carnivalesque has nothing to do with politics, when it is often found at the heart of revolutionary art, like the Day of the Dead sequence in *¡Que viva México!* (1932).

Brilliantly played by Walter Slezak, Willie embodies the prewar German culture that Hitchcock knew and loved—he and Slezak had both worked for UFA—but in Willie's hands that culture has become a sophisticated form of barbarism. A mini-battle of the bands ends when Joe's flute stops playing jive and, in Rittenhouse's hands, accompanies the Captain as he sings, while rowing, an artful pastiche of a folksong by Schubert, with words by Goethe:

> Once upon a time a boy saw a rose growing, a little rose on the heath, and it looked so sweetly fresh and dewy that he ran to see it closer, and looked at it with delight; it was a rose, a little rose, a little red rose on the heath.
>
> And the boy said: I'm going to pick you, little rose on the heath! But the rose said: I shan't let you, and what's more I'm going to prick you so hard that you won't ever forget me. So said the rose, the little rose, the little red rose on the heath.
>
> All the same, that rough boy picked the little rose on the heath; the rose defended itself and pricked as promised, but its cries of distress were in vain; it had to suffer. Oh, rose, little rose, little red rose on the heath.

I leave it to readers who have more German than I do to enjoy how Hitchcock handles that eerie Blakean ballad in the editing, which shows Slezak telling the other lifeboat passengers, in words they can't understand, where he is taking them. Connie understands the words but enjoys playing footsie to them with Kovak too much to think past the sexual innuendoes. Willie turns his eyes from her legs and their feet to impassively watch Gus profiting from their distraction to fish for saltwater to drink, an equally appropriate action for the macabre accompaniment he is singing. German culture has already become sinister to Hitchcock in *Suspicion* (1941), his second wartime film, when Cary Grant's silhouette carries the poisoned milk up to Joan Fontaine accompanied by Strauss's *Weiner Blut* (Vienna Blood).

Willie is Falstaff, Shakespeare's comic version of England's medieval Lord of Misrule—portly, witty, seductive—with the soul of Prince Hal (whom Orson Welles once described as a fascist): a Brechtian rewriting of the stereotypical Nazi swine who was educated at Oxford. His "resistible" rise must end in a blood sacrifice from which society can be reborn. Bazin suspected that the message of *Lifeboat* was the same as that of all American films made during the war, but *Lifeboat* dramatizes the message in a way that exposes it to scrutiny that made people uncomfortable in 1944 and no doubt always will.

While *Lifeboat* may be eternally stuck on the B-side of *Shadow of a Doubt*, the two films, made back-to-back when Hitchcock was at the height of his powers, are one of his double platinum discs. They also illuminate each other, as Rohmer was no doubt thinking when he described *Lifeboat* as an apologue in which the subtext of Hitchcock's earlier films is all on the surface, laid out like a theorem. Willie's counterpart in *Shadow of a Doubt* is Charles Oakley (aka the Merry Widow Murderer): a sporty visitor from the city who sets a small town on its ear, before Young Charlie, his niece, is forced to kill him in self-defense. The hero's final speech would have resonated with wartime audiences, in a film where the war is everywhere on the edges of the scenes but never spoken of: "[The world] goes a little crazy sometimes. Just like your Uncle Charlie."

Hitchcock was making anti-Nazi thrillers before he left England and continued making them while on loan-out from Selznick, but *Lifeboat* is his only war film—that is to say, his only film about war—and unlike more straightforward propaganda films, it takes its subject seriously enough to raise questions at every turn. Is fascism better than democracy? (No, because the lifeboat is headed in the right direction, arrived at by democratic discussion, before the Nazi tricks them into changing course.) Should Willie be killed or saved? Should Gus, who's dying anyway, keep using scant supplies? Is Joe allowed to vote?

Because of the heightened lucidity of *Lifeboat*, the allegorical justification of war and the loss of innocence it entails in *Shadow of a Doubt* raise fewer doubts than the blackboard version of the same idea, which begins with the sinking of an American supply ship and the shelling of the lifeboats and ends with the sinking of a German supply ship and the shelling of the lifeboat sent out to pick up the castaways. *Lifeboat* emerges from the gray fog that Steinbeck wanted at the beginning of the film, like the Stygian seascape littered with wreckage and corpses that Hitchcock's camera pans up from a floating life jacket to disclose, and the film never forgets where it comes from as it struggles to see clearly through the fog of war. There is no other Hitchcock film like it, but it has the visual and moral complexity of the great Hitchcock films and a sublimity worthy of its theme, which lift it above even the best films made during the war. "*Lifeboat* is circumspect," as an enthused reviewer writes, "and asks profound questions about war, and values, and vulnerability. It second guesses itself. It wonders."

Notations

Hitchcock's comment about the closet was shared by Robert Boyle in a February 2, 1982, roundtable discussion about the making of *The Birds*, "Ils ont fabrique *Les oiseaux*," *Cahiers du cinéma* 337 (June 1982): 36–48.

Crowther on *Lifeboat* is in the *New York Times*, January 13, 1944, page 17, and again on January 23, section 2, page 3. On *Dr. Strangelove*, he is in the *New York Times*, January 30, 1964. André Bazin discusses *Lifeboat* in chapter 5 of *The Cinema of Cruelty from Buñuel to Hitchcock*, ed. François Truffaut, trans. Sabine d'Estrée (New York: Arcade, 1982).

Barbara Harris's comment about Hitchcock is quoted on page 727 of Patrick McGilligan's *Alfred Hitchcock: A Life in Darkness and Light* (New York: Regan, 2003).

The Manny Farber comments on *Lifeboat* are in his chapter "Among the Missing: Hitchcock," in *Farber on Film* (New York: Library of America, 2016).

On Brecht's carnivalesque, see Hans-Peter Breuer, "The Non-Political in Brecht," in James K. Lyon and Hans-Peter Breuer, eds., *Brecht Unbound* (Newark: University of Delaware Press, 1995).

The comment about *Lifeboat* being circumspect is from D. C. Bruton, available at https://www.imdb.com/title/tt0370717/reviews?ref_=tt_ql_3.

10

Alfred Hitchcock

Dark Carnival

W HAT WE KNOW ABOUT *Aventure Malgache* (1944), the remarkable
short Alfred Hitchcock made to show how the flame of the
Resistance had burned brightly in the colonies, we owe to
Alain Kerzoncuf, who discovered that Jules François Clermont, the actor
who plays Clarus, the leader of the Resistance in Malgache (Madagascar),
had been a lawyer there before the war and had lived the adventure told
in the film—as if Pina, the heroine of Roberto Rossellini's *Open City*
(1945), had been played, not by Anna Magnani, but by a real heroine
of the Resistance. By 1944 Clermont had joined the Molière Players, a

troupe of exiled French performers assembled in London, because the
Allies could no longer employ him in a staff position during the coming
invasion of the continent. Having been on the stage before taking up the
law, he now went back to his first profession.

After meeting with Hitchcock, who had traveled in steerage to
London to contribute to the war effort, Clermont was commissioned
to write a script in tangy colloquial French with Hitchcock's future
collaborator Angus MacPhail, whom the director first met at Claridge's
in London during preproduction for this film and another, *Bon Voyage*
(1944), made to be shown in France when the Allies landed. (The opening credits address a specific "vous" that never saw the film: the French
people who had been living under Nazi occupation.) The collaboration
with the gifted MacPhail lasted until the writer died of alcoholism after
outlining the structure of *Vertigo* (1958) for Hitchcock. *Aventure Malgache*,
shelved until 1999 at the request of the French, who didn't care for its
portrayal of the political and economic contradictions at the heart of the
French Empire during the Occupation (for example, the black-skinned
servants whose wordless presence makes its own comment), didn't fare
much better, but both have now gotten their due. *Ars longa, vita brevis*.

The account of Clermont's war in *Aventure Malgache* cuts some
corners for reasons of budget. He was being shipped to a penal colony
when British warships stopped the convoy and freed him, setting him
up as Radio Free Madagascar on a ship in the Indian Ocean. Hitchcock,
who didn't have the money to film a scene at sea, built a dungeonlike set
for Clarus's maritime prison from which he could see the smokestacks of
British ships coming to save him. (His joyous exclamations are greeted
by a fellow prisoner's muttered "giveafuck"s, which are left untranslated
in the BFI's subtitles.) The British invasion of Madagascar, which is
shown in newsreel footage, then leads to the scene where Clarus has
the pleasure of broadcasting back to the man who imprisoned him, the
gangster and Vichy turncoat Michel (Paul Bonifas), that the British are
coming for him.

The film pays tribute to a hero of the Resistance by having him
reenact for Hitchcock's camera the daring subversion that made him
famous. Clarus introduces the show with a few words in Malagasy, the
language of Madagascar, then does the "knock knock" sound effect that
introduced all his broadcasts. Poverty of means spurs a wealth of invention. It's hard not to read this as a metaphor for *Aventure Malgache*, a
better film than *Spellbound* (1945), which Hitchcock put on hold when
he came to England, despite MacPhail's contributions to the latter when
he followed the director back to California: David O. Selznick spent lavishly on *Spellbound*, then lopped off MacPhail's opening sequence, set in a

mental asylum, and truncated the dream sequence planned by Hitchcock and another gifted collaborator, Salvador Dalí.

Selznick's tinkering paved the way for the psychoanalysis-on-skis sequence that would be Hitchcock's ludicrous first attempt to portray that impossible-to-portray process until he and screenwriter Jay Presson Allen finally nailed it with the psychoanalysis-in-the-boudoir sequence that resolves the mystery of the heroine's frigidity in *Marnie* (1964). By way of contrast, despite the gripes about too much dialogue from "users" and professional critics alike preserved on IMDb, *Aventure Malgache* deftly pulls off a psychoanalysis of the Occupation carried out in France's colonial unconscious, tucked away out of sight in the Indian Ocean, which anticipates the triumphs wrought by "talky" Hitchcockians ranging from Eric Rohmer to the Straubs long after *Aventure Malgache* had been consigned to the vaults.

The situation we see in the dressing room of the Molière Players (created to give French actors in exile a way to participate in the fight while hiding their identities to protect their relatives in France) is one that could really have happened: Clarus advising a colleague on how to play the villain in a play they're getting made up for by telling him about his personal nemesis in Malgache to enable him to get into the skin of a real-life Nazi.

While Clarus explains the character of Michel to this colleague as they prepare to take the stage—translation: to begin the film we're watching—the latter gradually dons the makeup that accompanies his inner transformation as he gets into character. Hitchcock stages the transitions so that, when we cut from the dressing room to the trial scene in the first flashback, Michel's back is to us, and we discover his features only gradually. The figure looming in the foreground of the trial sequence, whose face is also turned away from the camera, is Clarus, the witness—in reality and within the film—to everything that happens in this early Hitchcock experiment with single-point-of-view storytelling.

It would have taken a while for French spectators—had they been permitted to see the film—to realize that the actor playing the villain of the stage piece is the same one who plays Michel in the flashbacks.

Hitchcock has never been subtler, in fact. Clarus recounts, and the film shows, how the Resistance-friendly governor of Madagascar was forced by Michel to put a spy on Clarus's tail to uncover his Resistance activities. Back in the present of the film's narration, the other actors in the dressing room joke that Clarus must have been killed and ask how he could get away with anything while being tailed. "Nothing simpler," says Clarus. Cut to Clarus entering the cellar that is Resistance headquarters to address the troops, arm in arm with his tail. The ceiling of this odd little set is decorated with symbols from the Zodiac: Fate, looming like Wagner's Valkyries over the Resistance, will have to be overcome by guile.

As with the real and reel Michels, the spectator has to use his eyes to understand these gags, and the actor playing the part of the false spy doesn't make it easy. His dress and demeanor change considerably between the office of the governor, where we met him, and the cellar, and no dialogue hints that this is the same man come to the aid of spectators who haven't been paying attention. In *Bon Voyage*, Hitchcock's other wartime short, the action recounted in flashback happens at night, teaching the spectator a political lesson in how to read images. *Aventure Malgache*, which happens in bright light (including an uncanny scene of treachery illuminated through a sheet), is a lesson in how to see.

At the end of the film the nameless actor preparing to play a Nazi, who now sports Michel's moustache, picks a fight with the indignant Clarus, who realizes when the transformation is complete that his colleague has become Michel and they are talking to each other the way they did back in Malgache. They have become the characters they're playing, like Norman Bates in *Psycho* (1960), still sixteen years in the future. As they leave the dressing room to go on stage, "Michel" buttons the jacket of his Nazi uniform and Clarus dons the costume of a Resistance fighter. The flashback is over, but the struggle goes on.

Does the budget alone account for the bare-bones staging of some scenes, like the one with uncanny illumination where a hysterical woman whose motives are never explained in words picks up the phone to denounce Clarus, where the set is a bed and a gauze curtain with a light behind it? Perhaps, but the production seems to have had a dolly, a costly piece of equipment for a no-budget short, which the director uses here to pull back until the phone that seems to be controlling her actions, like the stolen money on Marion Crane's bed in *Psycho*, is in the frame. Other scenes where the dolly is being used in offbeat ways include the one with the pooterish Vichy general, during which the camera moves closer to the characters, almost imperceptibly, until Michel is center frame, then pans right each time the general paces nearer to the camera. There is also a rather modern quick dolly-in on Michel during the trial. For viewers who aren't hypnotized by the dialogue they hate (cf. those IMDb comments), there's quite a lot being done with the camera in this little film.

If *Lifeboat* (1944) is a film influenced by Brechtian stagecraft, *Aventure Malgache* is a Freudian miniature, with Michel occupying the place of Willie (Walter Slezak), the German submarine captain. "I see the type you mean," says Boniface, playing the nameless actor who is having Michel explained to him in preparation for his own performance as a Nazi he considers underwritten and opaque. "A rat like Laval" (a Vichy official executed after the war). "No," says Clarus, "he was a roly-poly man . . ." Surfaces are deceptive when the Unconscious is calling the shots.

Aventure Malgache also reproduces the mythical structure of *Lifeboat* by equating the rise to power of Michel, a gangster, with a period of misrule: a dark carnival that can end only when the Lord of Misrule who presides over it is killed. Although we don't see Michel go before a firing squad, we're assured that the British weren't fooled by him when they arrived in Malgache. He sticks his framed picture of Petain (shown in the first insert used in this little film) under the fridge, prudently stashes his bottle of Vichy Water—this is the second insert—inside the fridge, an expensive but invaluable item in the tropics in 1944, and puts up a picture of Queen Victoria where Petain had been.

The last dolly (a cut, actually: Hitchcock's own pricey equipment had its limitations) isolates the motto at the top of the painting: *Honi Soit qui Mal y Pense*, Latin for "Shame on anyone who sees evil in it"— an ironic motto that French spectators in 1944, who spoke a language descended from Latin, would have had no trouble parsing: Michel, who embodies Collaboration, would be quickly spotted and put to death by the Free French accompanying the British invaders, the way the enraged lifeboat passengers execute Willie when they realize he's steering them to a concentration camp.

Notations

Alain Kerzoncuf's "Hitchcock's *Aventure Malgache* (or the True Story of DZ 91)" is published in *Senses of Cinema* 41 (November 2014), available online at www.sensesofcinema.com.

Much is to be learned from François Truffaut and Helen Scott, *Hitchcock* (New York: Simon & Schuster 1967; rpt. 1985), and readers may also want to look at Bill Krohn, *Hitchcock at Work* (London: Cahiers-Phaidon, 2000).

Angus MacPhail had been driven to drink by dialogue writer John Michael Hayes, who should have shared screen credit for the script of *The Man Who Knew Too Much* (1956) with him but didn't because the ambitious Hayes was American and a dues-paying member of the WGA, founded in 1954 to look after the rights of American screenwriters but not of English writers working on American films—a situation that the Guild had not yet figured out, although Hitchcock imposed his own solution: he never worked with Hayes again. When *Aventure Malgache* was finally released in 1999, MacPhail was properly credited as the coauthor of the screenplay with Clermont. He was subsequently the credited screenwriter on such classics as *Dead of Night* (1945), *Whiskey Galore* (1949), and, for Hitchcock, *The Wrong Man* (1956). He is cited in books on the Master as the man who invented the concept of the MacGuffin.

On the psychoanalytic symbolism of characters facing away from the camera, see Stephen Heath and Janet Bergstrom, eds., "Cinema and Psychoanalysis: Parallel Histories," in *Endless Night: Cinema and Psychoanalysis, Parallel Histories* (Berkeley: University of California Press, 1999), 25–56. Heath discovers this figuration of the Unconscious in early films about psychoanalysis like G. W. Pabst's *Secrets of a Soul* (1926).

The eerie illumination in the scene where Clarus is denounced to the Gestapo recalls the scene with Judith Anderson and Joan Fontaine in dead Rebecca's dressing room (*Rebecca* [1940]). Hitchcock disliked *Rebecca* because he didn't have complete control when he made it (cf. the ham-fisted scenes with George Sanders), but for that very reason it seems to have haunted him, as we can see in this little scene in *Aventure Malgache* where the Unconscious is in the driver's seat.

Directors Who Started in Talkies

"All This Is So"

Orson Welles's Shakespeare Films

A FEW YEARS AGO IN A 1986 article on Orson Welles's television
work, "Welles, Television, and the Essay Film," I suggested that
Welles's oeuvre could be conveniently divided into two "radicals
of presentation," to borrow a term from the Canadian literary critic
Northrop Frye: drama and *epos*, by which Frye means the art of the
oral storyteller. Frye's radicals are not to be confused with what another
great Canadian called media—they are situations that can be imitated
in any medium. Frye lists four radicals of presentation based on varying combinations of three elements: author, audience, and characters. In

drama (the radical of presentation of the narrative film), the author is absent, while characters and audience are co-present; in *epos* (the radical of presentation of the essay film), the author and his audience are co-present, while the characters are absent.

Having already argued in that article for the existence of the invisible strand of *epos* in the Welles oeuvre, I now want to consider the other part of the drama/*epos* symmetry from the point of view of a problem I raised when I first proposed applying it to Welles: "What Welles did was to bring these twin arts of presence—arts that depend on the co-presence of performer and audience—into media where the audience is confronted with performers who are absent." My answer will focus on the inscription of the radical of presentation of drama in the three extant Shakespeare films, seen from a theoretical perspective supplied by André Bazin and by Welles himself, in a youthful essay on theater that I think deserves to be better known.

Theory: Bazin and Welles

Let's begin with Bazin, whose essay "Film et théâtre" (1951) fleshes out the idea of the dramatic radical of presentation, after taking an aggressive polemical stance on the subject of "presence." Bazin argues that we can explain the success of filmed theater pieces like Welles's *Macbeth* (1948) only if we "call into question the commonplace of theatrical criticism, 'the irreplaceable presence of the actor.'" What matters is the relationship created between the actors and the audience, and this finally comes down to the audience's attitude: "It is to the extent that cinema favors the process of identification with the hero that it is opposed to theatre." Bazin had echoed contemporary criticisms of the solitude and passivity of the film spectator in his 1941 article "Créer un publique," where he spoke of recovering "something of the human 'presence' of theatre." The way to do that, he argues in 1951, is through "an aesthetic of decor and decoupage": "If cinema cannot restore to the spectator the communal consciousness of theatre, a certain science of mise-en-scène will permit [the filmmaker] . . . to conserve the text's sense and effect[,] . . . that consciousness of the active opposition between spectator and actor that constitutes theatrical performance and which the architecture [of theater] symbolizes." For Bazin, the quintessential example of that symbolic architecture is the Teatro Olimpico built in Vicenza by Palladio at the end of his life, which happens to have been the last attempt by a Renaissance architect to reproduce, at a time when our modern picture-frame stage had already made its appearance, the theatrical space of a classical Roman theater. Only in such a symbolic space, Bazin argues, can the theatrical text properly resonate; transplanted into a conventional cinematic decoup-age, "the dramatic energy of the text . . . will lose itself without an echo in the cinematographic ether."

In the essay "On Staging Shakespeare and on Shakespeare's Stage" that Welles wrote for the *Everybody's Shakespeare* series he edited with Roger Hill in the early thirties, Welles offers a definition of theater made up of the same three elements that Bazin articulates to define the radical of presentation of drama in its original purity—an audience present in the same space as the actors, a space with certain architectural properties where that interaction occurs, and a text written to resonate in such a space. Welles argues that the Elizabethan theater is the proper home for Shakespeare's plays and blames the difficulties of staging them today on changes in theater architecture, but whereas Bazin's precepts for transposing theater to film embody the familiar Bazinian idea of the progress of the arts, Welles at eighteen is already recounting a drama of decline—typically Wellesian in that the author's attitude toward the drama is ambiguous, and told in two acts, which irresistibly invite us to write the third:

Act I: "England's stage . . . was simply an inn yard fixed up for a play but without the inn. The stage platform was made permanent with a roof over it to protect the actors but the rabblement still had to stand around this platform in the rain or sun. An inner stage with a curtain and a level above it like a gallery was added inside. Benches were built in the spectators' galleries where you sat if you had money. . . . Scenery, with only a few exceptions, and confined mostly to that little inner stage, remained in court ball-rooms for masques and musical spectacles where everybody thought it belonged."

Act II: Cromwell, Puritanism, the closing of the theaters, the Res-toration, and the growth of a new dramatic literature that had become, Welles notes cuttingly, "almost as immoral as the Puritans thought it was." He goes on to argue, however, that

> the methods of performing Shakespeare were most changed
> by the physical changes in the playhouses. . . . The forestage
> turned into what is called an apron, and grew smaller and
> smaller with the improvement of stage lighting. Certain of
> the Elizabethan gallants had been sometimes permitted to sit
> on the sides of the platform and show off, and this one early
> ostentation was inherited and developed into the stage box.
> Nobility was now framed in little stages of its own on each side
> of the big one. . . . Decoration was acutely elaborate . . . and
> the stage was not to be outdone by the auditorium. The

forestage having dwindled into an apron and stage-boxes, the playing space was now one gigantic inner-stage. This it has remained with the court-masque idea of literal and scenic effect having been gorgeously and quite irreparably enlarged upon.

Poetry has since then been neither necessary nor possible because when you can make the dawn over Elsinore with a lantern and a pot of paint there's no call for having a character stop in the middle of the action to say a line like, "But look, the morn, in russet mantle clad, walks o'er the dew of yon high eastern hill," even supposing you could **write** a line like that. You can't see and hear beauty, fully, at the same time.

"Before the Restoration," Welles concludes, "theatres were court-yards around platforms where you went to hear and to be heard. Since then they've been birthday cakes in front of picture-frames where you go to see and be seen."

Turn that picture frame into a screen for the projection of a spectacle from which the audience, invisible in the dark, is separated by the barrier that divides being from nonbeing, and we have our third act: the reinscription of the radical of presentation of drama in a medium where theater as the arena for actors and audience to celebrate the ritual of the text has become a fiction—that is to say, any narrative film, but particularly one adapted from a play. If my extrapolation of this youthful polemic has any truth to it, Welles in 1933, seven years before he became a film director, saw the evolution of Western scenography that had led to narrative film as a devolution, a loss of energy, a dangerous decadence— albeit one that brought with it compensating gifts: "To be fair . . . ," he notes after describing the tawdrier innovations of Restoration drama, "the theatre acquired on its return a new and considerable style." The same would have to be said of the discoveries that lay ahead for Welles in the medium he was to revolutionize, but it is worth remembering that from the outset he had reasons, fully spelled out in the Shakespeare preface, to be suspicious of the alienating power of cinema, a suspicion which I believe Welles the filmmaker never ceased to entertain.

Symbolic Architecture

Assuming that these were the contours of the problem as Welles saw it, how did he solve it, as a stage director and then as a filmmaker?

First of all, paradoxically, by aggravating the conversion of theater into spectacle. We see this in the *Everybody's Shakespeare* editions, which are themselves an attempt to recover for plays that pedagogues had exiled to the printed page the dramatic radical of presentation, complete with italicized indications of the gestures, expressions and intonations with which lines were to be performed. Despite his recommendation in the preface that students should try staging Shakespeare on a bare platform set up in the local gym, Welles illustrates the texts of the plays with drawings of sets, costumes, and scenic effects reflecting a philosophy of production that is anything but ascetic, and when he attacked the same problem in practice as a theater director, he showed no inclination to return to the simplicity of Shakespeare's Globe: contemporary accounts of the production of *Macbeth* he staged in Harlem three years after writing that preface, for example, describe a concatenation of scenic, lighting, and sound effects that make the musical version of *The Phantom of the Opera* seem as austere by comparison as a production of Beckett by the Comédie Française.

If Welles chose to assume and embody the condition of modernity he had deplored as historically inevitable in his preface, then film, an art of spectacle that had only recently learned to talk, was indeed the inevitable third act, and the way it made its first appearance actually recalls his account of the origins of theatrical spectacle: in his aborted plans for staging *Too Much Johnson* and the barnstorming stage production of *The Green Goddess*, that he did just before going to Hollywood, he attempted to use films projected onstage to achieve the kind of mute scenic effects that the Elizabethans had relegated to the curtained inner stage. When the genie was finally let out of the bottle in 1941, Welles chose again to accept and even exacerbate the "enlargement" of "literal and scenic effect" that he had described as "irreparable": *Citizen Kane* (1941) was a spectacle calculated to dazzle film audiences with effects they had never seen before.

But *Kane* was also a solution, which Bazin would immediately recognize, to the problem of reinscribing drama's radical of presentation in film, first of all by according priority to the spoken text as the element of mise-en-scène that preceded and guided all the rest, and by visually accentuating such signs of theatricality as long takes, scenes played in fixed shots and deep focus, and lenses and camera angles that emphasized the enclosed space of the set. Here already was that "science of mise-en-scène" which would permit the filmmaker to conserve the "consciousness of the active opposition between spectator and actor that constitutes theatrical performance."

Indeed, Bazin's analyses of *Kane* rendered superfluous any detailed analysis of that "science" when Welles elaborated it in his film adaptation of *Macbeth*, with more signs of theatricality to spell QED: obviously fake sets, an extraordinary ten-minute *plan-séquence* that Bazin regrettably

did not live to see, and actors performing to playback—to which would
have been added, if Welles had had his way, a stereophonic soundtrack.
This paradox is exacerbated in the Shakespeare films considered as a
series: from *Macbeth* to *Othello* (1951) to *Chimes at Midnight* (1965), the
element of spectacle increases exponentially, incorporating a panoramic
variety of practical locations, natural and man-made, and culminating in
the Battle of Shrewsbury; on the other hand, each film attempts, while
expanding the arsenal of cinematic expression, to recover in its own way
the radical of presentation of drama. This did not escape the attention
of Bazin. When he saw *Othello* at Cannes in 1952—a location film composed of machine-gun shot/reverse shot cutting that seemed to violate
every aesthetic principle he had ever expounded—he recognized it as a
confirmation of the essential argument of his 1951 essay. His review of
Othello from Cannes was a restatement of his theory of symbolic architecture, with the paradoxes underlined:

> I find in it once again the confirmation that the problem of
> adapting theatre to cinema does not reside in the actor but in
> the conception of the decor. The theatrical scene is a closed,
> centripetal universe like the inside of a seashell. The screen
> is a centrifugal surface, a *cache* applied to the unlimited uni-
> verse of Nature. The dramatic word is conceived to resonate
> in a closed space; it dissolves and disperses irrecoverably in a
> natural setting. Passing from the stage to the screen, the text
> should therefore find a dramatic space that can satisfy the two
> contradictory qualities of theatrical and cinematographic space.
>   Welles achieves this stunningly by creating a totally
> artificial dramatic architecture composed almost entirely of
> natural elements taken from Venice and the fortress of Moga-
> dor. Thanks to the montage and camera angles (which give the
> mind no chance to reassemble spatially the elements of the
> decor), Welles invents an imaginary architecture invested with
> all the prestige and all the beauty, deliberate and accidental,
> that only real architecture, shaped by centuries of wind and
> sun, can have. *Othello* takes place outdoors, but not in nature.
> These walls, vaults and corridors echo, reflect and multiply
> like mirrors the eloquence of the tragedy.

The suppleness with which Bazin responds to the way Welles stood
on their head the formal principles that had shaped *Macbeth* undercuts
any reductive interpretation of Bazin's aesthetic of realism, the paradoxes
of which are most forcefully deployed, it seems to me, in his writings on

film and theater, and in his writings on Welles. That parenthesis about disorienting the spectator is important: discomposed by the camera and recomposed in the editing room so that the spectator has no chance of reconstructing in his mind the spatial relations between its various elements—which in this case, anyway, are totally illusory—the space Welles creates for the text of *Othello* to resonate in is not a realistic space but a symbolic one, and despite the fact that they are constructed decors, it would be just as hard to draw a map of Macbeth's castle, or of Mistress Quickly's inn.

I think Bazin would have been the first to appreciate the symbolic function of the on-screen audiences who respond noisily to Falstaff's comic *tours de force* in *Chimes at Midnight*, particularly in the scene where Falstaff and Hal take turns playing Hal's father for an enthusiastic audience of "gentlewomen" led by Mistress Quickly, in a set whose design, glimpsed in pieces and at odd, disorienting angles that never add up to a view of the whole, nonetheless evokes the architecture and origins of Elizabethan popular theaters: an inn with upper galleries surrounding the playing area and a trapdoor for Falstaff to pop in and out of when the sheriff pays a call.

It is in any case entirely consistent with Welles's approach to the problem of filmed theater that these scenes at the heart of the film, where the dramatic radical of presentation returns in its original purity, compose not a filmed symbol of the world as a stage, like the Elizabethan theater in Olivier's *Henry V* (1944), but a cinematic world with the symbolic properties of an Elizabethan theater, one whose walls can expand to annex the real world of wind and sunshine, a Bruegel snowscape or a medieval village knee-deep in mud, birch trees like columns against a winter sky, and the greatest battle sequence in the history of cinema.

The Disappearance of the Audience

What Welles's preface adds to the Bazinian reading of his Shakespeare films is a perspective within which this evolution is also an irreversible devolution, to be computed by a subtle calculus of loss and gain. In keeping with this, each of the three films is marked in its own way by a loss that haunts them all, the severing of the existential bond between actors and audience, and each of them marks this loss in the same way, with a shot of an actor looking into the camera for which no reverse shot is possible: Macbeth ranting at the camera as if it were Banquo's ghost; Othello looking into the camera and seeing the death agony of Desdemona, whose point of view we cannot be sharing because her face is covered by the handkerchief that is suffocating her; Hal looking into the camera and saying "adieu" to Hotspur, who lies dead at his feet. Each of these shots is a scar that commemorates a separation and a birth: the navel of a new world that came into being when the actors were cut loose from the audience and arranged into a different kind of drama, where the illusion of presence has to be continually reproduced in monocular perspective compositions articulated according to the principle of the shot/reverse shot.

Welles already understood and used this basic law of film language when he made *Citizen Kane*, but in the first film he made of a Shakespeare play the effect I have just described—which occurs only once in *Othello* and once in *Chimes at Midnight*—is treated as a virtuoso series of variations on a theme that resolves itself by literally designating the machinery for creating the film illusion. Bazin described *Macbeth* as a film about a world coming into being, and the description fits in more ways than one. The theme is announced with a gag: low-angle shots during the execution at the beginning of the film show a drummer pounding, apparently, on the camera itself—a shot that becomes, when the drumming suddenly ceases, an image of the executioner's axe falling on Cawdor, followed by a high-angle shot from the point of view of the decapitated corpse. A few scenes later, Duncan and his son, who is describing to him the traitor's courage at the moment of death, participate in a shot/reverse shot with Cawdor's decapitated head, mounted on a cross. The shot of the drummer as executioner will be echoed, this time literally and with horrific effect, during the murder of Macduff's wife and child, when the camera becomes the child looking into the mad eyes of the masked, helmeted soldier who is killing him, an act which is symmetrically avenged at the end of the film with the quick shot of Macduff striking at the camera as he cuts off Macbeth's head.

These devices might be nothing more than shock effects, and so might the brilliant device Welles hit on for showing the materialization of Banquo's ghost in the banquet scene, but in the theoretical perspective suggested by the Shakespeare preface, that scene retrospectively unfolds the meaning of all the other grisly point-of-view tricks in the film, by reenacting the birth of cinema from the disappearance of the audience in a context that recalls the architecture of an Elizabethan court theater: Macbeth sits where the chief royal spectator would have sat; the courtiers on either side of the table become the audience, which would have sat along the sides of the hall, and Banquo when he appears in the place of honor at the other end of the table occupies what would have been the playing area. The analogy between a royal banquet and a royal theater may be just a coincidence, and an easy one to understand, but Welles's uncanny device for staging the apparitions invests this space and the drama enacted in it with symbolic overtones. When Macbeth sees the guests seated at the table, Banquo's chair is empty; when Macbeth sees Banquo's ghost sitting in the chair, the other guests at the table have disappeared. For Macbeth, and for us, Banquo and the guests can exist only in alternation with one another, because in this new kind of theater the actor can only exist as a specter who occupies the place of the vanished audience.

The consequences of this disappearance are then dramatized in two successive instances of the "camera look." During the "maws of kites" speech, when Macbeth, with the court now arrayed behind him, looks directly at the camera as if it were the ghost, we can still imagine, even though no reverse shot is shown, that he is seeing Banquo's image, but after he overturns the banquet table and recovers his senses, the effect is repeated without the hypothesis of a ghost to justify it. Again Macbeth sits with his back to the courtiers, never looking at them, turning his head from side to side as he explains to the listeners behind him the reason for his discomfiture:

> You make me strange
> Even to the disposition that I owe,
> When now I think you can behold such sights,
> And keep the natural ruby of your cheeks,
> When mine is blanched with fear.

On the phrase "such sights," Welles's look again intersects, fleetingly, the axis of the camera, which can no longer represent anything but the void to which the spectacle as a whole is now addressed. That shot appears on the cover of the volume of *Qu'est-ce que le cinéma* (*Le cinéma et les autres arts*) containing Bazin's essay on film and theater, with a double significance. On the one hand, the seated figure of Welles in full Shakespearean regalia staring into the camera evokes the dramatic radical of presentation embedded in film; on the other hand, the fact that the only possible object for the actor's gaze is the camera, and the void it represents within the symbolic architecture of the film, recalls the double loss that Bazin's theory of filmed theater attempts to supplement by a "science of mise-en-scène": the loss of the existential rapport between actor and audience, and the loss of what opponents of filmed theater had called "the irreplaceable presence of the actor," the transformation of the actor into a specter. This double absence, which the shot/reverse shot is designed to conjure away, is revealed in a privileged way by the "camera-look," for when an actor seems to look at us from the screen, two possibilities are being evoked: that the image will still be able to look at us after the actor is dead, and at other audiences when we ourselves are dead. "Death makes its promises to us in the cinema."

The spectral implications of the cinema of the shot/reverse shot—which Welles practiced in his own way, whatever critics may sometimes say to the contrary—are theorized in *Macbeth* and taken to their extreme in *Othello*, where the rigorous but deliberately excessive and dizzyingly rapid use of the shot/reverse shot; the elimination in many shots of depth of focus in favor of two-dimensional compositions that distort the shape and scale of the human body; a disembodied soundtrack that one unfriendly critic has compared to that of Dreyer's *Vampyr* (1932); and the frequent reduction of the actors to shadows and reflections creates a world of specters, where Bazin's metaphor of a structure built of mirrors could just as easily describe a universe of subjectivities madly whirling in their separate orbits, rarely allowed to remain in place, as subject or object, long enough to deceive us into thinking they exist. Even the richly corporeal world of *Chimes at Midnight* is framed by two camera looks which remind us that we are not in a theater of flesh and blood: the last image of the main title credits, in which a group of soldiers, with corpses hanging behind them, begin to kneel as if in homage to the camera, and the image of soldiers looking at the camera over which the end credits roll, where the ghostliness of the effect is enhanced by the fact that the shot has been printed as an endlessly repeating slow-motion loop.

The Text

What are the implications of this Wellesian skepticism for the third element in Bazin's ideal theater, the text? Resonant it may still be, but it can't resonate as it would in a theater when it is being performed in a haunted house. This is the point, I think, of Dudley Andrew's beautiful appreciation of the much-reviled soundtrack of *Chimes at Midnight*:

> Perhaps the greatest adaptation of Shakespeare that the cinema has yet produced, *Chimes at Midnight* is also the adaptation most difficult physically to hear. Lines are delivered at lightning speed, often over the shoulder, mixed with the dialogue or laughter of other characters, by quick turns bellowed, then murmured. . . . Instead of a text which comfortingly remains behind the scenes and outlasts the film, Welles gives us a voice disconcertingly disappearing over time. . . .
>
> Thus, the nostalgia expressed in the prologue ("Where have they all gone? Dead, all dead") comes through the soundtrack to haunt every moment of the film. . . . Far from

betraying theatre, cinema here bestows upon it a most intimate gift, to let its cultured speeches contend with the wind
of a truly open space, to test the human struggle in the vast
stretches of inhuman time. . . .

Welles is one of those few directors . . . whose over-
riding obsession with the past and death goes against the
grain of the medium even while it is best expressed in that
medium. . . . We watch Welles's films not as living artifacts
emerging into our present, but as traces of a power that once
was. . . . We are left with a nostalgia for a full-throated presence left in its echo in the soundtrack.

But the inauthenticity of this showman's technique still
serves as a great volume for the vibrations of life within
it. . . . He may no longer be able to touch the real life of
Merrie England, nor that of Shakespeare, but . . . he can
permit something of their sound to vibrate the empty space
he has fashioned around them.

Andrew is, of course, Bazin's biographer, and that last passage in
particular sounds to me like a revisionist footnote to Bazin on film and
theatre, although Bazin's thought is so intertwined with Welles's practice
that Andrew's emphasis on the way Welles foregrounds the illusory nature
of cinema, like my own reading of Bazin through Welles's Shakespeare
preface, may just restate the paradoxes that are already implicit in that
rich essay, which tend to come out of the woodwork whenever Bazin's
writings are brought into contact with Welles. What I am arguing, at
any rate, is that Welles knew cinema for a dangerous illusion before he
ever decided to devote his life to doing tricks with it that had never been
done before, while constantly reminding us, with a look or an intonation,
that the card has been up his sleeve the whole time (see Andrew's book).

I have saved my favorite "camera look" from *Macbeth* for last. It
involves one of Welles's most telling rearrangements of Shakespeare's text,
another liberty for which he has been frequently criticized. In the play,
act 4 begins with a long scene during which the witches show Macbeth
a series of mute prophetic apparitions that appear and disappear from
behind the curtain of that famous inner stage—a scene that Welles had
played to the hilt in the 1933 stage production, but reduces in the film
to a single stunning *plan-séquence* of Macbeth addressing the witches from
the top of a hill during a storm.

The line he delivers to the camera at the end of this sequence originally referred to the last and most disturbing apparition, a dumb-show
portraying the eight kings who will descend from Banquo, but Welles

makes it a general demand for reassurance that the witches' prophecies are true—a question that also inevitably refers in the context he creates for it, as it did in its original context, to the truth of the spectacle itself. It comes at the end of the long descending crane shot of Macbeth on the hilltop, half-swallowed up in darkness before the camera begins its descent, like a tiny figure at the bottom of a huge well, lit by a single spot and occasional flickers of lightning. He looks up as he questions the unseen witches, whose answers seem to come from the sky—the famous prophecies about Great Birnam Wood and "none of woman born," which are metaphorically true, but literally lies, designed to ensnare him further. The sequence ends with a tight close-up, and he addresses his last question directly to the camera, almost in a whisper, like a child who wants to believe something he fears can't be true: "What, is this so?" "Ay, sir," comes the answer, "all this is so." Macbeth is reassured, but we are not, because this answer, like the others, is both true and false, and we know it.

Notations

On the *plan-séquence*, see the notations to chapter 24.

My essay, "Welles, Television, and the Essay Film," appeared in the program to the American Film Institute's 1986 National Video Festival, December 4–7, 1986.

I refer to Northrop Frye's *Anatomy of Criticism* (New York: Atheneum, 1968), 247–251; and to André Bazin's *French Cinema of the Occupation and Resistance* (New York: Frederick Ungar, 1981).

Bazin's comment, "What Welles did was to bring these twin arts of presence . . . ," is from "Welles, Television, and the Essay Film." Bazin's comment, "It is to the extent that cinema favors the process of identification . . . ," is from *French Cinema of the Occupation and Resistance*, 69. In this early article, Bazin states the problem and proposes as a kind of solution the new custom of having filmmakers present their films in person at screenings in film schools and film clubs, which had led to the revival in these screenings of "the customary expression of the theatrical community. . . . applause."

Bazin's "Créer un publique" appeared in *Information Universitaire* 1185 (March 18, 1944).

In the late 1930s, Harper & Bros. published Shakespeare's plays in separate editions edited by Roger Hill, and these contained, as introduction, Orson Welles's essay, "On Staging Shakespeare and Shakespeare's Stage," from which his comment here on poetry is taken.

André Bazin's review of Welles's *Othello* appeared in *Cahiers du cinéma* 13 (June 1952), the month after the film showed at Cannes. André Bazin on *Othello*, a critique from 1952, can be found in R. J. Cardullo, ed. and trans., *André Bazin, the Critic as Thinker: American Cinema from Early Chaplin to the Late 1950s* (Rotterdam: Sense, 2017).

Dudley Andrew's appreciation is in his *Film in the Aura of Art* (Princeton: Princeton University Press, 1984), 164–168.

12

Ulmer without Tears

IT'S 1945. A DOWN-ON-HIS-LUCK piano player quits his job at the "Break o' Dawn Club" in New York and heads for Los Angeles to see his girl, using his thumb for transportation. Somewhere en route he gets into the wrong car. By the end of the film he's an outcast, wanted by the police for a bizarre double murder he didn't commit, cut off from the woman he loves, and condemned to wander like the Flying Dutchman along the back roads of America, where every jukebox in every hash house is playing "their song."

This essay first appeared under the title "King of the B's" in *Film Comment* (July–August 1983), available online at filmcomment.com/article/edgar-g-ulmer. It has been revised for this collection.

That's the plot of *Detour*, a B-movie that rose from fleapit obscurity to a spot on the Library of Congress's list of indelible American classics. Made in fifteen days for a little company called PRC (Producers Releasing Corporation) just before the end of the war, it is the testament of an émigré director named Edgar G. Ulmer, one of the legends of film history.

Historians have traditionally seen Ulmer as a man who took the wrong turn, and Ulmer, who identified closely with the hero of *Detour*, would probably agree with them. The metaphor seems sadly appropriate to a career that began with Murnau and Reinhardt and ended—almost—with *The Doris Day Show*, after passing through a series of films with Golden Turkey titles like *Girls in Chains* and *The Man from Planet X*, and films with stranger titles yet, like *Moon Over Harlem, Amerikaner Schadchen*, and *Zaporozhets zu Dunayem*.

Yet there is an element of myopia in this view. Critics have mainly focused on the films Ulmer made in Hollywood, often in idiotic genres, and excluded his European work and the films of his American "ethnic period" in the thirties, when Ulmer was working like an independent filmmaker on the European model.

He was born in Ulmitz, Czechoslovakia, sometime around the turn of the century, to Siegfried Ulmer, a Jewish wine merchant active in socialist politics, and a headstrong, passionate Viennese coquette named Henrietta Edels. Shortly afterward the family moved to Vienna, where Ulmer suffered the tortures of a Jesuit education. Rendered homeless by the First World War, he was taken in by the family of an old schoolmate, Joseph Schildkraut, through whom he became acquainted with the theatrical impresario Max Reinhardt.

Although he wanted to be an actor or a musician, Ulmer started off under Reinhardt designing and building sets, then did production design on films at UFA, where he worked with Fritz Lang and became one of F. W. Murnau's close collaborators. In the twenties he immigrated to America and went to work for Carl Laemmle at Universal, building sets and models and assisting William Wyler on a number of silent two-reel westerns. Wyler tells an anecdote in his biography that is as startlingly apropos, for the man who would someday make *Detour*, as the one about Hitchcock and the village constable. Apparently Ulmer was the victim of an elaborate on-set prank. An argument was staged, the lights went out, a gun was fired. "When the lights came on again," Wyler recalled, "one of the fellows was lying sprawled in his blood and Edgar stood over him, dumbfounded, with a gun in his hand. He didn't know how he had gotten the gun. As he stood there watching his 'victim' in horror, a studio sheriff, who was in on it, put a hand on his shoulder, telling him he was under arrest for murder."

Ulmer was frequently loaned to other studios during his stint at Universal; this permitted him to collaborate again with Murnau on all the director's American films, and also to return occasionally to Germany to work at UFA. During one of these trips he made the pseudo-documentary *People on Sunday* (1929) with Robert Siodmak codirecting, Billy Wilder scripting, and an uncredited Fred Zinnemann pushing the camera in a baby carriage.

In an interview with Peter Bogdanovich in 1967 and a work biography he dictated from memory in 1971, Ulmer recalled working in one capacity or another on films by Murnau, Lang, Lubitsch, Stiller, Pabst, Leni, Wegener, Curtiz, Griffith, Vidor, Stroheim, Walsh, De Mille, Mamoulian, Maurice Tourneur, Clarence Brown, Chaplin, Borzage, and Eisenstein (on *¡Que Viva México!*). Even allowing for faulty recollection, it's a remarkable list. Reinhardt, Murnau, and Lang, whose films list Ulmer in their credits, are more influences than most young filmmakers could comfortably digest, so it's no wonder that Ulmer's first solo effort, an all-star musical called *Mr. Broadway* (1933) produced by a New York film lab, came out in his own words "a nightmare, a mixture of all kinds of styles."

With his first two features, made independently and far from Hollywood, Ulmer had found his genres, melodrama and the musical, spiced by a penchant for eccentric projects. His next was *Damaged Lives* (1933), a limpid melodrama about syphilis produced by Harry Cohn's luckless brother Nat and filmed in eight days at Hollywood General Services Studios, in which a young upper-class couple afflicted by a premarital lapse on the husband's part are treated by the head of a sinister clinic to an illustrated lecture frankly reminiscent of the "Hôtel des Folies Dramatiques" sequence in *Blood of a Poet*. Behind a series of numbered doors are displayed crippled, *innocent* victims of the disease, frozen into grotesque postures or locked into infernal patterns of mechanical repetition. As in Cocteau, or a bad documentary, these shots are cut in as reverse shots with no attempt at spatial credibility, so that it is impossible to tell which of them, if any, is staged and which, if any, is real.

The same format—Anglo-Saxons honeymooning in the *Cabinet of Doctor Caligari*—is used in *The Black Cat* (1934). Made at Universal under the benign sponsorship of Carl "Junior" Laemmle, this Lugosi-Karloff horror classic was Ulmer's first—and last—picture made with the resources of a major studio, but far from being a youthful work it is a grand summing up of the decade of cinema that preceded it. Ulmer got the idea for *The Black Cat* from a grisly anecdote about World War

I told to him by Gustav Meyrink, the author of the novel on which
Paul Wegener's *The Golem* was based, and the film's warlock and master
builder played by Boris Karloff is named after Hans Poelzig, the great
German architect who designed the revolutionary sets for *The Golem*,
the first picture Ulmer worked on (as a "silhouette cutter"). Even in the
brief prologue, memories of a certain tradition come thick and fast: the
short-lived character of the cab driver (an emaciated double of Emil Jan-
nings in *The Last Laugh*) drives Lugosi and his young English friends to
their unexpected rendezvous at Poelzig's castle in a cab with side-flaps
instead of doors, recalling the phantom coach in *Nosferatu*.

At the same time the myths of expressionism are made new by
being married to the private mythology of Poe, with Karloff playing
the doomed artist figure—a fusion of American and European strains
of Romantic extremism that produced the only cinematic treatment of
Poe before Fellini's *Toby Dammit* (a.k.a. *Spirits of the Dead* [1968]) that
is not a travesty of its source. Ulmer was faithful to the letter of Poe,
to his symbols, which he manipulates with such sensitivity that Marie
Bonaparte's analysis of the Poe *Tales* could serve as a commentary on
the film as well: Bela Lugosi's cat phobia, the subterranean crypt, the
upright posture of the embalmed women, even the uncanny whiteness
of the castle walls à la Roderick Usher's painting of a vault whose walls
emit "an inappropriate and ghastly splendor," the especially morbid connotations of which are unraveled in Bonaparte's reading of *The Narrative
of Arthur Gordon Pym of Nantucket*.

While making *The Black Cat* Ulmer met his wife-to-be, who was
apprenticing on the picture as a script supervisor, present on set to preserve spatial and temporal continuity during shooting. Ironically, Shirley
Ulmer (whose book, *The Role of the Script Supervisor*, would be lavishly
illustrated with stills from Ulmer's films) was to perfect her craft under
the tutelage of a director with a passion for heterogeneity, who would
frequently change the lighting or the background of a shot over her
protests and in flagrant violation of all the laws of screen continuity on
the pretext that it was "right for the feeling" or that "no one notices
these things anyway." It was a collaboration that lasted forty years, during which Shirley worked on many scripts, although she received writing
credit only on films made between 1934 and 1940.

The marriage occurred during a seminal period for Ulmer, just
before his career as far as Hollywood was concerned came to an end,
and the legend began. Shirley had been briefly married to Laemmle's
nephew Max Alexander, and Ulmer's good fortune in winning her away
so outraged "Uncle Carl" that he forgot his soft spot for Germans.
Ulmer is one of the rare examples in Hollywood history of someone

who was blackballed not for politics, but for love. The newlyweds made one more picture before leaving Hollywood, a western called *Thunder Over Texas* (1934) produced, oddly enough, by Max Alexander, directed by Ulmer under the pseudonym John Warner, and starring Guinn "Big Boy" Williams, the amiable behemoth who played the villainous Mac in Murnau's *City Girl* (1930).

Few filmmakers have had less to work with than "John Warner" when he found himself on the B-western beat, but the mood of the picture is upbeat. Shirley drew heavily on Alexander Hall's *Little Miss Marker* (1934) for the scenes between Williams and the little girl he adopts, which are infused with a freakish sexuality. A trio of Yiddish comedians implausibly cast as Big Boy's sidekicks do imaginary radio broadcasts featuring their impressions of movie stars of the period, and stray expressionist conceits dart out like moonbeams from sequences of incredible platitude and technical impoverishment: a dialogue scene displaced onto shadows on a wall, a fistfight intercut with vertiginous shots of trees à la *Sundays and Cybele* (1962), a cascade of faceless riding shots that builds rhythmically until the horses seem to be plunging straight down the side of a cliff.

With the studios closed to them, the Ulmers moved to New York during the Depression. Shirley modeled hats and Ulmer sporadically worked as a cameraman for Pathé Newsreel. In 1936, producer William Steiner hired them to make a thriller under Canada's "quota quickie" system, starring Ruth Roland, the Queen of the Serials. Like *Thunder Over Texas*, the title Ulmer gave the film, *From Nine to Nine*, is an allusion to his high-culture background. A psychological thriller for which he had done some preliminary model work, *From Nine to Nine* (1936) would have been Murnau's last German film if William Fox had not called him to America to start work on *Sunrise* (1927).

Ulmer had a free hand to experiment with the sets on *From Nine to Nine*, which were built with ceilings for the sake of realism, and he was able to use the conventions of the fake-English detective story to paint a subtly corrosive portrait of Canadian high society. But the main interest of the film is historical. For the first time Ulmer adapted the formal principles of *The Black Cat* to the draconian conditions under which he would be working for the next few years: long takes played mostly in wide shots and intercut with carefully lit close-ups, pans substituting for the sinuous camera movements he always favored, and a musical structure based on repetition and variation that wrests stylistic advantages from a restricted number of set-ups. *From Nine to Nine* was shot in eight days during an especially terrible Montreal winter, and the Ulmers were paid so little that an attack of appendicitis that felled Shirley on the eighth day wiped out their earnings, sending them back to New York as poor as when they left.

Salvation came in the form of a "crazy Ukrainian" Ulmer met while shooting a newsreel at Coney Island. Vasile Avramenko, whose ballet troupe and dancing schools had popularized Ukrainian folk-dancing in the United States and Canada, now wanted to make the first Ukrainian musical film, and Ulmer, for a $50 advance, was hired to direct. Financed by a crude early form of presales devised by Avramenko, *Natalka Poltavka* (1937), shot for $18,000 in a Ukrainian village constructed overnight in the backwoods of New Jersey, was a huge success, making possible a more ambitious Ulmer-Avramenko collaboration, *Zaporozhets zu Dunayem* (*Cossacks in Exile* [1939]).

Even more important, Avramenko had shown Ulmer, who was a resourceful businessman, the way to a new career. Using the system of presale financing pioneered by Avramenko, he produced four films in the next three years for the booming Yiddish-language market, and one all-black feature, *Moon Over Harlem* (1939). He also made a series of short fiction films for the National Tuberculosis Association (now the American Lung Association), including three miniature versions of *Damaged Lives* (1933), with casts of blacks, Mexicans, and Navajo Indians. Ulmer told Bogdanovich that during this period, the documentarian Pare Lorentz dubbed him "the director of the minorities." An ad in one of the trades read simply, "Edgar G. Ulmer, Director: 723 Seventh Avenue."

Natalka Poltavka and the better-funded *Cossacks in Exile* are remarkable experiments. Although *Cossacks* was made in the middle of Ulmer's Yiddish cycle, it is very different from his *Yankel dem Schmidt* (*The Singing Blacksmith*), which was shot during the same summer of 1938 and on the same Jersey locations. Whereas *Blacksmith* is like a low-budget Hollywood musical, *Cossacks*, which is based on a Mozart-style operetta from the turn of the twentieth century, was an opportunity for Ulmer the frustrated musician to do filmed opera in natural settings. When the hero sings an aria in the middle of an open field, reverse shots of earth and sky and trees form a visual accompaniment. The first act, which climaxes in the burning of a Cossack village by the soldiers of Catherine the Great, filmed in color, is punctuated with shots of galloping horsemen straight out of *Thunder Over Texas*. These equestrian images are replaced in the second act by boats silhouetted against glittering expanses of water (reminiscent of the funeral sequence in *Potemkin* [1925]), symbolizing the melancholy sweetness of the Zaporozhian Cossacks' exile "over the Danube" in Turkey.

In his ethnic films Ulmer put his art at the service of oppressed minorities, so each film is first of all a collective statement, and a highly political one. *Moon Over Harlem*, unlike most black B-movies, includes whites in its worldview. White gangsters (seen in Langian back-of-the-head shots) telephone orders to their lackeys in Harlem, who are always discovered sitting fecklessly around the same table in the local saloon. The film ends with the hero proclaiming that "Harlem is a great town, but it needs a leader." At the end of *Blacksmith*, when the wayward hero has been saved by the love of a good woman, he remarks improbably that "workers create the wealth of the world." (This habit of shoehorning a Marxist moral into the last shot continued as late as *Ruthless* [1948], with its famous last line: "He wasn't a man, he was a way of life.")

More subtly, the first of the Yiddish films, *Grine Felder* (*Green Fields* [1937]), which was co-billed during its New York release with a documentary called *China Strikes Back*, adds to Peretz Hirschbein's charming play a discussion of "the union of Labor and Torah"—language that was not lost on the reviewer for the *World-Telegram*, who observed that the marriage of the scholar Levi-Iyzchok and the peasant girl Tzineh is "symbolic of the new Jew that is being born amid the stern realities of Europe." But in *Green Fields* the filmmaker has also portrayed his own relation to the collectivity in the character of the unworldly scholar who is adopted by an uncultured community of rural Jews and becomes the prize fought over by two peasant families competing for the honor of housing and feeding him. (Ulmer told Bogdanovich that while he was making *Green Fields* a fight broke out among New York's three Yiddish-language newspapers over which paper was going to sponsor him.) The utopian dream of *Green Fields* expresses Ulmer's own feelings of liberation: far from the haunted soundstages of Bavaria and Hollywood, he created a lyrical fusion of landscape and theatrical artifice where the long takes necessitated by an $8,000 budget evoke an invisible presence brooding over the natural world.

If *Green Fields* is Ulmer's song of innocence, then *Fishke der Krumer* (*The Light Ahead* [1938]) is his song of experience, and the village of Glubsk is the dark side of the happy peasant community in the earlier film. Beset by perpetual night, pieced together out of sparse, sharp-angled expressionist sets, Glubsk is a sinkhole of superstition, cruelty, and poor sanitation. The evening idyll around the dinner table from *Green Fields* is repeated, but this time the camera lingers ominously on the collective pot of slimy noodles into which everyone is indiscriminately dipping his spoon. When a group of young girls in white shifts go for a swim in the river, we know that the water is full of vermin, and even before the inevitable outbreak of cholera their innocent act is reproved as a sacrilege by the wife of the *shamus* whose black-garbed figure looming up in the landscape behind them is like a harbinger of the plague. In fact, religion is in league with the plague. Reb Mendele, the humane bookseller who advocates cleaning up the river and building a hospital, is upbraided for opposing the will of God, and the corrupt city fathers use religion as a club to enforce the backward, grim, unsanitary status quo.

This systematic inversion of motifs from the earlier film in part reflects Ulmer's growing involvement with New York's Jewish community, which was torn by class conflicts and dissension over the deepening crisis in America and Europe. But Glubsk ("Foolstown") also represents a spiritual condition, a particular state of the human imagination. In *Green Fields* the union of Tzineh and Levi-Iyzchok symbolized the marriage of the imagination and the forms of nature; here the imagination, too closely tied to nature, has lost all capacity for vision and sunk to the level of animal existence, engendering the mechanical round of work and ritual that is the horizon of life in any traditional culture. On the allegorical level the lame Fishke (David Opatoshu) represents that crippled imagination. His marriage—performed in a graveyard as a Saturnalian rite to ward off the plague—is a parody of the marriage at the end of *Green Fields*, and his bride Hodele—Nature—is literally bereft of vision, although Reb Mendele holds out the promise that her blindness can be cured by the simple act of leaving Glubsk.

After *The Light Ahead*, the religion of nature and the revolutionary hopes it had nurtured gave way to studies of the ills of modern urban life in 1939's *Moon Over Harlem* and *Amerikaner Schadchen* (*American Matchmaker*), which anticipate the films Ulmer would make in the forties when an accountant named Leon Fromkess invited him back to Hollywood to produce and direct for PRC. (*Moon Over Harlem*, made on location in Harlem, and *Strange Illusion* [1945], made for PRC in the forties, have many plot elements in common.)

The growing tragic element in Ulmer's vision is also visible in the little films he did for the National Tuberculosis Association despite the rationalistic premise of the series, which was to educate ethnics, working people, and children about the causes and cures of tuberculosis. Both *Let My People Live* (1938), a lovely all-black film shot in Alabama with a musical accompaniment by the Tuskegee Institute Choir, and *Cloud in the Sky* (1939), made in San Antonio with a cast of Mexican Americans, portray religion and science, the old and the new, as allies. While characters are tempted to rely on folk medicines or the consolations of prayer, it is always a priest or minister who recommends that they have a skin test. But *Another to Conquer* (1941), the last of the series, filmed with nonprofessionals on a Navajo reservation in Arizona, is a tragedy like *The Light Ahead*. Slow Talker, the revered grandfather who tells everyone to avoid the white man's medicine and stick to the old warrior ways, learns that he is the carrier of the "invisible worm" that has decimated his family.

Goodbye, Mr. Germ (1939), which fuses live action and animation, supplies a sardonic coda to the NTA films with a germ named Tee Bee bragging to the camera about traveling in a spoon of oatmeal that Aunt Mathilda thoughtlessly fed to "little Edgar" after tasting it herself. That unfortunate child is not the only Ulmer hero in this complex little film: the cartoon sequences inside the human body, designed by Ulmer and animated by H. L. Roberts Jr., strikingly anticipate the weird organic forms that imprison the characters in *The Cavern* (1960), one of Ulmer's last films. Tee Bee and his "tribe," as they are called, are really the most ancient "traditional culture" that Ulmer filmed during his ethnic period, and not the only one threatened with extinction at the hands of science and reason.

Two moments can serve to sum up the achievement of that amazing period. Perhaps the most beautiful moment in any of Ulmer's ethnic films is the funeral sequence in *Moon Over Harlem*, for which Ulmer seems to have filmed an actual wake. Singing and occasionally pausing to converse in low tones, the mourners sit in a semi-circle, with some chairs left vacant to permit individuals to circulate and quietly talk with their neighbors before rejoining the collective dirge—all filmed in a ragged, slow back-and-forth pan that counterpoints the Brownian movement of the bodies in the circle with its own searching gaze. This very modern sequence recreates in an urban setting the rhythms of the dinner scene in *Green Fields*, where Ulmer stationed the camera in the hearth with the women moving back and forth between it and the table where the men are seated in the background of the shot. Ulmer's ethnic films are full of ceremonies, often enacted by believers, but what shapes these "ethnographic" sequences is the arbitrary positioning and movement of the camera, which adds its own scansion to the text of the ritual.

For these films are not the work of an ethnographer. When Ulmer filmed a culture, he appropriated its mythologies and turned them to his own purposes, just as he appropriated the symbolic universe of Poe in *The Black Cat*. In *Another to Conquer*, for example, the white doctor explains that he can tell if a lung is sick by listening to it, and his young Indian patient observes that "warriors put their ear to the ground to hear the footsteps of their enemy." The warrior code is used to enlist the tribe in a war with an enemy who can be conquered only by taking to one's bed—a prospect that understandably horrifies Slow Talker. When Ulmer's imagination later espoused the codes of the B-movie in *Club Havana* (1945) and *Detour* (1946), the approach was the same, and the results were just as subversive.

In *American Matchmaker* Ulmer said good-bye to his ethnic period. It is the most mysterious of his Yiddish films, a comedy in which we see what became of Fishke·and Hodele's descendants in the city. Nat Silver, a wealthy and cultivated New York bachelor, after failing eight times to get married, grows resigned to his condition and sets himself up as a super *Schadchen*, or marriage broker, the trade pursued in the Old World by his uncle, which Nat proposes to update using the methods of modern business embodied in the "Schadchen Trust." Even when he meets a young woman who is perfect for him, Nat rigidly insists on finding her a younger, more suitable mate and pays for the wedding out of his own pocket, but she takes the initiative at the last moment and obliges Nat to lead her to the altar himself. *Matchmaker* is devoid of cinematic frills, but Shirley Ulmer's script, the only Ulmer original in the Yiddish cycle, is rich in comic stock-types treated as archetypes and used to explore the Jewish American psyche on the eve of World War II. Despite their glamorous appearances, Nat and the heroine are inhabited by cartoon identities that spawn a multitude of secondary characters: on her side, a series of childish, overly assimilated women and, on his, an eruption of old vaudevillians wearing beards and derby hats, seemingly triggered by a pre–Woody Allen nightmare of himself as a bearded, impotent match-maker in the Old Country. Only by exorcising these grotesque images can these two eminently eligible people form a couple.

But *Matchmaker* is also a very personal work, made around the time the director turned forty. Why should Nat Silver, self-made man, man of the world, and respected member of New York's Jewish elite, be unable to marry? The trouble really starts when Nat, dreaming of his impend-ing marriage to Number Eight, is rousted out of bed by an angry young man with a gun who reveals that only his own poverty has prevented the young woman—whose name happens to be Shirley—from marrying him instead. Recognizing his own unhappy youth, Nat renounces the chance for a new life not only because he is afraid of what he might become—everything he once hated—but also because, like Octave in *The Rules of the Game* (1939), he feels that he is already too old for anything new.

His marriage to a woman who represents everything new, after the comic detour of the Schadchen Trust, signals Ulmer's acceptance of his own new identity. During and after the war years he, became a work-ing Hollywood director, an ardent patriot, and a supporter of the free enterprise system, going so far as to make musical shorts for the armed forces and filming commercials for Coca-Cola. That acceptance could have come about only through the singular detour of the ethnic films, which permitted him to explore his own condition of exile and his mixed feelings about being the inheritor of an alien tradition—"the executor of the Murnau estate," as Andrew Sarris called him—confronted with a younger world already staked out by pioneers named Griffith, Vidor, and Walsh, to whom the ethnic films in their glorious primitivism pay tribute. Since any director is a matchmaker of sorts (and all these films, whether comic or tragic, end in marriages), *Amerikaner Schadchen* also announces Ulmer's readiness to finally become what he had set out to be seven years earlier: an American *filmmaker*, one who had found his own version of the American Sublime, but only after an exuberant and often downright wacky pilgrimage through all the cultures and conditions that had somehow gotten left out of the American Dream.

Notations

The William Wyler gun story is in Axel Madsen's *William Wyler: The Authorized Biography* (New York: Crowell, 1973).

Originally made in February 1970 over three sessions, the Bogdanovich-Ulmer interview is published in a longer version in *Film Culture* 58–60 (1974). A truncated version is in Todd McCarthy and Charles Flynn, eds., *Kings of the Bs* (New York: E. P. Dutton, 1975), and the interviews appear in full in Peter Bogdanovich's *Who the Devil Made It: Conversations with Filmmakers* (New York: Knopf, 1997), 558–604. Marie Bonaparte's *The Life and Works of Edgar Allan Poe: A Psycho-Analytic Interpretation* was published originally in London by Imago in 1949. All the films cited in this essay were at first, to put it mildly, hard to see. (I first saw *Moon Over Harlem* in a "theater" jury-rigged inside an abandoned Greyhound Bus station in New York City, which was accessible like a mythical speakeasy through a door with an eyeball peering out and demanding the password: "Joe sent me.")

Many Ulmer films are available on YouTube. Thanks to the work of Arianne Ulmer, that rarity of rarities, *Goodbye, Mr. Germ*, is on YouTube at aucipes@aol.com. I recently saw her, and she is very sharp at eighty-two and can spell out the reality to which my statement about the availability of the films alludes. For example, *Mr. Broadway*—a rare compilation of fragments—is not on YouTube, although *Detour* (referenced in this chapter) and *Damaged Lives* are indeed there, and so is *Cossacks in Exile* (also reference here); but *Natalka Poltavka* (referenced here, too) isn't, and *Amerikaner Schadchen* (also referenced) and *Another to Conquer* (referenced as well) are present only as clips. It's really amazing how much of Ulmer's work, once impossible to see, is there. You can see for yourself by skimming this playlist: https://www.youtube.com/playlist?list=PL2m98r5tZcXjF_TEN-89LCfdzUdZJ4FEks. Arianne, the National Tuberculosis Association, and the people who preserve Yiddish films have done an incredible job.

When I use the poetic concepts of Imagination and Nature and of Innocence and Experience, I am alluding to William Blake's *Songs of Innocence and of Experience* (1789–1794) as theorized by Harold Bloom in *Blake's Apocalypse: A Study in Poetic Argument* (New York: NCROL, 1970). The brief entry on Ulmer in Andrew Sarris's *The American Cinema: Directors and Directions 1929–1968* (New York: E. P. Dutton, 1966) stimulated my interest in Ulmer and is still required reading for anyone interested in the subject.

Two final notes. My comment about *The Black Cat* and *Toby Dammit* being the only good remakes of Poe onscreen may have been overkill. Roger Corman's *The Masque of the Red Death* (1964) is stunning. Avramenko delivered a copy of *Cossacks in Exile* to D. J. Turner in his office at the Canadian Film Archives. Turner also preserved *From Nine to Nine* and created the definitive Ulmer filmography.

13

Phil Karlson Confidential

PHIL KARLSON IS KNOWN FOR a handful of crime films he made in . the 1950s. That is a tribute to the strength of those films and a disservice to the director, who made over fifty features and won two Emmys for his television work, so the French Cinémathèque is putting on the first comprehensive Karlson retrospective ever in 2014.

Why so long after the fact? Ironically, the impact of the crime films may have hurt Karlson's reputation. "These pictures have been copied and recopied so many times," he once observed. "Unfortunately Phil Karlson never got the credit for it because I've never been a publicity hound." Shame, modesty, or self-preservation? Karlson's films have had their political detractors, while the crime films have been damned and praised for their violence.

Initially, Karlson was a left-wing filmmaker who liked filming in natural settings. His black-and-white crime films were made during five years at the height of McCarthyism. Emerging from that dark passage, he consigned his gangsters to TV and replaced them with juvenile delinquents, surfers, and even stranger "gangs" during the Vietnam years, although the paranoia induced by the witch hunts never receded. "We've all had to make compromises," Richard Widmark's sold-out Cold Warrior says to the Hungarian freedom fighters who just beat him to a pulp in *The Secret Ways* (1961).

Karlson once said in an interview that he liked having three acts in a movie, omitting to stipulate that each act should be completely different from the others. This is the first rule for understanding the most mysterious cinematic signature of the postwar era, and it applies to that signature's surprising history too. Just leave your preconceptions about Phil Karlson, that phantom, at the door.

Monogram

Born in Chicago in 1908, Philip Karlson, né Karlstein, was half-Jewish and half-Irish (cf. *There Goes Kelly* [1945]). His mother was an actress from the Abbey Players in Dublin who became a star on the Yiddish stage in America. He inherited her artistic bent and studied painting at the Chicago Art Institute, but his father insisted he get a law degree at a California college. Doing odd jobs at Universal while studying, he rose through the ranks, assisting on films ranging from Abbott and Costello comedies to A pictures with Marlene Dietrich.

We lose track of him between 1941 and 1944, when he reappears with *A Wave, a WAC, and a Marine*, his first film as a director and the first of fifteen films he made for Monogram, the B-movie company to which Godard dedicated *Breathless* (1960). Anonymously produced by Lou Costello, Karlson's Brechtian clown show about the relationship between Hollywood and the war soared over the heads of Monogram's rural audiences. So instead of making *The Best Years of Our Lives* (1946) and *Detective Story* (1951), he would make *Kilroy Was Here* (1947), about a man haunted by a ridiculous wartime phantom, and *The Missing Lady* (1946), a dirty Borgesian romp where the characters occasionally use the camera as a mirror to check their appearance.

Monogram took the name Allied Artists for the first time to distribute *Black Gold* (1947), which Karlson filmed for a year on location between shooting cheapies in Hollywood to get the colors of the seasons right. The company took the name again to release *The Phenix City Story* (1955), becoming a powerhouse independent after that success, then another true story, *Hell to Eternity*, in 1960. Only the studio where Karlson learned how to throw in a burlesque number to keep the second act from flagging would release a film where act 1 is the internment of Japanese Americans, act 2 an orgy in Honolulu, and act 3 the mass suicide of Japanese soldiers at Iwo Jima. During act 2 Karlson's camera, in the midst of war, tracks the libidinal currents in a room the way John Cassavetes would in *Faces* (1968).

Exterieur Nuit

The last film Karlson made for Monogram before the start of the Cold War was *Louisiana* (1947), starring the Singing Governor, Jimmy Davis, and a rainbow of Southern musicians playing themselves and filmed in the locations where Davis had risen to power from a sharecropper's cabin. Besides inventing the form Karlson would use in *Phenix City Story*, *Louisiana* introduced him to the South, a rich terrain for correcting the commercial miscalculation of *A Wave, a WAC, and a Marine*.

This was accompanied by the switch to location filming in natural settings for *Black Gold*, then in the programmers Karlson made in the fifties, often for independent producer Edward Small. In the 1950s westerns the exuberant colorist's palette darkens into the shades of film noir, while he indulges his love of Technicolor with romances set in the past but haunted by the same contemporary themes: conspiracy, men framed for treason, spies, imprisonment, the third degree, secrets passed to the enemy, and other facts of life during the Red Scare.

Karlson's scenes of sudden violence are already above and beyond the call of genre—there's an out-of-frame castration in *The Texas Rangers* (1951)!—although he learned at Monogram that less is more and never forgot it: a hat repeatedly knocked off, a sweater or petticoat ripped (*Key Witness* [1960], *A Time for Killing* [1967]) can be as jolting in the hands of a master as torture or rape.

The violence escalated in the 1950s, climaxing when the head of the Production Code Office wrote a letter after Allied Artists ignored five memos from his staff, asking "as a personal favor" that "the shot of the tire rolling over the little Negro girl's head be removed" from the *Phenix City Story* script. But while the Code had kept Karlson from reenacting Huey Long's assassination in *Louisiana*, now he would show the assassination of a political reform candidate in chilling detail, with the actor wearing the dead man's clothes.

The heroes of Karlson's crime films make a stand to rally the community to the Law—they are opposed to vigilantism. Lynchings were on the rise in the South because of the civil rights movement, and Karlson had been a militant antiracist since *Black Gold*, where he told the true story of a horse owned by Native Americans that won the Kentucky Derby, and added a Chinese jockey for good measure.

The shadows that enfold *Kansas City Confidential* (1952) and *99 River Street* (1953) are replaced by the sun-bleached surfaces of the Alabama city where the army battled the Mob in *Phenix City Story*, and that Sunbelt noir look was kept for crime films made on location in Miami, Reno, and Los Angeles. While those films are fictions, they scooped the A picture competition on PTSD (*5 Against the House* [1955]), police torture (*Kansas City Confidential*), and witness sequestration (*Tight Spot* [1955]). Later, Karlson's brutal actioners (particularly *Ben* [1972], the sequel to *Willard* [1971]) would hold a mirror up to the impact on America of the Vietnamese War of Liberation.

Who Is Phil Karlson?

To interpret this sinuous path we have to go to the films themselves, because Karlson moved through six decades of Hollywood history without leaving many traces, while assembling a cadre of collaborators and a galaxy of performers that makes Six Degrees of Phil Karlson the movie trivia game for the new millennium.

Another cloudy portrait can be assembled from all the material memes—gadgets, tricks, and gags—that recur without ever becoming themes. The geek in Karlson demanded real gadgets for his Bond parodies when the opposite would seem to be called for, but the modesty of the portable helicopter that is assembled and flown in *The Wrecking Crew* (1968) makes its own comment on the competition.

Our man loves technological progress, especially in the media. Telephone and radio, telegram and teletype, tape recorders, computers, television (and telethons!), phone tapping and surveillance screens are deployed as tools for the characters to communicate with, no social comment intended. The cinema of an artisan who doesn't want to be known as an artist.

Whatever he was doing during the war, this born filmmaker saw *Citizen Kane* (1941) and used brightly lit deep-focus sets with white walls in his first film, which pits the entire Jewish burlesque tradition against the influence of Welles. Without abandoning his love of comedy teams and black music, Karlson subsequently identified with Welles's master, John Ford (the Irish blood), and made *The Big Cat* (1949) ("my answer to *The Grapes of Wrath*" [1940]), which supplied the template for powerful social melodramas like *Gunman's Walk* (1958) and *The Young Doctors* (1961). After conquering the majors, he returned to independent production and the landscapes of the South for *Walking Tall* (1973) and *Framed* (1975), and they made him a wealthy man.

The formal system he invented at Monogram took the ostentatious use of deep focus (for example, young Charlie Kane seen through the window in the snow) and made it invisible by creating a little hole in the image, usually directly over the vanishing point, to isolate a piece of the background. Menaces, sexual opportunities, icons, paintings, phantoms, obtuse senses—an endless array of objects appear in The Hole. Its little music helps reduce the need for shot/reverse shot editing (that famous Karlson "speed") and summons up a camera that becomes a mirror for the characters (literally, in *The Missing Lady*, *The Brigand* [1952], and *The Brothers Rico* [1957]) in the off-space it projects.

This means Karlson's films are documentaries about their stars (Leo Gorcey, Thunderhoof the stallion, Dean Martin) made in complicity with them (Anthony Quinn and Katherine DeMille acting their marriage, Kay Francis playing a contented lesbian, Richard Widmark doing comedy, Dennis Hopper spouting poetic jive talk, Patricia Owens stripping). Sometimes the painter puts Hollywood fauna like Brad Dexter and Evelyn Keyes, or a big cat, next to the star to make the portrait more lifelike, and the mirror also captures magical presences: Sabu at thirty-nine, Ginger Rogers at forty-four. But a mirror leaves no recollection after we see ourselves in it, so Phil Karlson passed through Hollywood without being seen or remembered, until now.

Notations

The Phil Karson interview is with Todd McCarthy and Richard Thompson, and is available online at http://cine-resort.blogspot.com/2014/10/phil-karlson.html.

My thanks to Andy Rector, Aaron Graham, and the late Michael Henry Wilson, PHILologue extraordinaire.

14

Nicholas Ray

We Can't Go Home Again

NICHOLAS RAY's *We Can't Go Home Again* begins with a homecoming, like *The Lusty Men* (1952), where injured rodeo champion Jeff McCloud (Robert Mitchum) returns to the house he grew up in, only to realize that going home can be "like visiting a graveyard." Jeff has withdrawn from the fray, like the violent cop played by Robert Ryan in *On Dangerous Ground* (1951), who is sent to assist in a rural murder investigation to get him out of town, and the gunfighter hero (Sterling Hayden) of *Johnny Guitar* (1953), who has seen it all and has no illusions left when he rides up to Vienna's Saloon at the beginning of the film. Life has surprises in store for all of them, and for the filmmaker, who becomes a Ray hero himself in this cinematic testament.

The Hero's Return

After spending most of the previous decade out of the country, Nicholas Ray returned to America in 1969 to direct a film about the Chicago Conspiracy Trial. His voiceover narration at the beginning of *We Can't Go Home* gives a condensed version of his homecoming: getting tear-gassed, having his camera smashed, working with the Chicago Seven, then filming the blood-stained mattress on which Black Panther Fred Hampton was sleeping when he was murdered by Chicago police. "The confrontation had been too tough," the filmmaker notes tersely as the multiscreen montage sequence portraying clashes between antiwar protest-ers and the police draws to an end. "Most people started to disappear. What really made me wonder was: Where is everybody? So I thought I'd try to find them someplace else."

His search ended at Harpur College in Binghamton, New York, where he had been given a two-year contract to teach a filmmaking course. Nicholas Ray couldn't return to Hollywood, from which he was messily divorced, so in that sense homelessness was something he had in common with the disaffected youngsters in his classes, who were starting college near the end of the grim third year of the Nixon administration. "I don't want to go home to my parents," says one girl in the film. "They still think I'm a virgin. They *want* me to be a virgin all over again!"

Loss of innocence is punished by homelessness (vanished Eden), so in *We Can't Go Home* the commune formed for the purpose of making the film becomes a substitute family, one of many that sprang up during that era for many reasons. This one has been called into existence by the filmmaker's solitude and—although it isn't said—by the intimations of mortality that have begun to haunt him. This new Ray hero is named Nick.

Scenes

In *We Can't Go Home Again*, a film about the making of a film, we see scenes that the great director of actors Nicholas Ray directed his stu-dents in, invented from their own lives, and when Nick, his double, is onscreen, we see him directing them. *We Can't Go Home Again* exists in an in-between realm between fiction and documentary, between theater and life. Only the hundreds of hours of videotape archived by The Nicholas Ray Foundation are a documentary of Nicholas Ray teaching. What we see in *We Can't Go Home Again* is a fiction in which the character of Nick is shown teaching his art by practicing it with his student actors. It is an *ars poetica*; being a Nicholas Ray film, it is also a critique of the artist.

As the scenes we see in the film took shape, Ray helped his young actors overcome inner barriers against expression using techniques learned in the course of a life dedicated to hunting and confronting the unknown "other." The Stanislavski method was the most important of the techniques he had learned for doing this, but not the only one. He certainly was imbued with the discoveries of psychoanalysis. And doing theater for Frank Lloyd Wright at Taliesin he would have heard about the "rolls"—like player piano rolls—on which we store up our emotions, which Taliesin's spiritual *éminence grise*, G. I. Gurdjieff, had theorized around work done on oneself in a theater. If so, the resemblances with the method would not have been lost on Ray. But like any good student of Gurdjieff or Stanislavski or Freud he had come to his teachers with a question that was all his own, and had come away each time with a better version of his question: How can people—two people, or multi-tudes—love one another, to quote *King of Kings*?

Ethnology was another stream that fed the films. After getting his training in theater, Ray worked with Alan Lomax to record American folk artists, including jazz and blues musicians, and put them on the stage and on the radio in the 1940s. He was doing the same thing when he filmed the rodeo world as background for the story of *The Lusty Men*, or later when he filmed juvenile delinquents and Eskimos and gypsies in color and Cinemascope. Thanks to this alchemy, the Harpur film is as true a confection as *The Savage Innocents* (1960), which was filmed at the rim of the world and on English soundstages with professional actors playing Eskimos. That film was not a documentary, he said when asked to compare it to *Nanook of the North* (1922), but a fairytale.

Jean Douchet wrote in 1961 that the true subject of *The Savage Innocents* is the inevitable but not irreducible distance between the watcher and the watched, and in *We Can't Go Home* that distance keeps spilling over into the fiction. Halfway through Tom Farrell's monologue while shaving off his beard—a one-time event shown with very little editing—he is suddenly being prompted by off-screen cues from Nick, who guides the improvisation and obliges the actor to repeat lines with different intonations, even though he's in a very emotional state. At the same time, digital solarization effects are added to the image to enhance its expressiveness, while further estranging us from the illusion of unme-diated reality, which is restored as Tom, his face a soapy mess, haltingly improvises his speech again, with Nick in the off-space imploring: "Talk to me . . . Make me believe it."

In *Lightning Over Water* Ray describes to Wim Wenders how *We Can't Go Home*'s teenage star Leslie Levinson informed him that she'd just met a pimp who offered her money they needed for the film if she'd turn a trick: "I put I don't know how many students covering the area where this sonofabitch was going to meet her, and the rendezvous didn't take place. But the point is that, forty-five minutes after Leslie told me her story, cameras were in place and lights were rigged and we were shooting. I had let her tell me only the barest outline of the story, and she told me the rest of it on film. That's the way a good deal of this film was made."

That image is what we see: Nick with his back to the camera and Leslie with her face half hidden as he questions her. After a stormy discussion—jump-cutting over the failure of the pimp to turn up where Nick was waiting with his cameras—he encourages her to vamp a visitor who was dragooned into doing sound for the shoot and watches from offscreen as the timid novice inquires about her recent sordid experience. Sometimes it's Nick's voice asking the questions, intercut with the voice of the visitor asking the same questions. A trade reviewer attributed this to poor sound recording, but it is a rather sophisticated effect.

Later Nick leads Leslie, who says she has taken some "bad speed," into a little studio where he promises to help her "the only way I know how." Munching a tomato, he listens as she recounts another scenario that throws her into the arms of a creep. Then she tells it again with an abbreviated version of the same mise-en-scène. The original version of this Terry Southernesque tale ("Someone told me you have the clap. Would you give it to me?") may never have been filmed; what we see, twice, are staged re-enactments. Each telling ends with the actress getting pelted with tomatoes by Nick and her fellow students for being "sick," as a student explains to the camera between repetitions while the weary crew takes a break.

In the reverse shots of Nick listening to the clap story he has no expression, like the friendly cop named Ray (Edward Platt) in *Rebel Without a Cause* (1955), who maintains a professional concerned deadpan while a weeping Judy (Natalie Wood) confesses that her father made her feel ugly by refusing her kiss. The reverse shots of Nick directing in *We Can't Go Home Again* are downright sphinxlike. His eyepatch makes his expression hard to read; to make it harder, as Leslie's ribald tale nears its conclusion, he dons a second one. When she finishes her confession, he transforms the scene into a multiscreen extravaganza by yelling "Cut" with a slash of the hand across his throat, while one of the screens portrays him as the orchestrator of this violence, which the details from Picasso's *Guernica* on the left-hand screens amplify with historical and mythical resonances. This sequence dramatizes the violence that is part of Nick's art—the violence Tom denounces in their first scene together, when he sees Nick almost hit Leslie with a dart thrown to relieve his anger at the footage he has been editing about resistance to the Vietnam War.

The Hero's Death

Exploring the frontier between self and other is what Ray means whenever he uses the deceptively innocuous word *communication* in interviews, masking, among other things, the predatory face of the practice, which is joyously celebrated in Anthony Quinn's conversations with the prey he hunts in *The Savage Innocents*. Directing a scene of Nick directing, Ray shows him looking at Leslie the way he once looked at Natalie Wood while filming her confession to the cop named Ray. Looking is the crime—the ultimate violence—of which Nick is accused by Tom at the end of the film. After a touching scene where Tom and Richie invite Nick to come stay with them when he turns up on their doorstep after a faculty party that must have gone very badly, he seizes a camera and starts filming as soon as he enters the house.

Before Tom explodes at this, Nick gives a student who's leaving a hearty sendoff that brands him as a predator again, although the expression was coined by Woody Guthrie, with whom Ray had worked in radio: "Take it easy, but take it!" In *They Live by Night* (1948) Guthrie's jaunty expression becomes a thief's credo when T-Dub (J. C. Flippen) says it as he tells Bowie (Farley Granger) good-bye after the bank robbery that has set the boy on the road to infamy and an early death. In this palimpsest of a film, haunted by the memory of Ray's oeuvre, the echo of T-Dub's farewell points up the hollowness of Nick's bluff collegiality. Nick's eyepatch is overlaid on the image of T-Dub's volatile partner Chickamaw (Howard Da Silva) with his milk-white glass eye, and Chicamaw's Cyclops is superimposed in our memory on Nick's close-ups in the final scene, when he hangs himself, and Richie and Leslie watch him die. The eyepatch also makes Nick like a camera, with its single unblinking eye.

The director as predator is the hidden subject of *We Can't Go Home Again*, and the likely object of the recriminations the characters appear to be shouting in the barn scene at the end of the film without making a sound. The only voice that breaks the hush is the voice of Nick's hanging body, delivering his final lesson as if his strangled features were speaking from beyond the grave. The sound for this scene had been lost when it was shown at Cannes in 1973, and after finding it Susan Ray decided to follow Ray's instincts when he presented the scene without sound. An early observation of Jacques Rivette's about *The Lusty Men* applies just as well to *We Can't Go Home Again*: "Without any doubt, the most constant privilege of the masters is that of seeing everything, including the simplest mistakes, turn out to their advantage rather than diminishing their stature."

By a strange coincidence, while Ray was shooting these scenes, Orson Welles was shooting *The Other Side of the Wind* (begun 1970; finally released in 2018), which shows an old Hollywood director, Jake Hannaford (John Huston), playing God with the young actors in the avant-garde comeback film he is making, which he wrecks by seducing both his leading lady and his leading man. At the end of their respective films, Nick and Jake commit suicide. The death of classical cinema was happening in a hundred shapes during the 1970s. *We Can't Go Home Again* and *The Other Side of the Wind* (and Ritwik Ghatak's 1974 swan-song, *Reason, Debate and a Story*) enact it by sacrificing the auteur on the altar of his own last film.

François Truffaut, one of Ray's champions at *Cahiers du cinéma*, paid a less unruly tribute to classical cinema's passing in *La nuit américaine*, a film about the making of a film that opened the Cannes festival where the 1973 cut of *We Can't Go Home Again* premiered. Three years later the acolyte who wrote that "Nicholas Ray *is* cinema," Jean-Luc Godard, appeared for the first time onscreen as the maker of his own film in an homage to Ray's multiple screens, *Numéro deux*.

Nick's death is enacted three times in *We Can't Go Home Again*, the first time with a gigantic coffin like Falstaff's at the end of *Chimes at Midnight* (1967), associating the death of Shakespeare's tragicomic scapegoat—an indispensable bad influence on the young, to be discarded at the onset of maturity—with the mock death of Nick dressed up like a Binghamton poet who was run over hitchhiking in a Santa Claus costume: a more conventionally jolly Falstaff than Nick, who imitates him to stage his own death. Ray would do this again, for real, in *Nick's Movie* and *Lightning Over Water*, the two versions of the film he made with Wim Wenders.

In the scenes with Leslie the myriad transactions that occur when a filmmaker directs an actor or actress are laid out as if on a blackboard, whether the director is Nicholas Ray or Robert Bresson (to whom Ray's French admirers often compared him). But despite the uncanny poetry of an elliptical night scene by a lake when the Man in Red (the color of Nick, and of Saint Nick) becomes a Rabelaisian dirty old man, *We Can't Go Home Again* is not an indictment of Nick as the wielder of the "male gaze." The story of the professor and the students has the same tragic irony as Welles's version of the Henriad, with Tom and eventually the other students repudiating Nick as Prince Hal repudiates his dangerous tutor.

Screens

The multiscreen form of *We Can't Go Home Again* was not an afterthought. Ray had planned to use multiple screens as a narrative device in *55 Days at Peking* (1963), his last commercial feature, before it was taken away from him by Samuel Bronston, and he had done little experiments with multiple screens both before and after *55 Days*. For *We Can't Go Home Again* he planned his shots with the format in mind and started screening them using multiple projectors as soon as he could during production.

Today standard equipment in narrative filmmaking and televised news, multiple screens were certainly in the air during the psychedelic sixties and seventies: John Frankenheimer had used them in *Grand Prix* (1966); Richard Fleischer had used them in *The Boston Strangler* (1968); Norman Jewison's *The Thomas Crown Affair* (1968), a heist film, had used them; Michael Wadleigh's *Woodstock* (1970), a concert film, had used them; and simultaneously with the Harpur experiment, Brian De Palma was using them in *Sisters* (1972). Earlier he had used the split-screen technique in *Dionysus in '69* (1970). With the exception of De Palma's split screens, those diverse works had a common technical wellspring: films like Charles and Ray Eames's *Think*, projected on six screens at the IBM Pavilion during Expo 1964, and a similar installation Ray appears to have seen at a Dutch exposition during the early years of living in Europe after *55 Days*.

These films express the dream of panoptic vision that Alfred Hitchcock had critiqued with the multiple windows Jimmy Stewart spied on in *Rear Window* (1954) ten years earlier. Its ultimate outcome is our present-day culture of surveillance, which has turned public spaces in the United Kingdom, for example, into a multiscreen work being filmed 24/7 with 1.5 million closed-circuit video cameras. Ray's use of four and sometimes five screens in *We Can't Go Home Again* is diametrically opposed to this, nor can it be assimilated to the multiscreen experiments of the avant-garde, which was staking out its turf at Harpur College and saw Ray as an unwelcome intruder.

The origins of Ray's multiple screens are to be found instead in the cinematic tradition to which he had always belonged, until he rang down the curtain on it in 1973: they appear first in his Hollywood films, and before that in the first film of his great predecessor, Orson Welles. Ray made *They Live by Night* at RKO, where Welles had made *Citizen Kane* (1941) before the war, with Welles's former partner, John Houseman, as his producer. "Whispered comparisons to Welles might have daunted a lesser man," writes Patrick McGilligan, "but Ray felt confident, determined to make his own first film as great as *Citizen Kane*." He succeeded, and in 1957 Rivette described him as the leader of the revolution being carried out by the likes of Joseph Losey and Richard Brooks, both of whom—more obviously than Ray—were in Welles's debt.

Ray's internal frames are his love affair (in which a critique and correction are implied) with the first flashback in *Kane*: young Charles Foster Kane (Buddy Swan) playing in the snow, seen and heard through the window of the boardinghouse kitchen where his mother (Agnes Moorehead) is making plans to send him away to school.

The boy's cries are audible through the open window, and he continues playing in the vivid, snowy frame behind his parents as his fate is being decided. This will not be the last time we see Charlie Kane boxed in like this by Welles's expressionist mise-en-scène.

The sinister connotations of the device adhere to its use in Ray's films from its first appearance in *They Live by Night*. Bowie (Farley Granger) has escaped from prison, as the bars and slats framing him remind us from time to time; Keechie (Cathie O'Donnell) lives in a cluttered shack attached to a garage, where we see her framed by a glass partition that separates her from Bowie and his partners in crime when they first show up.

Windows, doors, and windshields are naturalistic equivalents of Welles's starkly contrasted internal frames in the poetic realism of Nicholas Ray's first film—during the first bank heist, for example, when Bowie is waiting in the getaway car. It is perfectly natural that the purchase of a convertible momentarily opens an unlimited vista behind the newlyweds, as it is that the reverse shot captures them again in the split screen of the windshield.

Even in their honeymoon cottage, the lines of the architecture suggest that their freedom is illusory. At the end of the film Bowie, looking through a screen window at the older woman who has betrayed him, misunderstands her anguished expression and walks into a fatal trap. His last glimpse of Keechie through the window of their motel room where she is sleeping is bait to help the police capture him. All these screens-within-the-screen compose a bigger trap, a world full of eyes looking for the hunted lovers, which is described with sadistic relish by the detective who is pursuing them along the lost highways of Depression-era America.

Ray continued using windows and doors as frames-within-the-frame—filming *The Savage Innocents* in the Arctic, he even managed to find them in igloos. The switch to Cinemascope in *Rebel Without a Cause* was an invitation to segment the screen horizontally: in the opening scene where the main characters are questioned in the police station, Geoff Andrew notes, Ray uses the glass partitions "to create frames within a frame, simultaneously to separate the three strangers *and* to connect them." Murray Pomerance stresses that the police station incorporates the panoptic dream: "the adolescents we are watching are being watched by others, too. What we are watching when we watch *Rebel Without a Cause* is the act of watching, itself, a systematic and controlling generalized state of surveillance."

Like the visual traps of *They Live by Night*, the screens-within-the-screen in *Rebel* and *Bigger Than Life* (1956) are part of a larger design—the web of social relations, the web of watchers—that separates people. Doors expose the colorblind decorating scheme dreamed up by Jim Stark's mother as vertical stripes of colors from a Mister Magoo cartoon, against which Jim Backus's performance is right at home, and his wife Lou's more tasteful verticals divide the horizontal images of *Bigger Than Life* like the axes of the geometrical grid on which Ed Avery's cortisone consumption is plotted. Susan Ray sees *Bigger Than Life* as a study in alienation, by which I construe her to mean all forms of separation imposed by society, including the "miracle drug" that gives Ed and his family the illusion that he will never die, even as the X-ray machine—a particularly macabre frame-within-the-frame—reveals the skeleton under his flesh. The scenes where Ed is subjected to endless tests only worsen that separation from his own body and then from his community and loved ones. But Ray has been using Lou's taste in wallpaper with discreet vertical lines to segment the space of the Avery home long before it becomes a grid where Lou (Barbara Rush) and her child Richie (Christopher Olsen) are prisoners kept under constant surveillance by a paranoid psychotic.

"Fences, walls, partitions, barricades and barriers of all kinds," writes John Hughes, lift the snowy landscapes in *On Dangerous Ground* "to the level of mental landscape" and "reach an epiphany in the homely kitchen wall of *Johnny Guitar*," with a window that frames the delighted reactions of Old Tom (John Carradine) to what's going on in the saloon. These shots typify Ray's practice of pulling in peripheral points of view (cf. the two silent girls in the scene where Dave talks about losing weight in *We Can't Go Home Again*), but putting them in an open window frame sets Old Tom up for the grim punch line, a cutaway when he is shot during a fracas in the saloon and drops out of the frame.

Hughes says that all these barriers and partitions symbolize the chains of inauthenticity the hero or heroine must throw off in his quest to achieve personal integration through the encounter with the Other, by which I assume he means the Lacanian Other: the protagonist's unconscious as well as the characters on whom its shadows are projected. In *On Dangerous Ground* the other characters, with a small "o," are pieces of the cop played by Robert Ryan, and a winter field crosshatched with snow becomes a feature of the mental landscape through which he has to make his way. The Other is mistrusted at first, then reached out to, even if love sometimes comes too late, as in the ending of *In a Lonely Place* (1950), where the watchers triumph over the couple and bring about their final separation.

Mirrors' flatness and weird optical properties are one example (television screens in domestic settings are another) of how Ray's internal screens took on a hallucinatory quality that makes them hard to overlook in the 1950s. Like every formal element in Ray's cinema, the frame-within-the-frame became more striking, pushing the limits of realism, during the musical and epic films he made in the last phase of his Hollywood career, exemplified by the shot in *King of Kings* (1961) where the shock of reality doesn't cancel the contrary impression of looking at a religious icon come to life when the Third Station of the Cross is shown through the barred window of Barabbas's cell.

Although there is a fascinating continuity in how Ray's cinema uses the frame-within-the-frame, which reaches its apotheosis in *We Can't Go Home Again*, that film turns the device on its head. The internal montage of screen against screen frees these forms from their earlier uses, creating a virtual loom on which forms are invented and reinvented, as Ray described when I interviewed him in 1977: "That's supplemental information which is peripheral to our thinking very often. Our thinking is not just pure straight-line thinking. There are other associations going on at the same time, and it helps fulfill that. Very often I use just a certain color, an area of the screen just in color that has no story significance, but it supplements my feeling about what the feeling is."

"*We Can't Go Home Again* is just another Ray film, dated 1973," wrote Serge Daney when he saw it in 1980, pursuing a reflection begun in an article on *Lightning Over Water* (1980). "Another film about fathers who aren't, who mimic Oedipus, fake their deaths, weave knots that we can never cut."

This new cinematic language is built up from simple juxtapositions: Tom shaving his beard while Nixon is being inaugurated on a small screen upper-right, or actors in masks miming the interactions of the characters on the central screen, occasionally synchronized with their words, so that the masks seem to be speaking; a quick shot from *Johnny Guitar* of the Dancing Kid (Scott Brady) getting drilled through the head when Leslie says that Nick must have a lot of money; or glimpses of what looks like a student play that appear and disappear in the upper-left corner while we are watching the silly film-school film the students are supposedly making—some kind of futuristic thriller.

Ray's cinema is shattered in *We Can't Go Home Again* and reborn as a new kind of thought, a new kind of vision. But the potential for creating this spherical vision, to use Susan Ray's term for it, was always there. The frames within the frame of the police station sequence, says Geoff Andrew, both separate and join the characters. Hughes makes a similar observation about *On Dangerous Ground*: the twisted tree form that divides Ida Lupino's living room joins her to Robert Ryan when their hands touch as they reach out and grasp it. Hughes calls the tree Nature; for Ray, speaking to the *Cahiers* in the 1950s, it was the kind of art piece he had seen at Taliesin. Whatever we choose to call it, it both separates people and joins them, a duality that Ray's montage within the frame exploits.

In *We Can't Go Home Again* the square frames that divide the image have begun to lose their definition, and they continue to overlap and meld as the film progresses, caught up in its steady, ineluctable unfolding. That rhythm, which is not the rhythm of a dramatic film, has been shaped by the principles of unconscious association, which we can read about in Freud's *The Interpretation of Dreams*: the dream work that fuses revolution and intimacy, big and small things, and keeps reshaping them until the final images of Tom Farrell dreaming his own film.

The screens in *We Can't Go Home Again* are like manuscript illuminations during the film's first half, becoming stained-glass windows in "the cathedral of the arts"—Ray's kenning for "cinema"—when light starts pouring through them after Nick's first death, as if they were shining the light of lost days on the students' graduation and subsequent attempts to "go home." This is just one ravishing example of how the interplay of screens represents thought in action: freeing our minds from the little boxes in which society has imprisoned them.

There is even a replica of the ragged peephole James Dean uses to spy on his parents at the police station, which serves as a fifth screen in some sequences, its crude outline suggesting that, unlike the four rectilinear screens, it is letting us see through the black matte in which the square images are embedded. What is really behind the matte, we soon realize, is a still photograph of an urban landscape at different times of day—the knothole is just an extra screen for 8-mm images. The illusory knothole, which at first recalls the original function of frames-within-the-frame as windows, turns into a form with nothing behind it before being devoured by the constant flux of metamorphoses that affects all the forms in the film. The last time it appears, it is fleetingly ghosted in over the head of Nick's hanging body, like a nimbus.

Overcoming separation is an action, like Jim reaching out to Judy to pull her back from the cliff's edge in *Rebel*. That is how Murray Pomerance wants us to use Ray's own term to describe scenes or sequences in his films "in which some felt line of action is carried through, rounded out, concluded with pregnant meaning for the story and the sensibility of the film." In *I Was Interrupted* Ray uses the word as Stanislavski had to teach dramatic form: "Each character in a play has one overall action, one thing he wants to achieve more than anything else." The discontinuous sequences of *We Can't Go Home Again* are actions—"Tom Shaves Off His Beard," for instance—that compose what Ray would call the overall action of the film.

In *Johnny Guitar*, the "homely kitchen wall" frames the nocturnal apparition of Vienna (Joan Crawford) in her wine-red nightgown while Johnny (Sterling Hayden) is drinking alone in the kitchen. She has to be torn out of that frame before she can tell him that she still loves him. Their kiss concludes the action they have been accomplishing, in secret from those around them and from themselves, all through the film's astonishing first act. But they will only be free to leave together when the saloon, the cage Vienna has built for herself, burns down.

If its images are a utopian farewell to the old cinema, why does *We Can't Go Home Again* end tragically? According to Bernard Eisenschitz the last act was mostly filmed in March of 1973. The scenes shot during this period when the production was wrapping are a coda that has its own coherence—its own overall action—even though the long take of Nick and Tom filmed then (establishing that Tom is in love with Leslie) is inserted earlier in the film. The coda concludes with the scene in the barn: "a moment directly echoing the deserted mansion sequence from *Rebel Without a Cause*," says Eisenschitz, "in its tranquility and crepuscular lighting as much as in its content." Why remake, after all these years, that nocturnal interlude from his signature film? And didn't Nick already explode like a Christmas piñata full of celluloid?

If he returns from the dead now (appearing first to Tom as an offscreen voice in the scene where he shaves his beard), he must have an action to perform, and that can only be to finish the film. So he tries a new ending. Wandering into a barn on the wintry property where the students have their commune after a very depressing faculty party (a reference to all the faculty politics Ray was subjected to during his Harpur tenure), Nick drunkenly weaves a noose in the hayloft, then thinks better of it and decides to sleep it off in the hay. The ensuing scenes inside the house where he is invited to live with his students expose the forces tearing this self-invented family apart, but the internal frames are superimposed to show that Nick is still part of the family, even though it no longer wants him around because of his obsessive need to finish the film.

His suicide by hanging is a Douglas Fairbanks stunt, using his falling weight to knock Richie off his ladder and into the hay with Leslie. Now he can prophesy, speaking to them from beyond the grave. At first we think the scene will end like the sequence in the deserted mansion where Jim (James Dean) and Judy cover their sleeping "son," Plato (Sal Mineo), with his own jacket and go off to "explore," leaving him to the tender mercies of Buzz's gang when he wakes up. But Nick's injunction to "Take care of each other"—a hardscrabble oracle about the eternal question of selves and others—rewrites the ending of *Rebel*. When Leslie and Richie seem to flee into the night, they're just getting a blanket for Tom. Following Nick's last direction, they will stay with Tom while he reenters his dream and wake him when it's time to wake up.

We Can't Go Home Again originally began with Tom's voiceover, speaking as a college freshman who had seen these scenes of protest and police violence on TV before coming to Harpur, but the restored version substitutes Nick's voice recalling his firsthand experience of the antiwar movement after returning to the States. So the film begins with Nick's voiceover and ends with Tom dreaming the present, shown in the same kind of melting multiscreen imagery that began it: a cinematic structure like a Moebius strip, acknowledging Tom's role as Ray's closest collaborator on the film and passing the torch between generations. When Ray said that his generation had betrayed the next one by embracing it, then abandoning it, he was speaking as the creator of *Rebel Without a Cause*. Almost four decades after *We Can't Go Home Again* we know that the students' generation failed in its own way, but the film ends not long before sunrise, when the old world is dying and a new one is trying to be born: the moment when the artist's work is done.

Notations

The Thousand Eyes was a publication from the 1970s, long defunct.

We Can't Go Home Again premiered at Cannes in May 1973. The restoration premiered at the Mostra in Venice September 4, 2011, and then October 2 of the same year, at the New York Film Festival.

Reading this essay really takes me back. My interview with Nick got me into the *Cahiers*. John Hughes (not the deceased maker of comedies for teenagers), who is quoted a lot at the end, committed suicide in Switzerland after I left New York in 1977. He was a good filmmaker.

John's quotes come from a mimeographed magazine called *The Thousand Eyes* or maybe *Rear Window*—the proprietors of *TTE* sold the title at some point to Sid Geffen, a real estate guy from upstate New York, and his wife Jackie Raynal, a high school friend of Serge Daney and a heroine of May '68 who organized the first Semaine des Cahiers at the Bleecker. Sid is dead; Jackie still lives in the apartment she inherited from him at Central Park South, which she rents space in to visiting dignitaries from Europe. She's a filmmaker too—her avant-garde film *Deux fois* (*Twice Upon a Time* [1968]) is featured in the first issue of *Camera*

Obscura. Her second, *New York Story* (1980), which ends with Sid falling down an elevator shaft and a close-up of a meatball representing the result, is a better example of Jackie's Basque sense of humor

Susan Ray commissioned me to write this piece. Nick had told her never to use volunteers. Tom Farrell is still in New York, as far as I know, and still devoted to Nick's ghost. I did a Q & A with Richie Bock and other student actors from the film at UCLA June 21, 2012, during which it became clear that they had no idea of the value of *We Can't Go Home Again.* That encounter was videotaped and is on YouTube at https://www.youtube.com/watch?v=Wlg3R1tSVk4, although *WCGHA* is available only to paying customers.

I have used as sources: Bernard Eisenschitz, *Nicholas Ray: An American Journey* (London: Faber & Faber, 1993); Patrick McGilligan, *Nicholas Ray: The Glorious Failure of an American Director* (New York: itbooks, 2011); Jacques Doniol-Valcroze, "Paul et Virginie se sont mariés la nuit . . . ," *Cahiers du cinéma* 5 (September 1951): 49–51; Charles Bitsch, "Entretien avec Nicholas Ray," *Cahiers du cinéma* 89 (November 1958): 2–14; Jacques Rivette, "De l'imagination," translated in Jim Hillier, ed., *Cahiers du cinéma: The 1950s: Neo-Realism, Hollywood, New Wave* (London: Routledge & Kegan Paul / British Film Institute, 1985), 104–106, and Jacques Rivette, "D'une révolution," *Cahiers du cinéma* 54 (Christmas 1955) is translated in the same volume, 94–97; Jean-Luc Godard, "Le cineaste bien-aime," *Cahiers du cinéma* 74 (August–September 1957): 51–53; Jean Douchet, "Harmonies de la Nature," *Cahiers du cinéma* 112 (October 1960): 54–56; Bill Krohn, "The class," *Cahiers du cinéma* 288 (May 1978): 62–67; Serge Daney, "Nick Ray et la maison des images," *Cahiers du cinéma* 310 (April 1980), in *Le Journal*, XIII.

John Hughes, "Man Alone: Reflections on Nicholas Ray," *The Thousand Eyes*, no. 4 (August 1974) (this is an extremely limited publication founded in New York by Sid Geffen and Jackie Raynal, now virtually unobtainable); Murray Pomerance, "The Hero in the China Sea," in his *The Horse Who Drank the Sky: Film Experience Beyond Narrative and Theory* (New Brunswick: Rutgers University Press, 2008); Murray Pomerance, "Stark Performance," in *Rebel Without a Cause: Approaches to a Maverick Masterwork*, ed. J. David Slocum (Albany: State University of New York Press, 2005); Geoff Andrew, *The Films of Nicholas Ray: The Poet of Nightfall* (London: Charles Letts, 1991); Nick Ray's own *I Was Interrupted: Nicholas Ray on Making Movies*, ed. Susan Ray (Berkeley: University of California Press, 1995).

This essay was enriched by input from Susan Ray, Tom Farrell, Andy Rector, Richie Bock, Charles Bornstein, and two friends who are gone: John Hughes and Jean-Claude Biette.

15

Robert Aldrich

Sodom and Gomorrah

WHEN THEODOR ADORNO happened to see one of Robert Aldrich's episodes of *Four Star Playhouse* about Willy Dante, a tough club owner in the lineage of Bogart's Rick in *Casablanca*, he was not aware that he was watching a film by Robert Aldrich or even that he was watching an early example of "TV noir," although the account of Aldrich's episodes of the series (which would have been called *Dante's Inferno* had it clicked as a spin-off) in *What Ever Happened to Robert Aldrich? His Life and His Films* makes it clear that the guy with the hat, the girl with too much makeup, and the "generalized atmosphere of crime" that

Adorno saw in this modest TV effort were filmed in a style—deep focus, long takes, and shadowy lighting schemes—that already anticipated the style of Aldrich's masterpiece *Kiss Me Deadly* (1955), which was made four years later, after the A-bomb and Senator Joseph McCarthy had imparted a new spin to the film noir tradition.

> When a television sketch is called *Dante's Inferno*, and when the first scene takes place in a nightclub of the same name, where a man with his hat on sits at the bar and, at some distance from him, a woman with sunken eyes, too much makeup, and her legs crossed high orders herself another double cocktail, then the habitual television viewer knows that he can look forward to a murder. If he knew nothing more than the title *Dante's Inferno*, perhaps he could be surprised, but he recognizes the show as a "crime drama," where care is taken to insure that horrible acts of violence will occur. The woman perched on the barstool presumably will not be the principal criminal, but she will end up paying for her careless lifestyle, and the hero, who has not even appeared yet, will be rescued from a situation all human reason would conclude is hopeless.
>
> Certainly experienced viewers will not translate such shows directly into descriptions of everyday life, but they are being encouraged to construe their own experiences just as rigidly and mechanically. They learn from watching TV that crime is normal because the dime-store romanticism of heinous deeds shrouded in mystery masquerades behind a pedantic imitation of the accessories of real life. If one of the characters so much as dialed a telephone number different from the one usually used in the series, the station would receive indignant letters from the audience, who are nonetheless ready to complacently entertain the fiction that a murderer is lurking on every corner. The pseudo-realism provided by the schema infuses everyday life with a false meaning whose duplicity viewers can't see because the nightclub looks exactly like the nightclubs they know. Even chance, when it plays a part in the drama, would be put down to "the accidental nature of everyday life." Nothing sounds more false than television pretending to let people speak as they usually do.

Could this analysis of "Television as Ideology" also serve as an indictment of *Kiss Me Deadly*, of Aldrich, and of film noir, whose traits would soon be imported into television, to be mass-produced in crime series like *Peter*

Gunn (USA, 1958–1950)? Scripts for Aldrich's *Dante* episodes, after all, were written by *Peter Gunn* creator Blake Edwards . . . Not really. Adorno emphasized not the "dime-store romanticism" of the worldview purveyed in *Dante's Inferno* but the "pseudo-realism" of television, with its "pedantic imitation of all the accessories of real life." The ultimate consequence of the ideological operation he was denouncing would be to jack up the American public's paranoia about crime (in the face of dwindling crime statistics), while the ultimate medium for infusing "empirical life with false meaning" by coupling "horrible acts of violence" with "pseudo-realism" would be local news programs, which would soon be dedicating much of their airtime to the local police blotter.

The way *Kiss Me Deadly* embodied the American psychosis was worlds away from the brainwashing delivered by the five decades of television crime shows that followed in the modest wake of *Dante's Inferno*. The baroque violence of Aldrich's masterpiece, which foregrounded the stylistic traits of film noir, and the mythical resonances of A. I. Bezzerides's script would never inveigle viewers to "construe their experiences just as rigidly and mechanically" as the givens of a genre. But the confrontation between Aldrich and Adorno is useful in situating an oeuvre whose best years were bordered on the left by communism and on the right by the paranoia of the Cold War era, which his films both embodied and denounced with their wonderful excesses.

By the time Aldrich undertook to make a biblical epic in 1961, he had enough artistic successes under his belt (notably *Kiss Me Deadly*) to earn him a reputation as one of Hollywood's leading auteurs. So much so that when *Sodom and Gomorrah* (1962) was finally released January 23, 1963, the British publication *Movie*, which had joined *Cahiers du cinéma* in championing him, felt obliged to apologize to their readers in their review of the film, adding that, happily, Aldrich had gone on to make *What Ever Happened to Baby Jane?* (1962) while the editing of *Sodom and Gomorrah* was being debated in the Italian courts.

Although sand-and-sandal epics were the blockbusters of their era, when Cecil B. DeMille enjoyed the prestige and revenues Steven Spielberg does today, they've aged badly, and *Sodom and Gomorrah* has all the drawbacks of the breed: wall-to-wall "history-speak" without slang or contractions; big scenes reduced to the level of a high school half-time performance by battalions of lumbering non-pro extras that stretch as far as the eye can see; idiotic costumes (the Helamite warriors sport shields covered with fur); pretty Italian actors playing Jews and Sodomites [*sic*] alike; special effects out of a Mothra movie; and a score by Miklos Rosza that is entirely composed of clichés, including woo-woo Indian attack music over shots of the Helamite cavalry.

The authors of *What Ever Happened to Robert Aldrich?* manfully attempt to rescue the film for the auteur theory by proposing Lot, the hero, as a typical Aldrich deluded-leader figure, and Aldrich told Peter Bogdanovich that he might have brought it off if he'd had "a guy you could believe was Lot." Instead he had Stewart Granger, and with Lot present in almost every scene, neither Anouk Aimée (fresh from filming *Lola* [1961]) nor Stanley Baker (warming up for Joseph Losey's *Eva* [1962]) could keep Granger's earnest performance from sinking the ship. Nevertheless they give it all they've got as a perverse brother-sister team (Aimée runs Sodom; Baker runs Gomorrah) whose legacy from their mother includes a penchant for S&M games learned in childhood. After a political argument establishes that Sis is still in charge, Baker lovingly bites her fingers, eliciting a wince of pleasure, but when she returns the favor he remains impassive. "You feel nothing?" says she, as it dawns on her that he no longer loves her. "Neither pleasure . . . nor pain," he retorts with a meta-sadistic smile.

"Unless I believe in a picture, I can't make it," Aldrich told an interviewer. "I'm the guy, remember, who spent two years"—an inflated number, fortunately—"making *Sodom and Gomorrah*. You've got to be an idiot to pretend to yourself that a film like that is worthwhile. But I did." His partner in delusion was Hugo Butler, a blacklist victim who had done an uncredited rewrite of Aldrich's first personal film, *World for Ransom* (1954), and would reteam with him later for *The Legend of Lylah Clare* (1968). Although there is no reason to revise contemporary evaluations of *Sodom and Gomorrah* today, Butler's script (preserved in the Arts Special Collection of the UCLA Library) is different enough from Aldrich's film that a closer study of what resulted from the director's year in the desert can be instructive.

A Marxist Parable

The sequence that unfolds under the credits—something Aldrich does as well as Sergio Leone, who is rumored to have created this one—gets things going with a bang: the camera dollies over a mass of intertwined, exhausted orgiasts until it comes to rest on a shot of one participant who is wide awake, Tamar (Scilla Gabel), the favorite slave of Sodom's queen (Aimée). A reverse shot shows us that Tamar is actually in league with the Queen's ambitious brother Astaroth (Baker). When he gives her the nod to get going, she mounts up and rides into the desert carrying a message to the Helamites, a band of nomad warriors with whom Astaroth has made a pact to seize power from his sister. As we follow

Tamar's progress we get our first view of the city, its salt mines, and the slaves who work them.

Leone was a second-unit director on the film, but the crisscrossing signatures we'll be examining are those of the writer and the director. The opening "after the orgy" shot, for example, though it was devised by Aldrich as a prologue to the action written for the film's opening by Butler, perfectly symbolizes Butler's intentions: the dolly over the tapestry of bodies instantly delivers on the sexual promise of the film's title, but it ends on wide-awake Tamar, whose lucidity is political.

Greatly expanding on the Bible's sketchy account of Lot's sojourn in the twin cities of evil, Butler's script is a Marxist parable about a wrong turn taken by a Hebrew splinter group on the way to the Promised Land. Because of a quarrel among their herdsmen, Abraham (never seen in the film) went to Canaan (also never seen—a boon to the film's budget of five million pre-Vietnam dollars) and his brother Lot to Sodom. After the prologue setting up Sodom, Butler begins with the arrival of Lot and his followers and proceeds to leave his biblical source far behind.

Butler's mouthpiece is Alabias (Feodor Chaliapin Jr.), a Sodomite [*sic*] abolitionist who is beaten by soldiers for denouncing both the salt trade as the foundation of Sodom's wealth and the need for a workforce of slaves to keep it going: "You who monopolize that one commodity more valuable in Africa than gold—salt!—who use the precious stuff to keep your cruel fingers tight on the heartstrings of a whole continent—who trade your salt for leather, jewels, perfumes, pig fat or gold, or that most precious of commodities—the only holy thing that exists—human flesh and blood. Your life based on this crime, how can you tell truth from lie, or right from wrong?"

Alabias's speech, written by Butler to be spoken in the film's opening minutes, subordinates the denunciation of Sodom's morals to a denunciation of the economic system that sustains the Sodomite empire and perverts its inhabitants' ideas of right and wrong. The sadomasochistic sexual practices shown in the film (scenes of torture) and the Sadean ideology that justifies them, expressed in such aphorisms as "Violence is useless unless it yields pleasure," are rooted in slavery, a practice necessitated by the salt trade. A bad economic system, in other words, nurtures twisted appetites.

This is where Aldrich and Butler begin to part company, for Alabias's speech gets rewritten in the film. Not surprisingly, the blasphemous notion that "human flesh and blood" is "the only holy thing that exists" is dropped like a hot potato, and the causality Butler was at pains to trace is reversed: in the film Alabias says that the Sodomites pursue the salt trade in order to buy slaves for their sadistic pleasures, which we are left to assume are an innate vice of the human animal. Twisted appetites and economic abuses are now both results of Original Sin, which has never played any part in Marxist-Leninist theory.

After that, the film preserves all the plot twists of Butler's political allegory while more or less stripping them of their original meaning. Although Lot forbids any Hebrew to cross the river separating them from Sodom when they first settle on its banks, he believes he is doing God's will when he decides, after stopping the Helamite invasion and discovering a huge salt deposit on the land they bought from the Queen, to move his people into the city and take up the salt trade: "We will show them that a society of free men can make more profit than a society based on slavery. God chose to turn my people from shepherds into merchants." (The line about a society of free men making more money than a society based on slavery, which was eliminated in the film, would have made Lot a prototype for the bourgeoisie as social revolutionaries, slated to be overturned at some later date by the laws of History.)

By trying to found a democratic and capitalistic alternative to Sodom, Lot turns his back on the primitive communism he invoked when he stopped one of his followers from buying surplus salt for purposes of trade: "Salt belongs to everyone—like air, like water." He also takes his first step on a slippery slope that will lead him and his followers from wanting to end slavery to tolerating it as part of their covenant with the Queen, which he believes is the "moral ground" for their presence inside the city walls, even though his honest lieutenant Ishmael (Giacomo Rossi Stuart) warns him: "We have no moral ground in Sodom as long as one man remains a slave."

Sounding like a nineteenth-century abolitionist with an economic bent, Lot replies (in the script) that accumulating wealth in the salt trade will enable them to "free future slaves, cutting off Sodom's labor supply while we out-produce them." When this policy is put into effect, however, economics will teach him a Brechtian lesson. One of the film's most powerful images is the cart that carries off dead slaves, the detritus of Sodom's economic system, to be dumped in the desert—a mirror image of the bodies at the orgy, which is underlined by a slave master's ironic reference to it (in the script) as "the marriage cart." When things go from bad to worse because the Sodomites are forced to drive their slaves harder to keep up with their canny new competitors, a slave complains: "Before the Hebrews came here there was only one cart a day."

Aldrich jettisons the irony but keeps the idea that the Hebrews have become complicit in the slave economy, as dramatized in an episode Butler wrote for the last act: when Ishmael leads a slave revolt and

Astaroth's men put it down, the Hebrews, good citizens of Sodom, refuse to give the fleeing slaves sanctuary in their homes. Unfortunately for the coherence of his film, Aldrich suddenly switches to black slaves at this point (a montage showing black hands and arms being thrust back by yarmulke-wearing Jewish householders as they slam their doors), attempting to assimilate this part of Butler's tale to the American civil rights movement, which was engaging in civil disobedience of the kind Lot's legalistic sense of propriety (and property) keeps him from endorsing.

While laudable, the attempt at a contemporary political allegory comes off as merely bizarre because the givens of the story oblige the director to show Jews as cowards who refuse to help, when in fact the American Jewish community was disproportionately numerous in the sit-ins and on the freedom buses that were mounting an assault on Jim Crow laws in the South.

Cinema and Sadism

Aldrich's attempt to replace Butler's Marxist critique of Lot's errors with a moral critique of his own, which makes Lot a surrogate for the film-maker, is more successful. When Astaroth (Baker) goads Lot into a duel by revealing in front of the Sodomite court that he has seduced both of Lot's daughters, Lot kills him despite pleas for mercy from one of the daughters and warnings from his wife (former Sodomite sex slave Ildith, played by Pier Angeli) that he is falling into a trap by yielding to the urge for vengeance. In the script the Queen imprisons Lot for killing a member of the royal family, setting the scene for a jail break engineered by two of God's angels before the destruction of the city, but Aldrich gives the scene a different twist.

"Congratulations," says the Queen, as it begins to dawn on the Hebrew leader what he has done. "How delicious it is to cause death, to see life leaking out of a body and to think, 'I did this.' You are a true Sodomite—welcome. Just look at your Hebrews"—cutaways show shame-faced Hebrews who have witnessed the duel. "Next only to the pleasure of giving death is the excitement of watching it. They were participants in every bloody moment."

This indictment of the sadistic pleasures of watching a spectacle like *Sodom and Gomorrah*, and of organizing one, comments retrospectively on the film's battle scenes (Helamites being shot with burning arrows and inundated with burning oil), which are on the same wavelength as the scenes of torture: a slave girl put in a cage with a blind warrior whose armor extrudes deadly spikes when his breathing becomes elevated; rebellious slaves being burned alive on a wheel; or a Hebrew traitor being roasted in burning oil after helping Astaroth sabotage Lot's strategy for defeating the Helamites, while noble Ishmael watches with a huge smile.

The Queen is even allowed to include in her indictment of Lot the drowning of the Helamites after he ordered the Hebrews' dam to be broken down—a desperate move brought about by the successful sabotage attempt. Without a word of protest, Lot permits the Queen to characterize his action as unmotivated cruelty, then condemns himself to prison. The illogic of her indictment and of his self-flagellating acts, added by the director, point up the real meaning of the Queen's description of the flood as an act of gratuitous sadism: if Lot is innocent on that point, Aldrich isn't.

In a sense, then, *Sodom and Gomorrah* is a victory for the *politique des auteurs*. Even though the director's very personal reading of the screenplay is erected over the bleached bones of Butler's Marxist parable—which still poke through in places—its denunciation of the DeMille syndrome implicit in the genre imparts a different kind of complexity to the film: "In the name of righteousness and your God," concludes the Queen, "you have abandoned yourself to the lust for blood."

We are not all that far from Aldrich's portrayal of Mickey Spillane's revenge-driven hero Mike Hammer as a sadist in *Kiss Me Deadly*, where the story of Lot's wife turning to salt after looking back at the destruction of Sodom is one of the cautionary myths Albert Dekker pretentiously trots out in response to an uncomprehending Gaby Rodgers's stubborn insistence on knowing "what's in the box." (It turns out to be a howling nuclear demon.) Rodgers's Pandora Complex, and its updated consequences, are replayed in their original archetypal context at the end of *Sodom and Gomorrah*.

To motivate that apocalypse, famously described in Genesis 19:24, Butler had written an earlier scene where Ildith, who was the Queen's mistress before she married Lot, is seduced by her after moving back into the palace as Mrs. Lot, for which purpose the Queen employs rather convincing arguments based on the Hebrews' decidedly prefeminist notions about the role of women in society.

The sex scene between Aimée and Angeli could have been part of the fifteen minutes Aldrich finally agreed to cut after a prolonged battle with the Italian producers, but if it had been filmed I doubt that anyone would have wanted to cut it—least of all the Italian producers. Instead Aldrich, canceling Butler one more time, had given Ildith his own non-biblical motivation for disobeying the divine injunction against looking back: she still doesn't share her husband's faith, preferring to believe that

Lot's achievements are his own, and looks back to prove to herself and to him that there is no God.

No matter. Aldrich's editing makes the climactic explosion that engulfs the city in a ball of flame the effect of Ildith's rapt, ecstatic gaze, shown in a tight close-up—a look of joy that turns to fear as her eyes follow the smoke rising from the flames to form a mushroom cloud—the emblem of Aldrich's fifties oeuvre—whose top we can't see.

Notations

First published as "Fernsehen als Ideologie" in *Rundfunk und Fernsehen* 4 (1953): 1–11, Theodor Adorno's "Television as Ideology" appeared in English, more or less, in *Critical Models: Interventions and Catchwords* (New York: Columbia University Press, 1998), a collection of critical essays by Adorno, one of the leading lights of the Frankfurt School, which appeared when much less Adorno was available in translation than there is now. In quoting it I've moved heaven and earth to make the translation read like English.

I was struck by the fact that Adorno's ideological analysis of a typical example of TV noir had overlooked the auteur behind the curtain. When he wrote his piece, he had never heard of Robert Aldrich. I seized on the Adorno piece as a means of debunking ideological criticism by means of the auteur theory. Like many fifties directors, Robert Aldrich started in TV and even used his TV crew to shoot his second feature, a nuclear blackmail thriller called *World for Ransom* (1954), before returning to the small screen to make *Dante's Inferno*, a Dick Powell episode of the anthology series *Four Star Playhouse* (1952–1956) that did not turn into a series as he had hoped it would.

His return to features via westerns eventuated four years later in *Kiss Me Deadly*, adapted from Mickey Spillane's gleefully fascistic novel by A. I. Bezzerides, a truck-driver-turned-screenwriter who also wrote masterpieces for Nicholas Ray and others during the McCarthy era.

Aldrich, a crusading liberal, occasionally used blacklisted writers like Butler, who was living in Europe when *Sodom and Gomorrah* was made there. He didn't employ Abraham Polonsky, who lost twenty years of his career to the blacklist, but Polonsky stood up in the audience at the wake for Aldrich held at the Directors Guild of America, the game-changing director's union he had founded, and read "Remember Me," the Christina Rossetti poem that is an important clue in *Kiss Me Deadly*.

By then I was living in Hollywood just up the street from the DGA, but I had learned to revere Aldrich from reading the *Cahiers* in New York in the 1960s and seeing his late masterpieces like *The Legend of Lylah Clare*, which cuts to a dog food commercial that Valentina Cortese is watching while waiting for Peter Finch to come home so she can shoot him, and never cuts back to "reality." The dogs running to wolf down the tasty treat in the commercial multiply and turn ferocious, terrifying the cute housewife who dished it up, and the film ends on a freeze-frame of their slavering jaws—a sardonic tribute to Aldrich's boob tube beginnings.

The paternity of *Dante's Inferno*—no relation to my essay of that name—is established by Alain Silver's meticulous *What Ever Happened to Robert Aldrich? His Life and His Films* (Brisbane: Limelight, 2004), 10, a Directors Guild of America publication with an introduction by Burt Lancaster. All this Hollywood background—which wasn't even on Adorno's radar when he came across *Dante's Inferno*, expecting perhaps a televised version of Dante Alighieri's masterpiece—was left out of "Television as Ideology," which represented for me when I wrote this piece the defects inherent in ideological readings of television, a subject much on my mind at that point in my life because of the political and aesthetic explosion of the TV movie format, where unabashedly political directors abounded.

My strategy in my pieces for the *Cahiers* at that point was the same that it is in this little squib: find the auteur (in modest films made for television by John Ford and Leo McCarey) and if necessary discover him (William A. Graham, Lamont Johnson, Joseph Sargent, and radical TV auteur Abby Mann). The masthead of *Cahiers du cinéma*, after all, had originally continued "et de la television," and television was part of the tradition I was attaching myself to, as exemplified by criticism like Eric Rohmer's appreciation of the televised Tokyo Olympics and practical applications like Jean Renoir's *Le Testament du Docteur Cordelier* (*Experiment in Evil* [1959]), heavily promoted in the magazine, which used multiple cameras to film and transmit "en direct" a new version of Dr. Jekyll and Mr. Hyde.

For general principles and specific points with respect to *Sodom and Gomorrah*, see Silver, *What Ever Happened to Robert Aldrich?*, especially page 22; Peter Bogdanovich, *Who the Devil Made It?* (New York: Alfred A. Knopf, 1997), 790. And please see, if it hasn't been misplaced, Butler's script in the UCLA Arts Special Collection. *Sodom and Gomorrah* is a turkey, but the *danse-contre-danse* between Butler and Aldrich in the passage from script to screen is a rare opportunity to study Aldrich's politics in action.

Even at the height of the palace revolution that had film critics the world over pretending to be bomb-throwing Bolsheviks in the 1960s, no one ever pretended that Robert Aldrich was a fellow traveler. A liberal who hid his candle under a bushel when McCarthyism ruled the roost in Hollywood, the man who made Times Square blockbusters like *The Dirty Dozen* (1967) in his heyday was more in danger of being denounced as a misogynist and a fascist by the eternal Lint-Headed Crybaby contingent who got their marching orders from the New York film critics. Even the *Cahiers* during its Red Years turned on him briefly for cranking up the weird sex in *The Grissom Gang* (1971) when the Red Brick Road to Moscow beckoned, but I'm pleased to report, after studying Alfred Hitchcock's afternoon screening schedule at Universal, that the Master liked *The Dirty Dozen* so much that he invited Alma to see it with him when he screened it again the next day.

Bits of then-contemporary theory cling to this piece, in particular the notion that shot–reverse shot editing can signify cause and effect, which is evoked at the very end. The same goes for the idea that watching a film could be a moral or immoral activity. The opposition between politics (Butler) and morality, including the morality of watching a film (Aldrich), seems to me to be of the same vintage.

Times Square as I knew and loved it no longer exists, but when I saw *The Dirty Dozen* there it was a great place for seeing films with a popular audience—Aldrich's audience—which was very different from any experience available to me today.

16

Blake Edwards

Skin Deep

THE SUCCESS OF *10* IN 1979 made stars out of Bo Derek and Dudley Moore and opened a new chapter in Blake Edwards's career. "Bankable" as something other than Peter Sellers's indispensable collaborator, Edwards left Europe, where he had been living, and took up residence again in Los Angeles, where he launched a productive decade that made his eclectic 1950s and '60s, nourished by the star system (four films with Tony Curtis, three with Jack Lemmon, seven with Peter Sellers), look old-fashioned in comparison.

This chapter was originally published as an article, "Ars Poetica," in *Cahiers du cinéma* 421 (June 1989): 13–15.

Working whenever possible without studio oversight and making do with Moore and a handful of newcomers from TV, Edwards and British producer Tony Adams made a dozen films in ten years, including three last-gasp additions to the *Panther* franchise without his deceased collaborator (Peter Sellers died in July 1980) and a number of critically acclaimed films starring his wife Julie Andrews, who was, of course, the biggest star in the world after *The Sound of Music* (1965) broke all box-office records. *Skin Deep* (1989), the unofficial follow-up to *10*, did not fall into either category. All the better.

Ironically, the only film Edwards and Adams were not able to get produced was a sequel to *10*, the one that started it all, although a script was written that was more akin to *The Godfather II* (1974) than to *Airplane II: The Sequel* (1982). At the beginning of the *10* sequel, the composer played by Dudley Moore, having realized that married life is better than casual sex with the girl of one's dreams, would find himself divorced, alcoholic, creatively blocked, and addicted to casual sex. This time his odyssey of self-discovery would be through darker terrain, shadowed by the threat of serious mental illness; the sexual episodes would be more daring, more grotesque, even life-threatening, and the eventual resolution would be more precarious (and less moralistic—I'm not a fan of *10*).

Perhaps it's not such a mystery that this project didn't get made until 1988, when it was resurrected thanks to a writers' strike that crippled the industry. Unable to develop any new screenplays, and seeing a chance to work with John Ritter, a gifted farceur whose commitment to the long-running TV series *Three's Company* (1976–1984) had made him unavailable before, Edwards dusted off the *10 II* script, assembled his usual collaborators, and shot it fast with Ritter under the working title *Change*. (Ritter plays a writer named Zack, not a musician, but he still sings a fair number of songs while pretending to accompany himself on the piano.) Released at the beginning of 1989 as *Skin Deep*, the film did well at the box office but displeased a number of critics who complained that it was a rehash of previous Edwards films (in particular *10*, *That's Life!* [1986], and *The Man Who Loved Women* [1983]), while others lamented that the main character was "an egotistical, unsympathetic, uncharitable, cold-hearted, narcissistic scoundrel." (Actually, that's an accusation leveled in the film by Zack at a dead friend, to which his ex-wife, played by Alyson Reed, replies, looking at Zack with unconcealed affection, "Nobody's perfect.")

We can infer that Edwards, unable to film a script that was close to his heart, used the idea of remaking François Truffaut's *L'Homme qui aimait les femmes* (1977) with Andrews and Burt Reynolds as a commercial pretext for treating some of the same ideas and situations, then went ahead and made a second sequel, *That's Life!*, in which the hero—now an architect played with maddening neurotic panache by Jack Lemmon—confronts a new set of problems caused by aging and the fear of death. (Edwards made *That's Life!* with his own money to avoid having interference from a studio.) Coming after *The Man Who Loved Women*, *Skin Deep* enabled Edwards to carry to their logical conclusion ideas that were only touched on there, offering us at last his shocking, hilarious portrait of a man experiencing midlife crisis at the height of the Sexual Revolution—a portrait for which *The Man Who* . . . was an unsatisfactory sketch, marred by a "Truffautesque" sentimentality that is nowhere in evidence in *Skin Deep*.

After this long development phase, *Skin Deep* was a film out of time, but it was in no way an anachronism in 1989, at the end of Ronald Reagan's presidency. Arriving when conservative sexual morality was being pushed by the government and the press alike, Zack Hutton's strange story carried a redoubled charge of provocation, particularly for younger spectators who preferred depictions of fantasy sex to the real thing. And the fact that it was made after *That's Life!*, an older man's masterpiece, gave it an objective quality that it would not have had ten years earlier. Edwards may have been Zack once, but he wasn't Zack now, and despite the warmth of the actors (Ritter in particular is much more likeable than the elfin Dudley Moore), the filmmaker seems to be viewing his hero at times from the vantage French critic Luc Moullet once ascribed to Fritz Lang in his late period: the point of view of Sirius.

I'm referring, of course, to the sexual episodes, when the film veers from its often grim examination of midlife crisis into slapstick. Edwards always uses slapstick to undercut his heroes' attempts to take themselves seriously (cf. the hospital scene in *That's Life!*), but here the alternation of farcical and near-tragic moments is so systematic that it becomes thematic. When Zack has his moment of satori at the end, framed by two particularly primitive slapstick stunts, it leaves him with the firm conviction that "God exists, and he's a gag writer!" Elsewhere Edwards's exhilarating tightrope act recalls the odd mixture of tones in the films of his mentor, Leo McCarey. McCarey, whose deepest feelings about the "battle of the sexes" were more perverse than is usually acknowledged, would have loved the scene when Zack seduces a girl in a bar (DeeDee Rescher) by singing a romantic ballad to her, then is almost torn apart by her in bed when she takes him home and reveals at the moment of truth that she is a bodybuilder with more muscles than Rambo.

At the film's two comic high points Edwards, as is his wont, turns his hero into a cartoon character: the sequence when Zack, subjected to electric shock by an angry ex-lover, undertakes a perilous journey through an underground garage, punctuated by spasms of electrostatic discharge, like Daffy Duck in a Robert Clampett cartoon, and the sequence in a darkened bedroom when Zack and a jealous rival who is chasing him both sport colored condoms that glow in the dark, an homage to the title sequences created for the *Pink Panther* series by another Warner Bros. cartoonist, Friz Freleng.

Logically, the glowing condom sequence, which is built around the rhetorical figure of synecdoche, or *pars pro toto*, became the image that represented the whole film in the consciousness of the media. (Edwards, in Paris for a press junket, thought he was dreaming when he woke up in his limo and saw a poster for *L'amour est une grande aventure* that looked like a public service ad for safe sex.) But it brings to a climax a larger sequence of the kind Edwards loves to orchestrate at the midpoint of his comedies (like the scene in Clouseau's bedroom in *The Pink Panther*), where small gags and large ones are interwoven with other story elements to create a film-within-the-film that mirrors the construction of the larger ensemble to which it belongs:

(1) Zack and Jake, his lawyer (Joel Brooks), meet in the bar of the Ambassador Hotel, and Jake informs Zack that his agent Sparky (Peter Donat) has committed suicide.

(2) While the two men are engaged in this dialogue about a dear friend's shocking death, a reminder of our frail mortal condition and of the pain that lurks beneath the civilized mask of our daily interactions, a waitress whose face we can't see enters the shot twice to take their drink orders, and each time the men pause in their conversation to watch her ass, invisible offscreen, as she walks away from the table.

(3) Jake leaves Zack to join his family; Zack, who has no family to join, signals to the invisible waitress that he would like a phone brought to his table. As he follows her with his eyes, his attention is caught by another woman seated across the room.

(4) They trade looks while Zack tries to get his ex-wife's phone number from information in order to tell her the terrible news. He picks up a pen to write it down, which turns out to be a swizzle stick, and throws it away, flashing a boyish, self-deprecating grin at his fetching new acquaintance. The voyeur has become an exhibitionist. The flirtation is intensifying.

(5) Still cradling the phone, he calls the waitress back and orders a drink to be brought to the woman's table—incidentally giving us our first look at the waitress's face: a dog!

(6) Dialing the number he got from information, he engages in a brief, puzzling conversation with the woman who answers before realizing that he has the wrong number. This discovery coincides with a more startling one: the girl has a boyfriend, with muscles, who returns to the

table just as the waitress delivers the drink there and points to Zack by way of explanation . . .

Twenty little gags and thirty-six observations of human nature later, Zack and the muscular boyfriend are transformed, by a process as gentle as it is gradual, into glowing emblems of male carnality, enacting what Zack describes as "a porno version of *The Red Shoes.*" What matters is not only the richness of the meanings implicit in this micro-ensemble, and the economy of means employed (e.g., the multiple functions performed by that waitress), but the process itself, which will carry Zack more than once, before he or we have realized it, into an enchanted realm.

This kind of thing is always happening in Edwards films, but never when we expect it, because he also loves to frustrate audience expectations. For example, the carefully prepared homage in 1983's *A Fine Mess* to Laurel and Hardy's Oscar-winning 1932 short *The Music Box*, about piano movers who demolish a neighborhood trying to get their payload up a steep flight of steps, which falls perversely flat in Edwards's film: this time the piano is delivered without incident. Toward the end of *Skin Deep*, Zack, in pursuit of his new dream girl, arrives at a black-tie ball inappropriately dressed as a djinn, but instead of a lyrico-comic apocalypse like the one visited on Inspector Clouseau (Peter Sellers) in his suit of armor during the party scene at the end of *The Pink Panther* (1963), the sequence turns out to be a throwaway. Embarrassed by his sartorial blunder, Zack gets swiftly drunk, crudely propositions the girl, who slugs him, and is hauled off by the police. We might as well be watching a documentary.

It only takes two shots to tell the story of Zack's relationship with the hot-tempered Molly (Julianne Phillips): (1) He serenades her at the piano while she serves dinner, her eyes full of love. There's a cozy fire in the fireplace, whose crackling is unusually audible on the soundtrack. (2) Sometime later he is still serenading her, a little nervously, as she goes over to the fireplace, takes matches and lighter fluid, and sets fire to the piano. Here the passage from one state to another is so abrupt (a quick cutaway to Zack telling his psychoanalyst [Michael Kidd], "I really thought Molly and I could have a long-term relationship") that when Molly, standing in the charred rubble of Zack's house, attempts to tell him what went wrong with the relationship, her angry words are less convincing than his terse explanation to the fire department: "Spontaneous combustion."

That answer—perfectly convincing in the context of the visual gag of the burning house—at least serves to get us to the next scene, where Zack explains to his best friend, Barnie the bartender (Vincent Gardenia), that "spontaneous combustion" means "excessive vicissitude."

It doesn't, of course, but "vicissitude" means "change," which was the working title of *Skin Deep* and a clue to the film's meaning: Zack thinks his problem is how to change, when in fact he is changing all the time. That's why the last thing we need are ex-post-facto attempts at the end of the film to explain the blinding revelation that enabled him to stop drinking. In *The Man Who Loved Women* Burt Reynolds's psychoanalyst, played by Julie Andrews, has a long discussion with her own analyst trying to understand why her patient has suddenly gotten better. Later she learns that it was because a small earthquake displaced a mirror in her consulting room allowing him to surreptitiously look up her dress. Similarly, maybe Zack finally decides to settle down because he needs a place to sleep. After he's thrown out of his house in the first scenes of the film the problem of where to sleep keeps coming up, and although we do catch a brief glimpse of the new house, still unfurnished, that he buys after his conversion, the party celebrating his "final" transformation six months later is held at Barnie's bar, a no man's land for men who don't want to go home.

So we shouldn't put too much stock in the scene that follows, which shows Zack, reunited with his wife, preparing to consummate their "committed monogamous relationship" in an anonymous setting that could easily be another hotel room, for change is the first principle of Edwards's system, of which this little film is the *ars poetica*—even though its characters are never more real, and more touching, than when they are trying to have the last word.

Notations

The anecdote about the French *Skin Deep* poster comes from an (unpublished) interview I did with Edwards for the *Cahiers* around the time of the film's release, which was March 1989. During that he revealed that "the Clouseau gene" runs in his family, all of whom are pathologically clumsy. Jean-Marc Lalanne was somewhat involved in that session.

Edwards made two more features after *Skin Deep*—*Switch* (1991), a body-switch movie in which Ellen Barkin plays a man in a woman's body, and *Son of the Pink Panther* (1993), starring Roberto Benigni as Clouseau's illegitimate son—but when we spoke he was toying with the idea of attempting a female Clouseau, and he was looking forward to doing a play with John Ritter as Satan, who seeks treatment from a female analyst because the human race has been blaming their bad behavior on him since time began. (Edwards's own analyst, Milton Wexler, cowrote *The Man Who Loved Women* and *That's Life!*) Ritter's untimely passing (September 11, 2003) stopped the writing of *Scapegoat* at the first draft, so the best scene can be told: when the incredulous shrink and her diabolical patient quit the stage at the end of the first act, a chorus of invisible devils breaks into a rousing rendition of "Row, row, row your boat."

17

Sergio Leone

Once Upon a Time in America

Adrian Martin's BFI monograph on Sergio Leone's long-awaited last film is a standout in a great series. Martin's writing never tips over into the kind of overwriting that marred David Thomson's BFI volume on *The Big Sleep*. Always at the service of its object, the last film of a great American director who happens to have been born in Italy, Martin's style blends interpretation with sensuous, felt evocation that mirrors Leone's.

For example, he plants this *memento mori* at the end of a paragraph describing Noodles (Robert De Niro) returning to Fat Moe's place in

1968—the year Leone unleashed *Once Upon a Time in America*—as an old man: "Part of the dark poetry of this lost hero's reappearance at Moe's bar derives from the fact that the establishment has previously been identified as "the joint that never closes," and here is Noodles, like some angel of death, instantly bringing down its shutters and closing its doors."

In Leone's valedictory film every image, to borrow a phrase from Andrew Sarris writing on John Ford, is haunted by its "memory image on the horizon of history." Ford is Leone's poetic master, even in this epic gangster movie whose plot pointedly recalls every film Raoul Walsh ever made about friends made foes by class divisions, and in *Once Upon a Time in America* Time is more than ever Leone's subject. Its images, treasures recovered from the shipwreck of Noodles's past, are particularly apt for evocation by Martin's critical style, which keeps the film before the reader's eyes throughout, sending us back to it at the end with its essential mysteries still intact.

Among those are the film's cruxes: the interminable scene in which Deborah (Elizabeth McGovern) removes the makeup from a face that apparently hasn't aged in over thirty years; the garbage truck that carries Max (James Wood) out of the film in 1968—ground up or still alive?— like the junk wagon that carried him into it in 1922, and the ghostly cavalcade of revelers from the 1920s that follows; the last zoom-in on Noodles as the opium kicks in and his face lights up in a savage grin.

That image is on the simplest level about "the brutish vulgarity of men," whose celebration Martin scrupulously recounts in his overview of the oeuvre before circling back to this film's melancholy with this observation: "Central to the film's portrait of masculinity is a feeling of torment, something ambivalent, tearing, wretched. It is a strange and plaintive moment in cinema history, this surge of male melancholia that reaches its peak with Leone's last film."

But the film ends with Noodles's smile, and Martin goes through all the answers given by Leone, screenwriter Stuart Kaminsky, and the film's critics to the question it poses—Why is this man smiling?—without settling on one, preferring to quote Leone on Leone: "I say it here, and I deny it here." Martin's final word on the subject, favored by coming at the end of a series of hypotheses, is that Noodles's smile is made possible by an act of repression, "the massive blocking out of what he has come to learn in the course of the film." He confirms that reading with a Leone quote about *Once Upon a Time in America*, which he described to an interviewer at the time of the film's release (1984) as a "dance of death in which a man moves toward forgetting."

Martin ends his reading of the film, not with Noodles's smile but with the scene that comes before the opium den finale. Max has offered

Noodles one last "contract": to kill his old friend and betrayer before his respectable identity as "Secretary Bailey" can be ground up by a looming scandal. When Noodles refuses, Max asks if this is his way of getting revenge, and Noodles says, "It's just the way I see things."

The low-key heroism of Noodles's reply is cold comfort in a film which, as Martin says, "exposes at every turn the fantasies, blind spots, masks and treacheries inherent in a drama of seeing." That sentence, which concludes Martin's reading, enables him to leave the question of Noodles's smile floating in the air like the film's final freeze-frame, just as he sidesteps the enigma of Deborah's eternally young face (quoting and then rejecting Michel Chion's interpretation of it as an Oedipal fantasy) by focusing on the looks that pass between the youthful versions of Noodles (Scott Tiler), Deborah (Jennifer Connelly), and Max (Rusty Jacobs) in the same sequence.

This interpretation of the film as a deconstruction of the "male gaze" permits Martin to read it at its highest level of formal abstraction, while concluding an argument that begins with the question of Leone's attitude toward men (that "ancient race" sentimentally evoked by Charles Bronson at the end of *Once Upon a Time in the West* [1968]). It's an eminently satisfying reading that even takes in, obliquely, the film's long production history (detailed in a chapter titled "The Mummy's Curse"), its tortured postproduction history, and its influence on subsequent films ("The Ashes of Time"). If the film is Leone's funeral for his own cinema, the mourning work will be interminable and ongoing, long after the filmmaker's death.

I was pleasantly surprised to learn, in an exchange of emails when I thanked the author for an advance copy of his book, that another interpretation of Noodles's smile had occurred to him, too, although it's an interpretation that belongs to a different tradition of criticism altogether, the theory of influence elaborated by Harold Bloom as a way of talking about Romantic poetry. That is my interpretation of *Once Upon a Time in America*, which I sketched out in my eulogy for Leone, in the *Cahiers du cinéma*, as a Romantic poet whose last film carries out the movement of internalization by which the Romantics—Wordsworth, Shelley, Keats—turned the quest romance of Edmund Spenser into an inner quest. This way of reading the ending of *Once Upon a Time in America*, I believe, averts a danger that Martin points out in the "upbeat, transcendent reading" of the film as Noodles's heroic quest, when in fact all Romantic quests end in glorious defeat.

The internalized quest of cinema's Romantics is a darker achievement than any portrayed in *The Hero with a Thousand Faces*, one predicated on "reduced expectations" with a vengeance. In *Once Upon a Time in America* a vision that encompassed Ford's Monument Valley, filmed by Leone in *Once Upon a Time in the West,* dwindles to the space between a gangster's ears. The central poem in the Romantic tradition, according to Bloom, is Robert Browning's ghastly poetic monologue by a failed quester, "Childe Roland to the Dark Tower Came," which was on Arthur C. Clarke's mind when he conceived the monolith at the end of *2001: A Space Odyssey,* another film that opened in 1968 and rivaled Leone's for its impact on filmmakers. Noodles is part of Roland's ill-fated band, and his smile is eerily reminiscent of the smile on the face of the Star Child at the end of Kubrick's film.

As Martin shows, the meaning of that smile hovers between fantasy (an opium dream?) and reality, between past (Noodles's childhood? the film we have just seen?) and future (a prophetic vision brought on by the drug?), with no room in the middle for a living present. He is describing the "ratio of misreading" (a defense mechanism for creative forgetting) that ends most post-Enlightenment poems, according to Bloom, who calls the ratio "transumption": the powerful act of repression by which a belated poet imagines that he is in fact the predecessor of the great predecessor whose work would otherwise cripple his imagination. Its closest Freudian analogue, according to Bloom, is not the Oedipus complex, but paranoid psychosis.

The way the Star Child transumes all human culture—the monolith was here before us, and continues to shape our ends—is reminiscent of Wordsworth's paradoxical assertion, "The child is father to the man," but Noodles's drug-addled moment of transumption is strictly personal. Hovering between past and future, he sees it all and embraces it with his savage smile. Moments of timelessness like this occur at the end of many Ford films—Lincoln walking into his stormy future, Roddy McDowall seeing his past rise up before him—but Leone's last variation on Fordean transumption evokes Nietzsche. In the Eternal Return, the past is the future, eternally recurring, and one must have the strength to will both future and past and laugh about it. Only in that sense does Noodles's quest succeed, but at the price of "nihilistic despair"—the last words of Adrian Martin's excellent, uncompromising book.

My favorite scene in *Once Upon a Time in America* is the moment when one of the young gang members, waiting in the hall with the creamy cake he has brought to purchase a neighbor girl's sexual favors, begins licking his fingers and ends up very gradually eating the whole thing. The scene has many meanings, at least one of which is macabre. The character dies in a brawl not long after, still a virgin, a life wasted. Scenes like this, that play on duration (another, described by Martin, is the scene where Noodles rivets his colleagues' attention by stirring his coffee with a spoon), are at the heart of Leone's cinema, and they have as much to do with an *arte povera* as they do with the epic qualities imitated by Leone's many admirers. That moment with the cake stops Leone's $30 million epic dead in its tracks for two minutes, and this little syncope from the characters' past somehow empowers the mysterious images of Time transcended that gather at the end.

Notations

When Sergio Leone unleashed *Once Upon a Time in America* in 1968, the American release had an impact on film lovers and filmmakers (at least in New York, where I was living at the time) comparable to the release of *2001: A Space Odyssey*. The genie was out of the bottle and couldn't be put back, and the shock-waves of its impact are still being felt and lamely responded to in America and in Europe. I considered Leone at greater length in "La Planète Leone," *Cahiers du cinéma* 422 (July–August 1989): 10–13.

Adrian Martin's book is *Once Upon a Time in America* (London: BFI, 1998). It was originally commissioned as a book review for the Australian online journal *Screening the Past*.

Directors Who Started in Television

18

Lucille Ball

I Love Lucy

No EVENT IN RECENT Hollywood history, which saw the deaths of legendary figures like Cary Grant and Fred Astaire, has provoked a greater spontaneous outpouring of emotion than the death of Lucille Ball, the undisputed star of 1950s television, immortalized in the series *I Love Lucy*. For once the media, accustomed to organizing this sort of farewell, simply listened to the masses. Even as I write, two weeks after the funeral, fresh bouquets of flowers left by fans surround her star on Hollywood Boulevard.

Lucy wasn't the first television star—she was preceded by the comic juggernaut Milton Berle—but she was the first star created for the domestic space of "situation comedy." For six years starting in 1951, Lucy and her husband, Cuban band-leader Desi Arnaz, enacted a comic version of their family life as "Lucy and Ricky Ricardo" on the TV screens of America. The highlight of the third season was the birth of Lucy Ricardo's second child, Little Ricky, on January 19, 1953, the date when Lucille Ball gave birth to her second child, Desi Arnaz Jr. During this period *I Love Lucy* became the most popular "sitcom" in the history of television.

According to the brief Chaplinesque obituary published in *People* magazine, Lucille Desiree Ball, the daughter of a telephone lineman in upstate New York, lost her father at an early age. (*People* omitted to mention that her paternal grandfather, who strongly influenced her political views, was a militant communist.) As a child, she remembered being tied to a tree in the backyard by the family that had adopted her after the loss of her father, while her mother, who had remarried, went on her honeymoon.

To keep her morale up she invented an imaginary playmate who told her she would be a movie star someday, and ran away from home for the first time when she was twelve to New York City, where she eventually settled when she was barely fifteen, earning her living as a chorus girl and an artist's model. She played small parts in films and signed contracts first with RKO, then with Columbia, to make B-movies. She even had her own CBS radio program, *My Favorite Husband*, the forerunner of *I Love Lucy*, which would also be broadcast on CBS.

When CBS reluctantly gave her a television series, her film career, which had not been brilliant, was almost over: she was thirty-nine years old. It was the fact that the endless separations imposed by her life as an actress were affecting their marriage that made Lucy and Desi want to work together on television, but her husband in the radio show was a WASP banker, and initially CBS wasn't enthusiastic about producing a TV series about a wacky redhead married to a Cuban. To convince them, the couple went on tour with Desi's orchestra, performing sketches before a live audience written by an associate of Desi's, "Pepito the Spanish Clown," who directed their rehearsals before they recorded the kinescope pilot of the show they wanted to do, financed with $5,000 of their own money. This modest pilot, where Lucy performed Pepito's best skits—including one with a seal playing a xylophone—impressed CBS, and they greenlighted the series with Desi as executive producer.

In his autobiography Desi recalled that familial concerns gave him the idea of using film for the series: at this time shows were broadcast from New York, then rebroadcast to homes in the western half of the country—which represented less than half the households watching television—in poor-quality kinescopes. But Lucy and Desi didn't want to move from their home in Hollywood to be near the CBS studios in New York, so they created a system that permitted them to perform before a live audience with three cameras. A new kind of studio was built for this purpose, a new kind of dolly was created, and the great cameraman Karl Freund devised a new system of lighting. Desi now had an editing table where he could project three images side by side, synchronized with a single soundtrack. He hired a director (Marc Daniels, who died, coincidentally, three days before Lucy) and a mixer who came from radio to record sound and simultaneously mix dialogue, music, sound effects, and audience reactions.

All these technical innovations raised the cost of the first episode of *I Love Lucy* to $95,000; by the end of the fourth episode the series was $220,000 in the hole. But by the end of the first season it was being watched in ten million homes. Moreover, the fact that it was recorded on film created the lucrative syndication market, where it could be rebroadcast *ad infinitum. I Love Lucy*, which Lucy and Desi ended up selling to CBS for $4.5 million, became the champion of the new genre. According to the statistics in trade publications, somewhere in the world, at any time of day or night, someone was watching *I Love Lucy.*

In 1958 Desi and Lucy had created a production company, Desilu, which they used to make a short film (intended as the pilot for a series based on stories by John Collier), *The Fountain of Youth*, written and directed by Orson Welles, which combined Sacha Guitry's first-person narrative technique with the "first-person singular" technique Welles had used on the radio, to create a new form of television narrative built around his presence on screen as narrator. (This experiment, which Welles biographer Frank Brady, quoting sources he hadn't bother to verify, claimed was very costly, cost approximately $50,000—less than the pilot for *I Love Lucy.*) The collaboration between Welles and Desilu came about because Welles, when he was at RKO, had given Lucille Ball the leading role in *The Smiler with the Knife*, a film adaptation of the antifascist thriller by Nicholas Blake (C. Day Lewis) that the Boy Wonder had prepared during the long production period of *Citizen Kane*—a thriller that was never made.

Welles later recalled that RKO hadn't taken Ball seriously, and I must say, having seen one of the B-movies she made there, costarring Jack Oakie, that I understand their hesitation. Limited by the analytic space of classical editing, her physical talents were almost invisible; it would have taken Welles's deep focus technique, a cinematic transcription of theatrical space, for them to be fully revealed. Only ten years later, when she and Desi invented a radically new TV space that combined the powers of theater and cinema, would she achieve stardom. In 1959 another inventor of new spaces for actors, Jean Renoir, adapted their discovery to cinema by shooting *Le dejeuner sur l'herbe* (released in theaters) and *Le testament du Docteur Cordelier* (broadcast on television) with multiple cameras to avoid breaking up the actors' performances by constantly calling "Cut!" Later, Jean-Marie Straub and Danielle Huillet would use the multicamera technique to film Arnold Schoenberg's comic opera *From Today Till Tomorrow* (Op. 32) for German television (*Von heute auf morgen* [1997]).

Like all great clowns, Lucille Ball threatened to explode the space that contained her, and in fact many of the stories used in *I Love Lucy* described her character's attempts to escape from the family home, which reflected the space of the small screen. Lucy Ricardo, jealous of her husband's success, was constantly devising schemes to get into movies, TV, or any form of show business that would have her, often resulting in immersions in liquids like wine or laundry starch. A famous episode paired her with an Italian knife-thrower whose instructions, spoken in an unknown language, she pretended to understand. Many episodes ended with her return—eagerly awaited by the TV audience—to the living room of the Ricardo home, her body petrified, frozen, flattened, enveloped, discolored, or otherwise metamorphosed by her misadventures in the outside world.

Loaded with sinister "ideologemes" organized around the proverb "A woman's place is in the home," *I Love Lucy* nevertheless inspired later generations of actresses (including feminists like Lily Tomlin) because of Ball's charisma. (Ball, for her part, said she was inspired by Carole Lombard.) Her abilities as a businesswoman also advanced the stature of women in the film business. When she divorced Desi in 1960 she bought his half of Desilu and became the first woman to own her own production company.

She also finally conquered Hollywood as an actress. In 1954 she and Desi starred in *The Long, Long Trailer*, directed by Vincente Minnelli, about the misadventures of a couple who buy a huge yellow trailer and hit the road, with predictably catastrophic results. This masterpiece and a supporting role in Gregory La Cava's *Stage Door* (1937), as well as her appearance in Tay Garnett's *Joy of Living* (1933) alongside Irene Dunne, were her only direct contributions to cinema, but she revolutionized television and used it, as Chaplin had cinema, to forge a powerful myth from the ephemera of a minor artform that in her hands became an art.

Notations

Lucille Ball died April 26, 1989. Arnaz's autobiography, *A Book*, by Desi Arnaz and Juan Pablo Di Pace (New York: Warner Books, 1977), supplied many of the details in this "Letter from Hollywood," which appeared in the July–August issue of *Cahiers du cinéma* in 1989.

A kinescope was a film of the image on a television screen, notably of low quality, and prior to the invention of videotape it was the only means of preserving a live broadcast.

I saw the actual cost of *The Fountain of Youth* in budgets that an employee of Desilu, Sandra Delaney, showed me after Desilu had been physically absorbed by Paramount.

Re: *The Smiler with the Knife*, see https://www.goodreads.com/book/show/1775438.The_Smiler_With_the_Knife.

19

Le Cas Wood

T HE MEDIATIZATION OF Edward D. Wood Jr., low-budget filmmaker extraordinaire, began when two critics named him "the
worst director in the history of cinema" and will climax with
the European premiere of Tim Burton's *Ed Wood* at Cannes [in May
1995]. But if Ed Wood becomes immortal, as I suspect he will, it will
be because of his films, which will not be in evidence on the Croisette.

Which films are we talking about? Wood made, as far as I know,
three masterpieces: *Glen or Glenda* (1952), *Plan 9 from Outer Space* (1956),
and *Final Curtain* (1957). Add to them *Bride of the Monster* (1955), which
we now know he directed; *The Bride and the Beast* (1958), which he
wrote but did not direct; and *Revenge of the Dead* (1958) and you have
everything that is likely to endure.

In short, although Wood's crime films, his westerns, and the pornography of his final period will continue to exert a certain fascination, what he did best were horror films—including *Glen or Glenda*, which treats transvestism as a form of lycanthropy, dished up with a pseudoscientific commentary. His best films were made between 1953 and 1958, when low-budget horror films with laughably unscientific science-fiction premises were rewriting the aesthetics of the American cinema, and his art flourished and died with the genre.

It was in the year 1953 that Jack Arnold's *It Came from Outer Space* launched the sci-fi boom to a chorus of sneers from the critics; the year of *Cat-Women of the Moon*, *Mesa of Lost Women*, and *Robot Monster*, three films that became classics because of their awfulness; the year of *Invaders from Mars*, which challenges received notions of "good" and "bad," "serious" and "funny," "intentional" and "unintentional" in much the same way as *Glen or Glenda*, which was released during the same amazing year.

All this by way of situating historically films which, at first glance, defy all criteria of aesthetic judgment. Although he has been singled out for his supposed incompetence, Wood's decision to save money by allowing his most glaring mistakes of mise-en-scène to find their way into the finished product was merely his way of pushing the limits of the aesthetic which better-financed directors were forging with their own work—a "carnivalesque" revolution that flaunted its indifference to the criteria of Hollywood filmmaking while subverting the sexual and political mores of the fifties for the delectation of adolescents and the underclass.

What Wood brought to the revolution was an excessively personal approach to low-budget filmmaking, which permitted him, in effect, to write his sexual autobiography on celluloid. It is no accident that, in terms of high art, his career as a director began one year after *Limelight* (1952) and ended, for all practical purposes, the year that Hitchcock brought transvestism out of the closet with *Psycho* (1960).

As Antoine de Baecque has noted in an article in *Cahiers du cinéma*, the formal principle that literally binds Wood's films together is his talent as a writer of voiceovers, which imbues all the disparate shots that make up the films with meaning. *Glen or Glenda* boasts two narrators: Bela Lugosi, declaiming in a laboratory that has nothing to do with the rest of the film, and a psychiatrist (Timothy Farrell) whose explanation of transvestism to a puzzled cop becomes the film's main voiceover—"documentary" in style, although it veers unpredictably into imitations and echoes of the incantatory style employed by Lugosi's sarcastic demiurge.

That style, wavering between incantation and parody, is Wood's signature as a writer, but his brilliance as a filmmaker shines through in the troupe of "acousmêtres" (Michel Chion's term) who haunt the diegetic space of *Glen or Glenda*: offscreen voices that are neither inside nor outside the film's ostensible story, beginning with the voice of a suicide note that narrates the sequence in which police find a transvestite dead by his own hand, and ending with eerie children's voices reciting phrases from a nursery rhyme about sexual difference during the film's climactic dream sequence.

Each of these voices has the power to effect narrative transitions, shape whole sequences, and, most important, to pull in an astonishing array of nondiegetic (purely symbolic) images. Even on-screen characters' voices are occasionally invested with this kind of power, as when the hero's fiancée innocently inquires if there is "another woman," triggering a shot of stampeding buffalo with a superimposed Lugosi chanting, "Pull the strings! Pull the strings!"

Glen or Glenda's vocal phantoms generate a structural richness unseen in narrative cinema since the early days of sound, when Fritz Lang was experimenting with these effects in *M* (1931) and *The Testament of Dr. Mabuse* (1933). In his later films Wood contented himself with getting a more restrained array of effects out of one offscreen narrator—a technique he brought to perfection in *Plan 9 from Outer Space* and *Final Curtain*, the failed TV pilot he made one year before Orson Welles made *The Fountain of Youth* (1958).

In *Final Curtain* Duke Moore plays an actor locked into a theater after hours. As he wanders around backstage, we see what he sees and hear his agitated thoughts, which endow an unremittingly banal series of sights with frightening implications. The character's compulsive odyssey ends in an encounter with a mannequin of a lady vampire that turns out to be alive. (The mad expression in the actress's eyes when the still figure suddenly grins at the unfortunate actor is the only genuinely frightening image in all of Wood's films.)

Wood reused whole chunks of *Final Curtain*, his *ars poetica*, in *Revenge of the Dead*, a self-conscious film in which real "mistakes" cohabit with contrived ones in scenes that seem for the most part to have been directed with a certain amount of care. This time Duke Moore plays a policeman investigating the activities of Dr. Acula, a phony medium who has set up shop in the mansion that burned at the end of *Bride of the Monster*. In the film's central section Moore moves through a darkened corridor behind the room where Dr. Acula holds his seances, opening the same series of doors and seeing the same sights, but now his thoughts are retrospective (remembering his previous visit to the house in *Bride of the Monster*) and deconstructive (debunking the phony medium's effects).

Moore's odyssey ends, again, with the discovery that the vampire is real, and Wood's farewell to the horror film ends with real ghosts closing in on Dr. Acula, who has unwittingly summoned them from beyond the grave. That horde of phantoms, which includes the film's narrator, the clairvoyant Criswell, are Wood's own voices coming back to haunt him one more time, embodied on-screen in flesh and blood.

Psychology, Freudian or otherwise, can't explain "Le Cas Wood." The films have to be seen in the light of anthropology. Retrieved from a laboratory and released after the filmmaker's death, *Revenge of the Dead* is the testament of a modern-day shaman for whom cinema briefly supplied the tribal support that was unavailable in fifties America, embodied in the ad hoc tribe comprised of Wood's infamous stock company: Moore, Criswell, Paul Marco as Kelton the Cop, Tor Johnson, and Vampira (Maila Nurmi).

Drunkenness and cross-dressing are tools the shaman uses to cross the boundary between life and death, for which he is accorded a special place in the tribe because he can communicate with the spirit world. These techniques figure prominently in Rudolph Grey's 1994 oral history *Nightmare of Ecstasy: The Life and Art of Edward D. Wood, Jr.*, which concludes with Wood, a lifelong heterosexual cross-dresser, drinking himself to death in a Hollywood motel, destroyed by spirits he could summon but not control. In return the spirits promised him the gift of immortality, which shamans and artists alike desire, and against all odds they have kept their promise.

Notations

Treated as jokes for too long by wise-guy film critics, Ed Wood's films were real films made by a committed actor-writer-director who took them very seriously. Studio space and equipment were rented to make *Plan 9*. Schedules and budgets were plotted out and met. *Final Curtain* was filmed, not in a play-house, but in a shuttered movie theater on the Santa Monica pier, which was a better setting for Wood's experiment with shot–reverse shot filmmaking than a legitimate theater would have been. The flying saucers in *Plan 9*, described as "pie plates" by fans of *Mystery Science Theater 3000* who haven't done their homework, were in fact constructed from a model kit popular when the first rash of UFO sightings gripped the American imagination, and the wires they were suspended from would not have been visible whenever the film was shown in the right aspect ratio.

In other words, these films were anything but jokes to the man who made them for all the usual reasons, including the desire to address hot topics of the day. The *Plan 9* trailer begins with a card reading "A Quote from Today's Headlines" over a shot of a flying saucer making a wobbly landing in a graveyard, followed by the narrator "quoting": "It is safe to say that the grandchildren of some of the people in this theatre will not be born on Earth." That may actually have come true in ways Ed Wood couldn't imagine in 1959, when alien abductions and gene-splicing experiments weren't going on, as far as we know, but he foresaw a lot, and so did his fellow low-rent visionaries.

Plan 9 was released on July 22, 1959, a month after a missionary in New Guinea saw a spacecraft land so that the occupants could get out and make repairs, an event that had already been foreseen in Jack Arnold's *It Came from Outer Space*. The premise of benign extraterrestrials stopping for repairs, taking over human instruments, and releasing them unharmed afterward is typical of the liberal politics that shaped Arnold's career, whereas *Invaders from Mars*, like Don Seigel's *Invasion of the Body Snatchers* (1956), was a full-bore exercise in Cold War paranoia.

On the other hand, the aliens in *Plan 9* (originally titled *Grave Robbers from Outer Space*), who reanimate dead bodies to stop humanity from deploying a weapon that will destroy the universe (another palpable hit: tradition in the UFO community has it that the saucers' aerial manifestations after World War II were prompted by concerns that hydrogen bomb tests would knock the Earth off its axis), are not hostile—just supercilious and understandably peevish. Arnold, who had launched his career with a docudrama produced by the International Ladies' Garment Workers' Union, and his ex-communist producer, William Alland, were putting Universal's money to good use, and Wood was doing the same with money squeezed out of his baffled Baptist investors. But if *Plan 9* had been noticed by HUAC, or anyone else, in 1959, Wood's service record in the Marine Corps (surreptitiously undermined by wearing bra and panties under his uniform during the Tarawa beachhead) and the seeming xenophobia of *Plan 9's* plot would have cleared him before he was ever called to testify—an event that would certainly have made television history had it come to pass.

Paranormal phenomena also loomed large in the public's consciousness when Wood was making his films. Criswell, the psychic who narrates *Plan 9*, actually spoke the words that kick off the movie ("Greetings my friends. We are all interested in the future, because that is where you and I are going to spend the rest of our lives . . .") on his TV show every week. They fit seamlessly into the quintessentially Woodesque voiceover that follows ("We are giving you all the evidence, based on the secret testimony of the miserable souls who survived this terrifying ordeal . . . Let us punish the guilty. Let us reward the innocent . . .") just as Criswell, spit-curled but straight, fit right into Wood's offbeat stock company, remaining with him until his film career sputtered to a halt at the end of the decade.

Communication with the dead was also, widely, a timely subject for film-makers. Not only did *The Search for Bridey Murphy* (1956), a best seller about past-life regression under hypnosis, spawn *The Undead* (1957), a Roger Corman quickie whose heroine relives a past life on the couch—it seems to have influenced Alfred Hitchcock's *Vertigo* (1958), in which Kim Novak's character is purportedly being driven to commit suicide by the ghost of a dead ancestor.

Last but not least, the fact that *Plan 9* presents itself as television is one more way Hitchcock and Wood crossed paths without meeting during the Fabulous Fifties. That decade saw the triumph of *Alfred Hitchcock Presents*, with a classic episode, "An Unlocked Window" (1955), in which an escaped lunatic dresses as a nurse to penetrate a household that has barred its doors against him, and ended when Hitchcock used his TV crew to make a black-and-white horror movie about a likeable cross-dressing killer.

Hitchcock, already a seasoned filmmaker when the fifties started, accepted television as the new matrix for cinema, remaking TV movies (*Dial M for Murder* [1954], *The Wrong Man* [1956]) while pointedly leaving television out of the new American landscape he was documenting—the Bates Motel must be the only one in the country without TV in its rooms. In comparison Wood, whose career began when television was chipping away at the audience for movies, was hyperrealistic: *Plan 9* addresses its audience from inside a TV set.

Wood made features, but he also made commercials (excessively personal, like everything he did) and TV pilots. *Final Curtain* was the unsold pilot for a series to be called *Portraits of Terror*, and Wood's first known film, *The Sun Was Setting* (1951), was a pilot with a premise as theoretical—and economical—as Welles's *Fountain of Youth*. It's set in one room, and if the heroine—seriously ill—leaves that room, she'll die. Actually, to keep the camera within those four walls Wood has her perish as soon as she dresses up to go out on a date. "We almost made it," she sighs to her boyfriend when he appears at the door, expiring in his arms.

Antoine de Baecque's article on Wood appeared in *Cahiers du cinéma* 487 (January 1995): 15, before the world premiere of Tim Burton's *Ed Wood* at the 1995 Cannes Film Festival, and my piece appeared in the next issue.

The term "carnivalesque" was proposed in the twenties by the Russian critic and anthropologist Mikhail Bakhtin in studies of Dostoevsky and Rabelais that tracked the subversive power in high literature of popular forms derived from the medieval Carnival. Rediscovered in the 1970s, Bakhtin influenced *Cahiers* readings of filmmakers like Fellini and Welles in the aftermath of the magazine's Red Years, a strand of *Cahiers* thought to which I contributed with my eulogy for Welles, "The Force of the Work" (part of "L'Héritage"), *Cahiers du cinéma* 378 (December 1985): 2–32.

Support for my anthropological interpretation of "Le Cas Wood" can be found in G. G. Bolich, *Transgender History & Geography: Vol. 3, Crossdressing in Context* (Raleigh: Psyche's Press, 2007).

Michel Chion is a musician and a *Cahiers* film critic who has focused his attention on the overlooked role of sound in cinema. His theoretical work appears in many volumes, including *Le son au cinéma* (Paris: Cahiers du cinéma, 1985) and Claudia Gorbman's English translation of his work, *Audio-Vision* (New York: Columbia University Press, 1994), with a preface by Walter Murch, who won an Oscar for Sound Editing on *Apocalypse Now* (1979). Chion draws considerable attention to the *acousmêtre*, who is heard but never seen, and Wood's masterpiece, *Glen or Glenda*, is held together by an array of voices with no visible source in the image.

My title, "Le Cas Wood," refers jokingly to André Bazin's defense of the unfashionable (supposedly "uncinematic," i.e., talky) Provençal filmmaker Marcel Pagnol in his piece "Le Cas Pagnol," in *Qu'est-ce-que le cinéma?* (Paris: Éditions du Cerf, 1975).

20

Robert Altman

Prêt-à-Porter

R OBERT ALTMAN'S COMEDY ABOUT the French fashion industry *Prêt-à-Porter* (1994) resurrects a device he used in *Nashville* (1975). There an English reporter named Opal (Geraldine Chaplin) questioned the characters preparing for a big country music broadcast; in *Prêt-à-Porter* an American television journalist, Kitty Potter (Kim Basinger), questions the participants in the annual *défilé de mode* where Paris's leading designers unveil their new creations.

This chapter originally appeared as "Le système de la mode," *Cahiers du cinéma* 489 (March 1995): 69–70.

The roving reporter in these two films is more than a device for telling a story, or creating the semblance of one. Opal is looking for the meaning of America in the era of the Vietnam War; Kitty is looking for the meaning of fashion. Both will be traumatized when they find what they are looking for.

Almost thirty years ago, Roland Barthes's *Système de la mode* asked Kitty's question and answered it by analyzing the connotations of the "written garment" of fashion magazines. Today, if Altman's film is right, the center of gravity for the fashion world is the image, represented by Kitty and by a sought-after photographer who humiliates the editors of three magazines who are vying for his services.

But when Kitty questions the designers who have created this year's fashions, their answers suggest that the connotations haven't changed. The fashion garment still signifies, globally, Fashion, and more minutely, the World. Barthes's favorite example of the latter ("Prints win at the races") has today given way to more grandiose significations: "the media," "the street," or "the sexual subtext," to quote some of the answers given by Kitty's flattered subjects, or all else failing, by Kitty herself.

But is there any reason to think that Robert Altman cares about the Paris fashion world, any more than he did about country music? What Opal twenty years ago and Kitty today give voice to is the relatively free play of connotations generated by the images of these films, and by Altman's own system: improvisational direction of actors chosen for their eccentricities, a layered soundtrack, overlapping dialogue, games with what is shown and what isn't, relentless intercutting among several stories.

A system whose power to surprise us has diminished with time: while Opal's delirious free associations mirrored the unexpected effects that Altman could still sustain for a whole film in 1975, Kitty's running commentary on the fashion scene, which is being read from cue cards, rings hollowly in a film that is short on surprises and devoid of charm.

Opal in *Nashville* has a double, a sinister political operative named Triplette (Michael Murphy), the behind-the-scenes organizer of the film's climactic concert, which will pair country music's leading male star and female star under a big American flag to endorse an ambiguous presidential candidate. Opal and Triplette are symbols of the formal principles that are generating the film: the elephantine skeleton of a classical narrative with a big climax and a big message to match, and a relentlessly gnawing termite nourishing herself on odd associations, stray surrealisms, and moments of unexpected beauty found in the corners and margins of the image.

Triplette's equivalent in *Prêt-à-Porter* is Olivier de la Fontaine (Jean-Pierre Cassel), president of the designers' union and organizer of the *grand défilé*, but Olivier dies for no particular reason ten minutes into the film, leaving the spectacle to unfold without him, which it does. The film's only narrative aim will be to reveal a few banal sexual secrets, before the climactic sequence in which an angry designer sends her models parading in the nude, to the chagrin and puzzlement of Kitty Potter, who turns the microphone over to her cue-card girl for the benediction: unashamed nudity is the deepest meaning of Fashion.

Or maybe it isn't, for Robert Altman shows no sign of being interested in the subject of his new film, which he seems to have made almost against his will. If *Prêt-à-Porter* is about anything, it is about Altman's cinema, whose decline began with *Nashville*. A final symptom of that decline: a filmmaking system whose greatest successes were loony versions of Hollywood genres lazily alludes today to famous scenes from *Ghost* (1990) and *Yesterday, Today and Tomorrow* (1963) as shorthand for love scenes the director can't be bothered to film.

The *Ghost* reference is part of a story about two reporters who fall in lust when they have to share a hotel room, which is punctuated throughout by a flow of sounds and images on TV, randomly selected by whichever lover happens to have the remote control in hand. A film that has almost no reason for existing, *Prêt-à-Porter* still boasts two: a confession, that the filmmaker who dazzled critics with his innovative narrative strategies has become just another zapper, and Anouk Aimée, the only living person in a gallery of faded caricatures.

Prêt-à-Porter is, in a curious way, a very honest confession from the creator of *McCabe and Mrs. Miller* (1971), *The Long Goodbye* (1973), *California Split* (1974), *Popeye* (1980), *Vincent and Theo* (1990), and other films that advanced the techniques and aesthetics of American cinema for over a decade, before exile and growing cynicism about filmmaking ways and means all but quenched the flame. Let's hope that his new project, a jazz film set in his hometown of Kansas City, will give him a chance to make it shine again.

Notations

I returned to Altman in a less skeptical way in "Altmanville," *Cahiers du cinéma* 619 (January 2007): 55–56.

Altman's jazz film is *Kansas City* (1996).

21

Stanley Kubrick

Full Metal Jacket

FIRST MOVEMENT: AT A MARINE boot camp on Parris Island, a squad of young recruits are brutalized by Sergeant Hartman (Lee Ermey), a horrifyingly funny drill instructor whose face and voice dominate the film's first section so completely that only two other characters emerge as individuals, a wiseass named Joker (Matthew Modine) and a

---

An earlier version of this chapter appeared in *Zone 6: Incorporations*, ed. Jonathan Crary and Sanford Kwinter (New York: Urzone, 1992), 428–435.

dumb farm boy named Pyle (Vincent D'Onofrio), whose propensity for screwing up makes him the main target for Hartman's brutality, until he goes mad and shoots his persecutor in the latrine.

Second movement: cut to Da Nang, where Joker and a gung ho newcomer named Rafterman (Kevyn Major Howard) have drawn easy duty as correspondents for the army newspaper *Stars and Stripes*, and suddenly the tension of the first part dissipates, the structure of the film loosens to the point of entropy, and the narrative is set adrift, as if we were watching outtakes from a film whose story we haven't completely understood. We follow Joker and Rafterman from the placid corruption of Da Nang, briefly interrupted by a curiously anemic sequence showing the Tet Offensive, to the countryside around Hue, where they join a seasoned combat unit called the Lusthogs for an assault on Hue, overrun by the Vietcong. The drifting, fragmentary, antidramatic feeling of these sequences is heightened in the aftermath of the assault, when a television crew films the characters speaking in choreographed succession like actors in a bad Broadway play about Vietnam, then addressing the camera directly in interviews that recall a famous episode of TV's *M*A*S*H*.

It's only during the last minutes of the film that some kind of story kicks in again. As the Lusthogs patrol the streets of Hue, they find themselves pinned down by an invisible sniper who turns out, when Joker penetrates her stronghold, to be a teenage girl. Cut down by Rafterman's bullets, she is slow to die, and Joker is the only member of the squad who's willing to put her out of her misery with a bullet to the brain. Afterward we see American soldiers marching at night silhouetted against a fiery landscape, singing the Mickey Mouse Club theme song, while Joker, barely distinguished from the horde by the last of a sparse series of laconic voiceovers, informs us that he is no longer afraid.

Is *Full Metal Jacket* (1987) an antiwar film, as the critics have assumed, or is it, in the words of an indignant Samuel Fuller, who saw it with me, "a recruiting film"? Fuller, a World War II veteran who made brilliant war films, had every right to be angry, and his anger did more to point up the slippery quality of *Full Metal Jacket* for me than all the raves predicated on the notion that Stanley Kubrick had made another *Paths of Glory* (1957), the film about a suicidal attack ordered by a mad general during World War I that put him on the map with critics. Throughout his career Kubrick depicted wars—from a generic war that looks like Korea in *Fear and Desire* (1953) to the Cold War (*Dr. Strangelove* [1964]) and the Thirty Years' War (*Barry Lyndon* [1975])—while rejecting messages in order to purify his art. *Full Metal Jacket*, which returned to the booby-trapped terrain of the war film per se, was the end point of that process. He made only one more film, *Eyes Wide Shut* (1999), before his death, revisiting the subject of *Lolita* (1962) and *The Shining* (1980): the war between the sexes, his other great theme. We can see Kubrick evading facile interpretations of *Full Metal Jacket* by comparing his shooting script with the film he finally made. Two scenes were eliminated that would have made the drill instructor a monster: one where he nearly drowns Pyle in a bowl of urine and one where he orders a recruit who has cut his wrists to clean up the mess he's made before reporting to the doctor. Instead, due in no small part to Lee Ermey's mesmerizing performance, his character remains human-size, by turns outrageous and sympathetic, even seductive. So it's not difficult to understand Fuller's rage at the way Hartman is portrayed, or his distrust of any film that includes a scene like the one where the recruits, transformed by the agonies of boot camp into proud members of the Corps, parade to the strains of the "Marines' Hymn" while Hartman's voice tells them they are now part of an indestructible brotherhood. The producer of *Merrill's Marauders* (1962) had tacked a scene like that onto Fuller's film to turn it into the kind of war film described by Roland Barthes in "Operation Astra," an essay anthologized in *Mythologies*: "Take the Army; show without disguise its chiefs as martinets, its discipline as narrow-minded and unfair, and into this stupid tyranny immerse an average human being, fallible but likeable, the archetype of the spectator. And then, at the last moment, turn over the magic hat and pull out of it the image of an army, flags flying, triumphant, bewitching, to which, like Sganarelle's wife, one cannot but be faithful although beaten." In fact, that's an excellent description of what happens in *Full Metal Jacket* until Pyle shoots Hartman. Then another kind of film begins, and by the time the image of the triumphant army returns at the end, the conventions of the (anti)war film have been transformed into something else altogether.

The best theory of Kubrick I know is Gilles Deleuze's observation that all of his films portray the world as a brain, one fated to malfunction from both internal and external causes. The little world of the training camp on Parris Island is a brain made up of human cells thinking and feeling as one, until its functioning is wrecked first from within when a single cell, Pyle, begins ruthlessly carrying out the directives of the death instinct that programs the organ as a whole, and then from without by the Tet Offensive, the external representation of the same force. Kubrick's camera describes a double movement: in the first section, as it follows the constant parading of the recruits and their instructor, movement is from the interior of the screen out; in the second section, beginning with a striking dolly forward on the miniskirted ass of a Da Nang whore, camera movements into the screen, toward the vanishing point, predominate. But the film's two parts describe a single movement with a single end point—the encounter with a fellow human being whose face, in Hartman's memorable phrase, has become a "war face," the face of death.

For the first time in Kubrick's cinema the narrative itself begins to malfunction in *Full Metal Jacket* after Pyle has turned his rifle on Hartman and then on himself, as if eliminating the antagonists whose repeated confrontations made a story possible has condemned the film to wander into regions bordering dangerously on nonsense, until a new antagonist erupts in the encounter with the sniper, which permits the filmmaker to start turning the screw of suspense again, imparting a linear and dramatic coherence in time to arrest the fatal drift.

Kubrick told *Newsweek* that he wanted to "explode the narrative structure of film," and in *Full Metal Jacket* the first casualty of the explosion is the conventional notion of character. *Full Metal Jacket* is a film without a hero. Its protagonist is a group-mind whose formation is shown in the boot camp scenes, most of which portray the process of indoctrination, with little reference to combat training per se. Then, in the second section, we follow scattered pieces of the group-mind as they are set adrift in a world where scene follows scene with no apparent dramatic or thematic necessity, so that even Joker, whose acts and motives were starkly delineated by the constricting circumstances of boot camp, seems to withdraw from us, becoming a cipher as the film unfolds, thanks to the unsparing labor of purification by which Kubrick during the year-long shoot stripped away the elements in his own script that made Joker someone with whom the audience could identify: his voiceovers reduced finally to four or five; the instinctive revulsion that impels him, in a scene that was either cut or never filmed, to kill an ARVN colonel who is murdering prisoners during the helicopter ride from Da Nang to Hue, and Joker's death and burial, which would have concluded the film on an elegiac note, which Kubrick replaced with the group shot of soldiers singing the Mouseketeer anthem that was originally planned for an earlier scene, after the assault on Hue.

Paradoxically, the mute, expressionless faces in the film's opening sequence—wordless close-ups of recruits getting their first Marine Corps haircuts—seem emotionally closer to us than the faces in the montage of TV interviews, which distance the characters at the very moment they are being permitted, for the first time, to "express" themselves, with all the method acting, mock hesitations, and other signals of sincerity on the part of the actors that "expression" implies. In the second section of *Full Metal Jacket* we meet a whole new cast of highly individualistic characters who are imbued with the full range of human emotions, but cut loose from their narrative moorings they appear as opaque fragments of a larger whole, their acts legible only as behaviors (to borrow a term from the science of operant conditioning) in which are embedded, with horrible monotony, the traits—racism, misogyny, machismo, and homicidal mania—that govern the group-mind, even in its malfunctioning, although this doesn't keep us from feeling sympathy for them. Sympathy is necessary, in fact, if we are to read the subtle, often nearly imperceptible gestures and expressions in which the drama of the group is being played out.

One striking effect of Kubrick's narrative experiments in *Full Metal Jacket* was to oblige alert critics to reconsider their unqualified adulation of Oliver Stone's *Platoon* (1986), because Kubrick had eliminated every scene or action that might have served as a handhold for the spectator in search of easy edification, constructing his film as a parody of all edifying and unifying fictions. Watching the last scene, where Joker, made fearless, is swallowed up by the marching throng, calls to mind Stone's proclaimed intention of bringing Americans together and healing the nation's wounds, to which the only proper reply is Alex's last line in *A Clockwork Orange* (1972): "I was cured, all right!"

The alienation effects that Kubrick uses in the Vietnam section of his film are a superior form of realism to *Platoon*'s scorched-earth naturalism, which is largely based on effects of déjà vu: Stone, who was there, has portrayed the Vietnamese War of Liberation in images copied from contemporary TV coverage and other war films, so that the shock of discovering a new reality is mediated by images that are believable because they're already familiar—as in his *Salvador* (1986), where the photojournalist played by John Savage says, not that he wants to take a picture that shows the reality of war, but that he wants to "take one like Capa."

Kubrick's formal strategy in *Full Metal Jacket* is to create moments of utter strangeness that have the shock of fresh perception. Brecht's alienation effect and Freud's idea of the Uncanny, which Kubrick spoke approvingly of in one of his rare interviews, resonate with one another if we hear the "strangeness" implicit in "estrangement effect," a translation for Brecht's *V-effekt* that fits Alex DeLarge (Malcolm MacDowell), the protagonist of *A Clockwork Orange*, like a glove. Alex is a machine made of living tissue—a clockwork orange—because he's programmed by the drugs he takes in the first part of the film and by the Ludovico technique used on him by the Minister of the Interior [*sic*] in the second part.

In his 1926 play *Mann ist Mann* Brecht himself had described the programming of army recruit Galy Gay, an ancestor of Joker inspired by the horrors of World War I. Deleuze discusses Kubrick in the second volume of *Cinema*, his comprehensive classification of film images and signs, initially assigning him to one of the two stylistic camps into which he divides modern cinema, the cinema of the body (Godard and

Cassavetes) and the cinema of the brain (Resnais and Kubrick). Deleuze's poetic rewriting of philosopher of science Gilbert Simondon turns out to have many applications, for as that diversified roster of modern film-makers suggests, Deleuze intends it to be more widely applicable than he indicates. It turns out, in fact, that the cinema of the brain is not just one type of film in Deleuze's taxonomy of modern cinema—it represents the whole terrain to be mapped. This means that the films of Resnais and Kubrick, which take Deleuze's new model as their subject, are exemplary. By dispersing its narrative and making classical narrative one element in a structure that implements another logic, *Full Metal Jacket*, like other modern films, is exploring the cerebral processes that found the new aesthetic of what Deleuze calls *l'image-temps*, but, by portraying as parts of a brain the stock characters of a genre that could stand for all of classical cinema ("A film is like a battlefield"—Samuel Fuller, 1965), Kubrick is staging, in a peculiarly literal way, an allegory of modern cinema.

I don't want to leave the impression that Kubrick, because he succeeded "making it new," was without masters. He had one, whom he proudly acknowledged: Max Ophuls, who is as present in *Full Metal Jacket* as he is in an obvious pastiche like *Lolita*. Hartman's first appearance, for example, visually duplicates the opening sequence of *Lola Montes* (1955), with Peter Ustinov's ringmaster spieling to the backward-tracking camera as he advances past a line of acrobats standing at attention. William Karl Guerin in his book on Ophuls has taught us to be suspicious of this Mephistophelian figure and his twin, the Master of Ceremonies in *La Ronde* (1950), who subject the other characters and the spectator alike to the seductive rigors of a mise-en-scène designed to illustrate "a sinister conception of man." Traditionally, critics have tended to identify these director surrogates with Ophuls, and Kubrick, who revises his predecessor by killing off Hartman in the middle of the film, might agree with them, but all the ambiguities of *Full Metal Jacket* are already deployed in Ophuls's late films, where, as Guerin has shown, a single close-up (Simone Signoret in *La Ronde*, Martine Carol faint and perspiring before her final leap in *Lola Montes*) is sufficient to derail the Master of Ceremonies' infernal machine. In *Full Metal Jacket* the close-up of Pyle, insane, signals the imminent death of Kubrick's Master of Ceremonies, which liberates images and characters from the machine of the narrative, and when the narrative begins to function again during the assault on Hue, the close-up of the young sniper shatters the spell, leaving us with those concluding images of the marauding horde, which recall the Dionysian mobs of *Le Masque* and the end of the *Maison Tellier* episode of *Le Plaisir* (1951): images of a world without a Master of Ceremonies.

Notations

Regarding Sam Fuller's reaction to the Kubrick film, I later learned from Sam's wife Christa that after he got over his initial anger he had decided *Full Metal Jacket* was a good film.

The Roland Barthes quotation is from Annette Lavers's translation of *Mythologies* (New York: Hill and Wang, 1972), 41. I've corrected the translation in a few places to make it more colloquial.

Deleuze's observation about Kubrick is in *Cinema 2: The Time-Image*, trans. Hugh Tomlinson and Robert Galeta (Minneapolis: University of Minnesota Press, 1989), 205–206.

On operant conditioning, see B. F. Skinner, *The Behavior of Organisms: An Experimental Analysis* (New York: Appleton-Century-Crofts, 1939).

In *Platoon*, the hero (Charlie Sheen) has a good angel and a bad angel played by Tom Berenger and Willem Dafoe, harking back to the didacticism of medieval morality plays, but Stone's first films, *Seizure* (1974) and *The Hand* (1981), were horror movies. Paradoxically, it was only when he returned to body horror in *Born on the Fourth of July* (1989), and to the mixture of film stocks and spectral highlights from his early experiments in *JFK* (1991), that he became a political filmmaker, one of the greatest.

The Kubrick interview is in Michel Ciment, *Kubrick* (New York: Henry Holt & Co., 1984).

Regarding Deleuze's rewriting of Gilbert Simondon, see the latter's *L'individu et sa genèse physico-biologique* (Paris: PUF, 1964), 261.

Samuel Fuller's quote about films and battlefields is in Jean-Luc Godard's *Pierrot le fou* (1965).

Regarding Kubrick "making it new": Kubrick is famous for creating films that don't look like anything ever seen before, but in my monograph *Masters of Cinema: Stanley Kubrick* (London: Phaidon-Cahiers du Cinéma, 2010) I argue that, paradoxically, his creative method was based on repetition. "Everything has been done," the modest demiurge once confided in Jack Nicholson. "Our job is just to do it a little better."

Robert Capa (1913–1954) was an American war photographer. He is viewed by many as the greatest war photographer in history.

On Ophuls and a "sinister conception of man," see William Karl Guerin, *Max Ophuls* (Paris: Cahiers du Cinéma, 1988).

22

John Frankenheimer

Jonah

Continuities

D IRECTORS TRAINED IN TELEVISION are a special breed and should have their own chapter in the promised new edition of Andrew Sarris's *The American Cinema*. If and when that chapter is

This essay appeared as a slightly different version in Murray Pomerance and R. Barton Palmer, eds., *A Little Solitaire: John Frankenheimer and American Film* (New Brunswick: Rutgers University Press, 2011).

written, Robert Altman and Sidney Lumet will be at the top of the list and John Frankenheimer somewhere in the middle with Spielberg, achieving varying degrees of aesthetic success but never rising above a certain level, while churning out a very long list of films, testimony to these TV wunderkinds' secret weapon: stamina. The scenes of Gene Hackman's bout with heroin in *The French Connection II* (1975) are overlong and bathetic, but Gene Hackman's pursuit on foot of Fernando Ray making his getaway by boat is far more engaging than William Friedkin's famed *French Connection* (1971) car chase. Out of shape after his detox, dodging through Marseille crowds with his eye on the boat he isn't even sure contains his quarry, almost too exhausted by the end to clamber over a low barrier when he finally sees an opening onto the water, Hackman squeezes off two shots as Ray emerges onto the deck, sure that his Droopy-like adversary has been left far behind. Bang bang!—Ray, startled, tumbles back and the film is over. Frankenheimer's career was like that chase.

We know how it began: a director he was seconding on a live episode of *Danger* (1954) saw himself on-camera, cried "Save me!," and threw up on his assistant director, who proceeded to finish the show. Promoted to director, the assistant soon found himself doing prestige dramas and, when the Young Turks of the cathode tube hit the pavement in the late 1950s, arty movies. That *Danger* episode was about an escape from a German prison camp, which set one of the topical templates for the subsequent career. Frankenheimer's next big break came when he was hired to replace the director of *Birdman of Alcatraz* (1962) and saved the film. (Prison was now locked in as a Frankenheimer "obsession," although like many directorial obsessions, it was acquired by accident.)

The offscreen substitution must have also lodged in his subconscious, because it's the basis for the Commie plot in *The Manchurian Candidate*, a book he selected to make when he was riding high: the Red-baiting Democratic candidate for vice president is supposed to replace his running mate when he's slain by a hypnotized drone during his victory speech to the TV cameras. Senator Jordan's (John McGiver) observation that "If John Iselin were a paid Soviet agent, he could not do more harm to this country than he's doing now" is a classic liberal line, and Frankenheimer was nothing if not a classic sixties liberal. When Frank Sinatra called President Kennedy on behalf of worried United Artists executives to get his okay before proceeding with *Suddenly* (1954), JFK, a rabid cold warrior who kept trying to have Castro assassinated, said it was one of his favorite books, along with the James Bond series.

Then JFK was assassinated, and after Frankenheimer had devoted himself body and soul to RFK's 1968 primary campaign, which was supposed to end with a victory dinner at his home in Malibu, Bobby was assassinated too by a real-life hypnotic drone, with a second gunman administering the killing shot. Bobby had asked Frankenheimer to stand with him on the platform when he made his victory speech, but Frankenheimer demurred, thinking it would look bad for the candidate to have a movie director next to him. "The man standing next to him was shot too," he told Charles Champlin. "If I'd been with him, that would've been me." But in a way, it was as if it had been.

"Bobby's assassination is when it all fell apart," Frankenheimer later said. He fell into depression and drink, and his career went south, with occasional oases of commercial success. His films also changed, keeping abreast of the times. The early Frankenheimers are made up of Welles shots reconfigured into contrasty black-and-white images that would stand out on the small screen and certainly do on a big one. One habit he never kicked was deep-focus shots of big heads looming in the foreground while homunculi in sharp focus listen in the background.

But this had already undergone modifications before the second Kennedy assassination: a car nut like Kenneth Grahame's Mr. Toad, Frankenheimer had discovered auto racing and broadened his palette to include multiple screens with *Grand Prix* (1966). After the assassination he studiously blended into the Hollywood New Wave, so that he had the distinction of figuring prominently in two Manny Farber fatwas against two completely different schools of cinematic hotshots: "Hard Sell Cinema," about the New York School of the 1950s and '60s, and "A New Breed of Filmmakers," where other, bigger targets included Francis Coppola and Martin Scorsese.

He achieved success with *French Connection II* and again with *Black Sunday*, an impersonal film by one of those "artist businessmen" Farber railed against in "Hard Sell Cinema." *The Manchurian Candidate* (1962) with a happy ending, Robert Harris's best seller is about a Vietnam vet who is programmed by Arab terrorists to blow up the Super Bowl. The film (1977) is more of a comic book than the novel, where the Mossad agent who would be played by Robert Shaw compares himself to Hitler for using torture to obtain information. In the film version he has no self-doubts, and nothing in Frankenheimer's history suggests that he would ever have been inclined to raise any. In fact, the bomb-laden dirigible targeting the Super Bowl on New Year's Day is a blue-screen descendant of the Soviet sneak attack, scheduled for Christmas Eve, that is portrayed with stock footage in *Forbidden Area*, Frankenheimer's first *Playhouse 90*, aired in 1956.

The debut episode of that distinguished series, *Forbidden Area* is no *Judgment at Nuremberg* (1959). "Pick a time, like when free men are worshiping the Prince of Peace, then strike!" intones the voice of the series' producer, Martin Manulis. The scene where the Soviet agent played by Tab Hunter is interrogated about baseball by his invisible handlers follows an uncanny opening sequence (scripted by Rod Serling) where a discussion of baseball in a Chicago bar becomes increasingly sinister until we realize that the bar is somewhere near Moscow and the seemingly banal conversation about sports statistics is part of a final exam for saboteurs. The stunning opening of this forgotten broadcast may even have given Frankenheimer the clue for how to film the sequence in *Candidate* that goes back and forth between a lecture on hydrangeas happening somewhere outside New Orleans and a blood-curdling demonstration of brainwashing happening somewhere inside Communist China—a scenography that is implied in only the vaguest terms by Condon's novel.

The director's use of stock footage in *Forbidden Area* is certainly every bit as clever as his merging of real and fake fans in *Black Sunday*'s climax, and some of the sets, like the cardboard shrubbery with an irregular patch of turf on a process screen peeping through it when the saboteur drowns the inconvenient "Cookie" (Jackie Coogan) offscreen, are modern art masterpieces. "La Mer" playing over the underwater shot of a frogman who is supposed to be Tab Hunter emerging from a Soviet sub to infiltrate the Strategic Air Command adds a wonderful touch of low-rent highbrow poetry reminiscent of the diving scenes with a puppet in a fish tank in Edgar G. Ulmer's *Isle of Forgotten Sins* (1943), which are accompanied by a theme from *Das Rheingold. The Manchurian Candidate*, for all its supposed paradoxes, puts on the screen the paranoid fantasy that underwrote the Vietnam War, but like the best moments in *Forbidden Area*, it "hallucinates" the ideology of Cold War liberalism in the same way that Eisenstein's *The General Line* (1929) "hallucinates" Stalinism, to use Jean Narboni's formula for that film's double-edged quality. Frankenheimer would continue to mirror the ideology of liberalism by crawling inside its paranoias until the very last phase of his career, when paranoia and its consequences became the subject of his most lucid film, *Path to War* (2002), but the hallucinatory quality of the early black-and-white thrillers would be replaced by realism, with the megacephalic signature shots continuing to lurk around the edges of the mise-en-scène. Like *Jaws* (1975), *Black Sunday* appears to be happening in the real world. And on September 11, 2001, it did.

Reluctant Prophet

Interviewed on the set of *The Island of Dr. Moreau* (1996), Frankenheimer identified the stylistic unity of his work in the 1990s as follows: "The look of this film is very similar to the look of my last four movies—a very fluent style with lots of moving shots and depth-of-focus shots. It's a very realistic look." Counting backward takes us to *Year of the Gun* (1991), a feature film that is rarely talked about in conjunction with the director's triumphant return to television except as the last of the series of genre efforts whose dismal box office performance made it necessary. But Frankenheimer is right: *Year of the Gun* did contribute to the evolution of the dynamic, in-your-face camera style used in *Against the Wall* (1994), a style powered by the invention of the Steadicam, which had an obvious appeal for a director who once wrapped a camera cable around a fountain on the set of a live TV drama until the camera could barely move.

What's more, *Year of the Gun* is also thematically related to the series of films kicked off by *Against the Wall* because it is about revolution. Set in Italy in 1978, this adaptation of a best seller by a journalist for *Newsweek* recounts fictional events surrounding the kidnapping of Italy's former prime minister Aldo Moro by the Red Brigades, a clandestine revolutionary organization that was making headlines throughout the 1970s.

A Malibu liberal with close ties to the Kennedys, Frankenheimer seems an unlikely filmmaker to be obsessed with revolution. But the one hundred days he spent working for Bobby Kennedy had been a revolutionary experience within the fluid confines of the electoral process, not because RFK was leading an insurgency against a sitting president of his own party (who had already withdrawn from the fray), but because that one-of-a-kind campaign, happening at a once-in-a-lifetime moment, channeled the energies of diverse groups looking for an alternative to politics as usual, which in this case was Johnson's veep, Hubert Humphrey, who ended up losing to Richard Nixon after RFK was assassinated. Remarkably, Humphrey's existence is not even alluded to in *Path to War*—hardly a structuring absence, I'd say, because very few people watching the film seem to notice it. No one in the film notices it either.

The coalition that came together around the Kennedy campaign in the spring of 1968 included civil rights activists and Black Panthers, Cesar Chavez's farm workers' union and Democratic machine politicians, blue-collar workers and Wall Street protesters, drawn together by the Kennedy legacy and the mantra "Peace in Vietnam"—just about everyone but the outraged supporters of the donnish Eugene McCarthy, who had been the first Democratic candidate against the war. RFK himself was a changed man after his brother's death: the enforcer with the brass knuckles emerging reluctantly from the shadows, quoting Aeschylus and Camus in his last speeches and daring death while generating an outpouring of popular fervor unlike anything America had seen since the end of World

War II brought down the chilly consensus of the Cold War.

That had been Frankenheimer's revolution—one of many that briefly took shape in the 1960s, only to be co-opted or blown away—and he spent the rest of his life trying to figure out what had gone wrong. In *Year of the Gun* Andrew McCarthy plays David Rayborne, a disillusioned sixties radical who gave up on politics after being implicated in a fatal explosion in a bomb factory. He's in Italy to finish a novel about the Red Brigades that unfortunately outlines a plan to kidnap Moro, who is forging an alliance between the center-left Christian Democrats and the Italian Communist Party, and the revolutionaries take this MacGuffin very seriously when the manuscript falls into their hands. In one grimly comic scene, when they stake out Moro's apartment, they find Rayborne in the bushes doing the same thing.

Emerging intact from the ensuing bloodshed to peddle a best seller on the *Dick Cavett Show*, Rayborne sees his prophecy come true—Moro's kidnapping is reenacted by Frankenheimer as an anticlimax to his thriller plot. Moro ends up dead like Robert Kennedy, and it is Frankenheimer's sense of having been an accidental prophet, or catalyst, for both Kennedy assassinations that gives weight to the portrayal in *Year of the Gun* of the relationship between a fictitious thriller in the tradition of *The Manchurian Candidate* and a real-life terrorist act. The fact that Moro's death in his captors' hands had long been a subject for conspiratorial speculations in Italy—his "historical compromise" scared the United States as much as it did the revolutionaries—would only have made the parallels more interesting to Frankenheimer when he tackled the subject in 1991.

Misconstruing the film's highly personal reflections as a standard-issue rant about the complicity of the media in political violence, critics praised Frankenheimer's depiction of a country in the grip of a revolutionary struggle but found Andrew McCarthy and Sharon Stone out of place in any story with pretenses to realism. (Is that why they hide in a movie theater displaying Italian *Star Wars* posters when they're escaping from the Red Brigade goons?) So for his next film Frankenheimer would focus on realistically portraying the Attica Prison uprising and relegate his stars, Samuel Jackson and Kyle MacLachlan, to supporting roles.

Revolution and Utopia

The Attica Prison uprising (commencing September 9, 1971) was the subject of a radical documentary made at the time by Cinda Firestone, and the politics of *Against the Wall* are not that different from Firestone's, even if the dramaturgy is traditional, interweaving with the depiction of events parallel stories of characters played by a white and a black star.

The thesis, which was confirmed by a hearing and a lawsuit after the event, is that the order by New York governor Nelson Rockefeller and his commissioner of prisons, Russell Oswald (Phillip Bosco), to take the prison back by force caused the deaths of twenty-nine inmates and nine prison guards who were being held hostage, all mowed down by the guns of the local police. Frankenheimer presents the uprising as a revolution, part of the larger revolution that was brewing in America in the late 1960s—the head guard played by Frederick Forrest says this to the new guard (MacLachlan) who is our surrogate, and an upstate New York cop announces that retaking the prison will be payback for the hippies and black revolutionaries who are causing him sleepless nights, just before joyously slaughtering everyone in sight.

Most of the leaders of the uprising saw themselves as revolutionaries with limited, reasonable aims: reform of Rockefeller's prisons and amnesty for the takeover of Attica, and their ally in the film is Commissioner Oswald. This well-meaning man insists on negotiating even though the warden, whose callousness and brutality has caused the uprising, wants to retake the prison immediately before the situation gets out of hand. Oswald is supported by Rockefeller (shown only as a beaming headshot) for four days and obtains twenty-eight concessions demanded by the convicts, but when negotiations break down over the issue of amnesty and a personal visit from "Rocky"—and when Oswald himself is almost taken hostage—he and his boss order the fatal onslaught. By leaving open the tactical question—was immediately retaking the prison a better option than negotiating, then attacking?—Frankenheimer shows that the contradictory behavior of Rockefeller and Oswald was the worst option of all. Rockefeller was the most prominent example in the 1960s of that now-extinct species, a liberal Republican, and he still harbored presidential ambitions for which he was ready to sacrifice the lives of the working-class guards and the black convicts to avoid looking soft to the electorate. The film not only sides with the limited revolutionary aims of the prisoners; it uses a revolutionary situation to shine a critical light on the liberal alternative. That is exactly what happened in the United States in the late 1960s and early '70s, which left us scathing exposés like Phil Ochs's "Love Me, I'm a Liberal" as a reminder of how having the idea of revolution on the table once blew open the airless enclosure of our national politics.

Frankenheimer always planned to do a film about Bobby, but the family, more risk-averse than its male scions, entrusted the job to its court painter, David Wolper. So Frankenheimer's next film for HBO, *The Burning Season* (1994), told the story of another revolutionary stopped by a bullet, Chico Mendes, who built a union of Brazilian rubber-tree tappers to block the deforestation of the Amazon and was assassinated by one of the big ranchers whose plans for expansion he was opposing.

At one point Mendes (Raul Julia) is flown to the United States by a filmmaker who wants to portray him as the leader of a green revolution, to which he mildly objects that he wants to save the trees for the rubber tappers, not for a bunch of tree-humpers in Beverly Hills. This facile self-flagellation is of a piece with the film's insistence on giving equal time to the viewpoint of the fascist ranchers—which is to say that the whole project is handicapped by the script Frankenheimer inherited from executive producer David (*Chariots of Fire* [1981]) Puttnam, particularly when it keeps shoving an old woman with what is known in Hollywood as "a great face" in the forefront of every scene showing Mendes's unionists. Perhaps that is also why Raul Julia's ironic, passionless Chico Mendes is more like Eugene McCarthy than he is like Robert Kennedy.

Frankenheimer bounced back artistically with *Andersonville* (1996), produced by Ted Turner. While theoretically on the same end of the political spectrum as Puttnam, the southern mogul who tried to color-ize *Citizen Kane* (1941) is no Goody Two-shoes, which is probably what makes him a better producer than Puttnam. The story of the hideous prisoner-of-war camp for Union soldiers in Andersonville, Georgia, had been something of an ideological football in the 1950s. Novelist MacKinlay Kantor, who also wrote Curtis LeMay's memoirs, won a Pulitzer for his 1956 best seller about the prison that implicitly evoked memories of the Shoah, with much time devoted to exonerating innocent farmers living on the outskirts of the compound, in support of America's postwar alliance with Germany against the threat of communism. Saul Levitt's 1959 Broadway play, *The Andersonville Trial* (later filmed for PBS in 1971, at the height of the Vietnamese War of Liberation), was a revisionist take on the story that portrayed the sadistic commandant, Henry Wirz, as a tragic scapegoat.

The script Turner commissioned from veteran TV writer David Rintels for his follow-up to the hit TNT miniseries *Gettysburg* (1993) went back to prisoners' diaries for its source and focused on doings inside the prison. Echoing the view that Andersonville had been the American Auschwitz, Frankenheimer told Charles Champlin that he hesitated to take on the massive project because he "was becoming the mavin of prison movies." But he found an incident in Rintels's script that links Andersonville with *Against the Wall* as a film that uses its prison setting for reflections on revolution: the armed revolt of prisoners that brought an end to the reign of the Raiders, a group of blue-shirt kapos in league with their jailers who had been living high by preying on their fellow prisoners. Once the Raiders have been disarmed in a fierce battle, Com-mandant Wirz (Jan Tříska) (straightforwardly portrayed as a loon) allows them to be tried for murder and thievery in hopes that the concession will help him maintain order. During the trial in the prison yard, which is the dramatic centerpiece of a four-hour epic of starvation, disease, and cruelty, the debate turns on the legality of hanging prisoners who have committed crimes against their own, given that Federal Army law has no force in the prison setting—an ambiguous situation recalling the short-lived revolutionary community led by a Black Muslim (Jackson) that springs up in the yard at Attica. These scenes of "the other Andersonville Trial" set forth an ideal of justice where Revolution is reconciled with Law, like the public tribunals set up after the Cuban Revolution to curb popular reprisals and punish wealthy landowners, state officials, police, soldiers, straw bosses, and hired thugs for crimes committed during the Batista era. The prison-yard court is a dramatic situation for representing the utopian ideal of any revolution that aims at founding a new society after the shooting is over.

The Island of Dr. Moreau

The history of the film that marked Frankenheimer's return to features after *Andersonville* is murky, and that may be why it is the most interesting of his unofficial quartet of films about revolution. The young South African–born writer-director Richard Stanley was replaced in mid-production at the behest of the film's star, Val Kilmer, and Frankenheimer brought along the screenwriter of *Against the Wall*, Ron Hutchinson, who had already done a rewrite for him on *The Burning Season*. (Legend has it that Stanley stuck around disguised as a dogboy extra and watched the film being finished—IMDb lists him as the uncredited actor who played the "Melting Bulldog Boy.") When the film subsequently tanked, everyone but the special effects artists scattered, casting blame in all directions and making it impossible to assign responsibility for specific details, but my guess would be that *The Island of Dr. Moreau* is a Richard Stanley film largely shot or reshot by Frankenheimer and patched up by Hutchinson with a voiceover to cover gaps created by Kilmer, whose erratic behavior had been a problem for all concerned.

In his allegory of Darwinism, H. G. Wells predicted not only gene-splicing, which substitutes for vivisection in this version of the story, but that other modern invention, the concentration camp, ruled over by a Mengele who is operating on his experimental subjects without anesthesia in the House of Pain. That horror becomes an obstetric hospital in Stanley's rewrite, and Moreau becomes another in the gallery of villains Brando played at the end of his career. The anti-imperialist actor makes him a caricature of the White Man's Burden, who is wearing sunglasses and covered with what looks like SPF 200 sunscreen when we first see him: a sweet, dotty benevolent dictator who wants the beast-men to call him "Father." Unlike Wells's Moreau, he is not the amoral embodiment of the blind evolutionary process but a believer in the perfectibility of Man who forbids his subjects to eat meat, keeping them under control with injections of hormones and endorphins, boring sermons from the Speaker of the Law (Ron Perlman), and electrical implants that he uses to zap them when they disobey, permitting him to grandly forgive transgressors after a showy public trial instead of killing them.

Moreau's cagey reactions when it begins to dawn on him that Hyena (Daniel Rigney) and his henchmen have not come to his compound in the middle of the night on a friendly visit (Hyena has torn out his implant . . .) set the comic tone for a series of violent scenes—beginning with Moreau being eaten alive by his creations—that portray a revolution where Murphy's Law rules. When Hyena gets his hands on a machine gun, he handles it with all the aplomb of Pedro Armendáriz's general delightedly trying out his first Gatling gun in *The Wild Bunch* (1969). (An uncredited Walon Green was one of Richard Stanley's cowriters.) "Burn it!" cries Hyena, setting fire to the dock and ship that are the island's only link to the world. (He is echoing "Let it burn!" shouted by the nihilistic leader of the uprising in *Against the Wall* played by Clarence Williams III.) Rather than fall into the hands of Azazello (Temuera Morrison), her "father's" dogman major-domo, who has started to regress in a particularly unpleasant way, the panther girl Aissa (Fairuza Balk) imitates Mae Marsh's "brody" off the cliff escaping from Gus the black rapist in *The Birth of a Nation* (1915). "Brody" is slang for *jump*, dating back to 1886 when Steve Brodie leaped from the Brooklyn Bridge. Moreau is Kurtz in clown face (Michael Herr was another uncredited collaborator on Stanley's script), so that Kilmer's character doing his impression of Moreau is a travesty of a travesty, and so on.

The flurry of film references, which is probably the work of film school graduate Richard Stanley (except for the self-quotation by Frankenheimer and Hutchinson), reduces the dyad of Third World insurgency and enlightened imperialism (which is still official US policy as I write, under the deluded rubric of "nation building") to a carnivalesque riot of clichés, but that dyad was Frankenheimer's too. After playing thoughtful variations on it in three films for television where the Law is the utopian horizon of Revolution, he films it masterfully as an impossible contradiction at the end of *Moreau*, where the Law is a ghastly joke: "A series of propositions they called the Law battled in their minds with the deep-seated, ever rebellious cravings of their animal natures," says Wells's narrator. "This Law they were ever repeating, I found—and ever breaking." *Plus ça change, plus c'est la même chose.*

The ending of the film feels like something Frankenheimer might have devised with Hutchinson to go out on a positive note: the Speaker, a dogboy, and the tiny sloth-man watch Douglas (David Thewlis) sailing away on a makeshift raft, after the Speaker has refused his offer to help them stop their regression to bestiality: "No more scientists," the Speaker says, which puts the emphasis on the old wheeze about the dangers of tampering with nature, but after I saw Frankenheimer's rough cut some-one added a pessimistic epilogue from H. G. Wells. A lawyer who was on a peace-keeping mission for the United Nations when a plane crash stranded him on Moreau's island, Douglas fears his fellow men when he returns to civilization, recognizing in them the same unstable mixture of reason and instinct he has seen in the beast men. I assume that Fran-kenheimer, who after all put his name on the film and signed it with his visual style, at least OK'd the epilogue and the documentary montage of violent images accompanying it, which echoes the first images of *Against the Wall*, where peace demonstrations alternate with violent repression (the assassinations of Martin Luther King and Robert Kennedy, Kent State) to frame a historical context for what happened at Attica.

George Wallace and *Path to War*

In between his last two films for television, Frankenheimer made two more features, both thrillers, the genre that had kept him working dur-ing the years of his alcohol-fueled breakdown. Critics spoke of a return to form in *Ronin* (1998), and that's just what's wrong with it: the scenes of the heist being planned are textbook examples of what Manny Farber meant by "Hard Sell Cinema," tailored to the tube and wildly overstated on the big screen. Because Frankenheimer is still trying to make the antagonism that sixth-billed Sean Bean feels toward Robert De Niro the instant he joins the group perfectly legible on an eight-inch screen, Bean indulges in expressions of loathing and impotent fury so outrageous every time he gets his close-up that you wonder why he isn't drummed out of the group on the spot. Then at the end, Mr. Toad takes over and finally gets to stage a car chase better than the one in Friedkin's *French Connection* (1971).

But *Ronin* made money and *Reindeer Games* (2000) cratered, shot down by the same critics who had adored the efficient mechanics of Mr. Toad's last wild ride (unless we count the car-chase coda in *Ambush* [1950], made appropriately enough as a commercial for BMX). Particu-larly after seeing *Reindeer Games*, one of his most personal films (with a superb understated performance by Ben Affleck), recut by the studio and trashed by the critics, one can understand why he kept going back to the freedom of television, as he did after first experiencing the slings and arrows of feature filmmaking while doing *The Young Stranger* (1957). On that occasion he proceeded to make television history by directing forty-two episodes of *Playhouse 90*, an experience he harked back to in his last two television films.

Although *George Wallace* (1997) originated with TNT, it strikingly recalls Frankenheimer's 1957 *Playhouse 90* episode "The Death of Manolete" in one respect: that docudrama was written by bullfighting expert Barnaby Conrad, who had written a book with the same title, and a young TV writer, Paul Monash; four decades later Monash teamed with Marshall Frady, the author of *Wallace*, to write *George Wallace*. Frankenheimer said he was surprised when he read the script, which drastically rewrites the story of one of the worst villains in the civil rights wars of the 1950s and '60s, and he would say the same thing about the script HBO sent him for *Path to War* after Barry Levinson dropped out of the project, which portrays Lyndon Johnson and his advisors as more conflicted about the escalation of America's war against North Vietnam than they admitted at the time they were pursuing their ruinous policy.

While stopping short of exonerating Wallace and LBJ, Frankenheimer portrays them with sympathetic understanding, which is particularly justified in the case of Wallace by the transformation he underwent after being crippled by Arthur Bremer. During the period after Wallace had been born again and reconciled with Alabama's black community, who helped elect him to his fourth term as governor, he invited the paroled Bremer to the governor's mansion so he could forgive him, but Bremer demurred. The potent Sirkian melodrama of the scene where Wallace (Gary Sinise) spontaneously goes into Martin Luther King's old church on a rainy night and asks the black congregation for forgiveness has been exaggerated in the film, but it also really happened.

The real agenda of these last two docudramas is political, however, because Wallace, like Johnson, was a liberal Democrat at the start of his career. A protégé of Governor Big Jim Folsom (Joe Don Baker), he was a liberal judge who ran for governor promising to improve the lot of Alabama's poor, black and white alike, only to be defeated by the Klan's opposition to any candidate who didn't stand up for the cause of segregation, a system under fire from the Supreme Court decision to integrate public schools. That's when Wallace won office by becoming a virulent segregationist, then went on to campaign three times for president on a tacitly racist platform that found a receptive audience among traditionally Democratic voters in the North, and still did in its Karl-Rovian variant. As Frankenheimer put it in his interview with TNT: "Wallace is the

Faust of our generation, a tragic hero who sold his soul." He is also a key figure in the realignment that created the present divided political landscape, although his daughter Peggy supported Obama in 2007 and thinks her father would have, too, had he lived to see that campaign.

This is obviously great dramatic material, and Frankenheimer squeezes out every drop of emotion, showing Wallace's second wife Cornelia (a young Angelina Jolie) dancing with him in his wheelchair and trying to coax an erection, and the black prison trustee Archie (Clarence Williams III) bathing his body with its pipe-stem legs and back covered with bedsores. Archie is an invented composite character who seriously considers driving an ice pick into Wallace's skull when they're alone in the kitchen one night. But at the end it's Archie who wheels the governor into the Dexter Avenue Baptist Church to make his speech of repentance and wheels him out again: a deep focus shot of the tiny figure coming up the aisle while members of the congregation reach out to him as he passes by and the choir sings—appropriately, for once—"Amazing Grace."

Frankenheimer called his version of Lyndon Johnson (Michael Gambon) in *Path to War* "a modern King Lear," but that's probably because he was reluctant to admit to having created another Faust story, although Gambon, who outroars the storm whenever LBJ is having one of his famous rages, obviously took the *King Lear* analogy to heart. (Other Frankenheimer films are Faust stories, most obviously *Seconds* [1962].) Another liberal Democrat from the South, Johnson was elected president in 1964 by the biggest majority in history, with plans to complete FDR's New Deal by eradicating racial injustice and poverty in America. Many of his programs were passed into law, including Medicare and the Voting Rights Act of 1965 (Sinise does a cameo as Wallace paying Johnson a visit and meeting his match in the great bull-thrower), but the "Great Society" was derailed, and Johnson's presidency with it, by America's disastrous involvement in the Vietnamese War of Liberation. *Wallace* and *Path to War* are a diptych about the decline and fall of American liberalism, embodied in bigger-than-life Faustian protagonists whose tempters are, respectively, the Ku Klux Klan and Robert McNamara (Alec Baldwin).

Frankenheimer and screenwriter Daniel Giat take a few liberties of their own in *Path to War* to preserve a strong emotional curve, like cutting from the day after the inauguration to the first bombing raids on North Vietnam, thereby leapfrogging over the Gulf of Tonkin incident. Johnson inveighs against McNamara and the generals for telling him to escalate, but always does, with Clark Clifford (Bruce McGill) playing the reproving chorus in every meeting, until the leader of the free world is stumbling from escalation to escalation as his advisors desert or change their minds, and his freedom of action dwindles to zero. The construction recalls Northrop Frye's description of tragedy: the hero is free to do whatever he chooses until he chooses to jump off a cliff—then gravity takes over. The second half of *Path to War* is a zombie movie, populated by figures drained of life and purpose, mechanically reacting to the latest optimistic projections from two buffoonish generals, Westmoreland (Tom Skerritt) and Wheeler (Frederic Forrest), with more troops and bombs, until Johnson makes his decision to resign.

Visually, these are very different films. *George Wallace* is filmed with a Steadicam like *Against the Wall* and sprinkled with punchy baroque compositions, as if Frankenheimer relished the chance to finally remake *Citizen Kane*, although the time scheme is actually pretty straightforward, beginning with the day of the shooting and following Wallace's downward spiral and eventual redemption while flashing back to show his rise to power, also told in chronological order. What gives this scheme its cumulative power is the collision and superimposition of images that it makes possible—repeated premonitory landmarks like King's church and the Edmund Pettus Bridge, and eerier juxtapositions: Archie's brother telling him that he "can strike the blow" before Bremer does it for him at the Laurel Shopping Center; Luraleen Wallace (Mare Winningham) meeting the trophy wife who will replace her after her death from cancer when Cornelia is just thirteen, and already sizing up George; or Big Jim stumping around on a bandaged foot during a tirade at the mansion when he comes to ask for a pension increase, brandishing a crutch, just before we see Wallace in his wheelchair for the first time, with spinning wheels of destiny supplying the transition. The film is happening inside his head, and the repeated black-and-white images of Klansmen in white and marchers under a blazing sun are ghosts, intercut with tight close-ups of his eyes.

The narrative of *Path to War* is linear but elliptical, and the visuals pass the sobriety test with high marks. Employing very little shaky camerawork, 90 percent of the scenes take place in rooms at the White House and the Pentagon with white men sitting around big conference tables earnestly debating their next plan of action while the consequences of their decisions appear on TV screens . . . and once through an office window when a shocked McNamara watches the Quaker protester Norman Morrison (Victor Slezak) set fire to himself on a wall facing the Pentagon. (Baldwin puts his hand over his mouth like a spinster who just heard a four-letter word.) When Johnson impulsively bundles his war cabinet off to Vietnam on a tour of inspection, they are like pale, blinking, wizened school children on a field trip to a hell of their own making.

"The aim was to emotionally involve the audience in the picture, without . . . calling attention to the camera or anything like that," said

Frankenheimer at the time. "I wanted to make it as real as I possibly could. And there's a lot of depth-of-focus stuff in there, because there's just so much going on in the background"—much of it involving Johnson's younger aides: Dick Goodwin, Bill Moyers, and Jack Valenti, the last played by the real Valenti's look-alike son. The "hard-sell" style carried over from television is back where it belongs, shaping the drama unobtrusively through mise-en-scène—"through what you put on the screen. A two-shot rather than a close-up, a sympathetic portrayal of a character, rather than an unsympathetic one. A flattering camera angle, rather than an unflattering one. . . . Just the design of a set, how you want the set to look. How you want a scene photographed. All kinds of things." *Path to War*, which ends with a high-angle shot of the shaken television crews that just covered Johnson's resignation speech slowly starting to pack up, is a brilliant final summing up of the aesthetic Frankenheimer carried from television into features.

McNamara in particular is put through visual changes. When he looks up at the portrait of his predecessor James Forrestal and talks about how the man committed suicide after Truman fired him and hung a decoration on him, Alec Baldwin's head swells till it looks like it might pop; when he is about to be fired himself, the portrait looms in the foreground; and when he accepts his medal, the camera stays tight on his sweating face as he flashes back to the dogmatic pronouncements he made while leading the country into a quagmire. Without adopting the avant-garde strategies of the historical films Roberto Rossellini made for television, *Path to War* achieves the same aims—the fact that Johnson and McNamara are portrayed as well-intentioned men (liberals almost always have good intentions) does not spare them being examined like bacteria under a microscope. The airless choreography of talking heads in plush rooms is as expressionistic as the subjective stylings of *Wallace*, and a marvel to watch.

Oddly enough, it may have been *George Wallace* that enabled Frankenheimer to finally exorcise the ghost of RFK by recreating the assassination he only heard about with Wallace as a stand-in for Kennedy. He noted tersely in an interview that the two days he spent shooting at the shuttered Ambassador Hotel (a popular location for period recreations until it was torn down) were his first visit to the scene of the crime since June 5, 1968. He even brings Kennedy (played by Mark Valley) back to life briefly for a tense confrontation with Wallace, which ends in a tie. After that, in *Path to War*, Bobby is Banquo's ghost on television stoking Johnson's paranoia about the Kennedys, whose advisors he blames for giving him bad advice, then turning on him. The ultimate cause of the war, the film implies, was Johnson's fear that Bobby could use any faltering in his resolve about pursuing John Kennedy's policies in Vietnam to destroy him—an interesting motive for the protagonist of a dark tale whose labyrinthine complexity recalls Middleton and Webster more than Shakespeare. *Path to War* is visually a labyrinth, and Johnson's paranoia is the minotaur at the center.

As a cinematic Jonah who was almost destroyed by the prophecy of *The Manchurian Candidate* coming true the second time—like Senator Jordan in *The Manchurian Candidate*, Senator Kennedy was shot in a kitchen—Frankenheimer was simply recording his own experience in these two films where the invisible destiny pulling the characters' strings occasionally shows its hand in eerie flashes. What remains to be seen is whether the reluctant prophet's last vision, *Path to War*, describes the fate still awaiting the country in Afghanistan, but the auguries are not good, and the entrails are starting to give off a nasty smell.

Notations

Andrew Sarris died in 2012 without ever producing a new edition of his 1968 book *The American Cinema*. But *The American Vein: Directors and Directions in Television* (New York: E. P. Dutton, 1979) by Christopher Wicking supplied filmographies and broke them down into categories that paid *The American Cinema* the compliment of imitation. More is available in Stephen B. Armstrong's *John Frankenheimer: Interviews, Essays, and Profiles* (Lanham: Scarecrow, 2013).

John McGiver's Senator Jordan and Senator Eugene McCarthy: Matthew Frye Jacobson and Gaspar Gonzalez observe that "[Senator Jordan] is recapitulating a most powerful—and common—denunciation of McCarthy," in their book *What Have They Built You To Do? "The Manchurian Candidate" and Cold War America* (Minneapolis: University of Minnesota Press, 2006), 45. President Truman, they note, once referred to the other famous McCarthy, America's Witchfinder General, as "the greatest asset the Kremlin has" (96). Jacobson and Gonzalez have written a very good book, but in my opinion what they call the contradictions of America are mostly the contradictions of Cold War liberalism, which continued to ravage the administration of Barack Obama as it kept on waging George W. Bush's War on Terror under another name, whereas the supposed contradictions of the American Right are simply hypocrisy—the Right is rarely in contradiction with itself.

Jean Narboni's formula "Le hors-cadre décide de tout," is in *Cahiers du cinéma* 271 (November 1976): 20: "Eisenstein *délire* la politique stalinienne . . ." Jacobson and Gonzalez could easily adopt Narboni's formulation to sum up their searching interpretation of *The Manchurian Candidate*.

Fans of *The Manchurian Candidate* can be forgiven for thinking that the real authors of the events that fulfilled Frankenheimer's second unintentional prophecy were seeking "powers that will make martial law look like anarchy," to quote Raymond Shaw's mother, which they already had conveniently drawn up and tagged with a stentorian acronym, USA PATRIOT Act (Uniting and Strengthening America by Providing Appropriate Tools Required to Intercept and Obstruct Terrorism Act of 2001). That 342-page document, written in the early days of the George W. Bush administration, was an extension of the Antiterrorism Act, which a Democratic president, Bill Clinton, asked Congress to pass in 1996, and it is still the law of the land.

The Steadicam, a camera stabilizer mount, was created by Garrett Brown and introduced in 1975.

I mention *Year of the Gun* as invoking the relationship between a fictive thriller and a real-life terrorist act. The inconclusive evidence that Lee Harvey Oswald may have seen Frankenheimer's 1962 film is summed up in *Oswald's Trigger Films: "The Manchurian Candidate," We Were Strangers, Suddenly?*, by John Loken (Boonton, NJ: Falcon Books, 2000). This controversy of course assumes that Oswald was the assassin.

Regarding America's alliance with Germany against the threat of Communism, see Jeffrey Neal Smithpeters's doctoral dissertation, "To the Latest Generation: Cold War and Post–Cold War U.S. Civil War Novels in Their Social Contexts" (Louisiana State University, 2005), https://digitalcommons.lsu.edu/gradschool_dissertations/2933/, particularly chapters 1–3.

My access to the rough cut of *The Island of Dr. Moreau* stemmed from the fact that I wrote the production information for the American release of the film, based on the strangest collection of on-set interviews I've ever seen. From what I read there, *The Island of Dr. Moreau* came closer to being a film without an author than *The Manchurian Candidate* (the Greil Marcus hypothesis, deftly skewered by Jacobson and Gonzalez). That it ended up being a John Frankenheimer film anyway is a tribute to Frankenheimer and a pyrrhic victory for *la politique des auteurs*.

Regarding LBJ being portrayed by Frankenheimer in *Path to War* as conflicted about going to war with North Korea, all quotes and other information about this film and *George Wallace* come from the production information posted by TNT (http://alt.tnt.tv/movies/tntoriginals/wallace/prod.credits.notes.html) and HBO (www.hbo.com/films/pathtowar/).

Whether George Wallace would have supported Barack Obama is of course unknowable. But see http://www.cnn.com/2008/POLITICS/11/03/wallace.kennedy.obama/index.html.

The Ambassador Hotel, where Frankenheimer shot parts of *George Wallace*, and where he was waiting to collect Robert Kennedy when the senator was shot, was on Wilshire Boulevard in Los Angeles and was demolished in 2005. "For several scenes, the production took over the famed Ambassador Hotel in Los Angeles, a monument to a tragic moment in history that Frankenheimer remembers well." But which scenes?

23

Monte Hellman

Iguana

MONTE HELLMAN'S *IGUANA* TELLS the story of Oberlus (Everett McGill), a harpooner on a nineteenth-century whaling ship who flees to an uninhabited island in the Galapagos chain to escape persecution at the hands of his shipmates because of his monstrous appearance. Oberlus, who has been deformed from birth, has been afflicted with a face that appears to be half-human, half-lizard. Recaptured and tortured by his chief persecutor, Captain Gamboa (Fabio Testi), he escapes again and declares war on mankind. He captures and enslaves four sailors stranded on the island who become his subjects in a kingdom built on force and terror, and he also captures a woman, an aristocratic Spanish libertine named Carmen (Maru Valdivielso), with whom he has a sadomasochistic love affair that becomes the emotional core of the film.

The Melville Connection

But the stability of Oberlus's kingdom is menaced by two events: Carmen's father decides to lead a mission to the island to find his daughter, and Gamboa's ship returns to the harbor. Stealing aboard in the middle of the night, Oberlus captures Gamboa and burns the ship, and when Gamboa attempts to escape in his turn, Oberlus kills him in a savage duel. As the rescue party closes in on his hiding place, Oberlus prepares to lead his surviving subjects off the island in a small boat, at the very moment Carmen is about to give birth to a child. The film ends with an extraordinary gesture by Oberlus that reaffirms his status as a man resolved to live outside any laws but his own. The last shot recalls the ending of Fritz Lang's *Moonfleet* (1955).

When *Iguana* opened, it had been ten years since we had heard from Monte Hellman (b. 1932, New York). His last film, *China 9, Liberty 37* (1978), had been a western full of strange and wonderful surprises, and with *Iguana* he brought back to life an *imaginaire* of sailing ships, pirates, smugglers, and South Sea desert islands previously embodied in the films of Lang, DeMille, Jacques Tourneur, Allan Dwan, and Raoul Walsh, who would have been right at home with this story of a proletarian hero-villain in love with a beautiful aristocrat.

But like *China 9*, whose story resembles a folk ballad about loving and killing more than a Hollywood western, *Iguana* renews the mythology of the sea adventure by a return to its literary roots: not the novel Hellman adapted, a best seller by the Spanish writer Alberto-Vázquez Figueroa, but Figueroa's unacknowledged source, which was Herman Melville.

For while the film's hero is based on a real nineteenth-century figure, Patrick Watkins, it was Melville who gave Watkins the name Oberlus when he told his sordid story in "Hood Island and the Hermit Oberlus," the ninth sketch in the series of sketches of life in the Galápagos called *The Encantadas, or Enchanted Islands*. Hellman learned of the Melville story only once the film was finished. Nevertheless, it is the spirit of Melville, caught in the pages of Figueroa's sensational novel, that informs *Iguana* from the first shot of the tattoo on Oberlus's forearm. In the blue-filtered night scene when we first see him praying to the gods of Haiti, Oberlus's face recalls the tattooed face of the heathen harpooner Queequeg in *Moby-Dick*, although it's Ahab he comes to resemble in his tyrannical conduct and his self-annihilating quest for revenge. This tragic interpretation of the character also originated with Melville, who saw the failed ambitions of the misanthropic Oberlus as a mirror of his own condition, after the twin disasters of *Moby-Dick* and *Pierre*.

And Monte Hellman? I have no wish to add to the overly dark portrait that his admirers have painted of him. It suffices to quote what Hellman himself said in Serge Le Péron's brief interview for our March 1982 "Made in USA" issue of *Cahiers du cinéma*, "Le solitaire de Laurel Canyon": concerning the state of Hollywood ("Vous êtes venu enquêter dans un desert" / "You have come to investigate a desert") and his own situation ("Je n'ai aucun ami dans le cinéma américain" / "I haven't got a single friend in American cinema"). To measure the terrible force of those words, one thing must be understood: they were spoken by the most gifted American filmmaker of his generation after Cassavetes, whom he resembles in his solitude.

A Laconic Cinema

Hellman first made a name for himself in 1965 with two westerns, *The Shooting* and *Ride in the Whirlwind*, made back-to-back, each on a six-week schedule—early masterpieces that were preceded by apprentice work: a war movie and a thriller, *Back Door to Hell* and *Flight to Fury* (both 1964), made back-to-back in the Philippines on a similar schedule, and two horror films produced by exploitation maestro Roger Corman, *Beast from Haunted Cave* (1959) and *The Terror* (1963), the latter of which Corman codirected and signed. Then in 1971 came *Two-Lane Blacktop*, a road picture about car freaks that benefited from more press attention than all of Hellman's other work combined, thanks to a studio promotional campaign and the work of a smart press attaché. *Esquire* magazine actually published the script while the movie was being made, announcing on its cover that *Two-Lane Blacktop* was going to be "the most important film of the Seventies," but when it flopped despite good reviews, the same magazine gave itself a "Dubious Achievement Award" for jumping the gun. Between *Two-Lane* and *Iguana* came two films: *Cockfighter* (1974), a picaresque tale about the South produced by Corman, and *China 9, Liberty 37*, a western produced by an Italian company and filmed in Spain in 1978. A detail worth noting: Hellman made five films with Jack Nicholson before he became a star and four with Warren Oates, to whose memory *Iguana* is dedicated.

Two articles in the *Cahiers du cinéma* by Sébastien Roulet on the early westerns and by Pascal Bonitzer on *Two-Lane Blacktop* convey the excitement these films provoked among European cinephiles when they first appeared. (The two westerns were released theatrically in France and sold to TV in the United States.) From one film to the next, whatever the subject or genre, a style and a vision were being elaborated within the great tradition of American cinema (Hellman is still a lover of Howard Hawks)—a style and vision that were nonetheless radically new: characters without psychologies who came from nowhere, wanderers without fixed destinations; American landscapes seen as if for the first time, nameless and mythic; a decoupage that respected real time and made its slow unfolding, unpunctuated by climaxes, undistorted by "psychological" montage, the true subject of the film; an anti-melodramatic dramaturgy that substituted the encounter—uncertain, shifting, always a little humorous—for the duel that had been the master rhetorical figure of classical American cinema; open endings like the famous ending of *Two-Lane*, when the film burns in the projector gate. Hellman's is an existential cinema in many ways like that of Wim Wenders, but Wenders didn't make his first short until 1967, and his first feature until 1970. And Wenders didn't make westerns.

One trait characterizes the Hellman hero from the beginning: his reluctance to speak. Willet (Oates) in *The Shooting*, unlike his young friend Coley (Will Hutchens), knows when to keep his mouth shut, while Wes (Nicholson) in *Whirlwind* is more than once annoyed at the need of his older friend Vern (Cameron Mitchell) to pass the time with pointless conversation. Wes and Willet survive, and their companions perish. We know in advance that the heroes of *Two-Lane* (James Taylor and Dennis Wilson) will win their cross-country race with the blabbermouth GTO (Oates), because they are laconic in the extreme; when they do talk, it's only to discuss technical matters pertaining to their car. (Hellman himself is the kind of filmmaker who is most at ease when he is talking about technical matters. Before he showed me *Iguana*, he regaled me with an elaborate demonstration of his new videotape recorder, and after the screening we talked about his obsession with direct sound and his respect for the abilities of his postproduction supervisor Cesare D'Amico, who enabled him to use dialogue recorded in close proximity to crashing waves.) Even the unheroic Marty (Richard Sinatra) in *Beast from Haunted Cave*, the only member of the gang of bank robbers making their getaway on skis who ever sees the Beast that is pursuing them (a giant spider), refuses to tell the others what he has seen, on the improbable pretext that they "wouldn't believe him" if he did—and just as improbably, when the Beast attacks the group at the end, Marty survives.

In the early films, this trait is first of all the sign of the hero's difference, which it was tempting to interpret as a state of spiritual election until Hellman made *Cockfighter*, a film that radicalized the trait and finally made its significance clear. The hero of that film, a professional cockfighter named Frank (Oates), is completely mute by choice—a choice based, logically in view of the rest of Hellman's oeuvre, on the fear that talking brings bad luck. Before the beginning of the film Frank lost his chance to win the coveted "Cockfighter of the Year" award because, on the eve of the contest, he bragged too much about his chances and was forced into a premature test of his champion cock's mettle, during which the cock was killed. (Frank's braggadocio may have reminded the filmmaker of that disastrous *Esquire* cover.) Now Frank has vowed silence until he wins the award. The hero's silence, however, can't be read as a sign of election, because it is broken by intermittent voiceover thoughts that undercut any spiritual interpretation (but not the magical one: Frank does indeed go on to become "Cockfighter of the Year"). Instead, as we savor Warren Oates's performance, we discover a whole language of gestures that Frank deploys to communicate with others, ranging from mimed proverbs (literally "burying the hatchet" to signify the end of a match) to the shocking symbol that concludes the film, when he twists off the head of his champion cock and forces the woman he loves to take it in her hand—a hieroglyphic language which, in a film that uses the resources of cinema this cannily, it is impossible not to read as "cinema" (= "writing with images"). In retrospect, the silence of Hellman's heroes is revealed to be an aesthetic choice: the refusal of overt or overly facile messages.

An anecdote: when a mutilated version of *Cockfighter* opened in Los Angeles, it played the bottom half of double bills with another Corman production, *Jackson County Jail* (1976), whose director, Michael Miller, had used every cliché of movies about the South to tell a heavy-handedly "feminist" tale of rape and revenge, ending with a shootout under the American flag, and that film actually got a better review from the *New York Times* than *Cockfighter*. When I asked Roger Corman why he thought that was, he replied that the film's commercial failure may have resulted from the fact that "Monte made a quieter film than I had anticipated." The adjective has always struck me as absolutely accurate, but the refusal to be governed by the ready-made connotations (implicit significations) of one's material does not imply a refusal to "write." On the contrary, it takes a kind of mastery rarely found today to stem, select, and channel the stream of connotations automatically unleashed by a subject as loaded as cockfighting in the state of Georgia into an optimistic film about America where little surrealisms (a bathtub full of dead cocks, a robber of cockfighters wearing a Nixon mask) can just pop up without the ponderous sociological significance they would have in a Jonathan Demme film.

Oberlus

All this serves to emphasize the paradoxical quality of the double gesture that defines the hero of *Iguana*.

On the one hand, Oberlus, illiterate at the beginning of the film, forces one of his subjects, an educated sailor who is keeping a diary, to teach him to read and write. All that we see of Oberlus's skill, however, is two scenes where he refers in passing to *Don Quixote* and the *Odyssey* and one shot of him alone on a rock holding a spyglass—another symbol of his newly won power—and writing. Pointedly associated with the act of seeing, Oberlus's writing, like Frank's language of gestures, is a metaphor for cinema.

And indeed in *Iguana* Hellman deploys, more overtly than in his previous films, a whole system of "writing" that begins with the literal mark of difference on the hero's face (like Lang in *The Big Heat* [1953], where Gloria Grahame's character has one side of her face burned with scalding coffee, and Preminger in *Tell Me That You Love Me, Junie Moon* [1970], where Liza Minnelli plays a character whose face has been scarred by acid, Hellman is inspired by filming a face that is divided between beauty and monstrousness, humanity and bestiality) and extends to every variety of difference and repetition: the parallel montage of scenes at the beginning that establish Oberlus and Carmen as twin monsters in the eyes of society; the use of music to underline the similarity of the opening and closing credit sequences, and the terrible circularity of Oberlus's voyage (all the voyages in Hellman's films are circular); the presence of reflections in mirrors and water in the scenes where Carmen manipulates the men in her life; and rhymes like the scar on Carmen's father's cheek ("A little Freud for the critics," says Hellman drily), or the red cover on the bed in the scene where we see her with her husband, which reappears mysteriously on the bed in Oberlus's cave. Like Hellman's previous films, but in a much more overt and self-consciously symbolic way, the film is "written" from the first shot to the last: *Iguana* is Monte Hellman's first art film.

On the other hand, Oberlus speaks, quite a bit. In fact, from the moment he declares, "From now on, I will make my own gods and devils," the main instrument by which he constructs his new world is speech. He enacts laws and enunciates the basis of his power to do so; he compares and contrasts his actions to those of "real kings"; he calls his subjects his "children" ("A little Freud for the critics . . ."); he explains to Carmen, in the crudest terms, the nature of her own masochistic enjoyment; he argues that he and she are both "monsters" but also explains the difference between them; he defines his own nature by talking about himself simultaneously in the first and the third persons; he engages in a refined moral calculus with Gamboa; he predicts his own last action, and explains his reasons before performing it. Everything the film shows, Oberlus *says*, and always in the same harsh, even, bitterly rational voice.

Which considerably subverts a fundamental law of the filmmaker's chosen "genre." One example: Art-house audiences may enjoy reading the heroine's masochistic pleasure in her face during the scene of the rape, but when the rapist takes the time to explain to her (like a true Sadean libertine), "You liked being my slave and getting screwed in the ass. You'll have trouble finding someone else like me," their own pleasure is blocked, or worse: turned to derision. Combined with a new self-consciousness about the act of writing, this massive return of denotation creates a singular form, as if the voiceover from a militant film of the early seventies had been added to, say, Louis Malle's *Au revoir les enfants* (1987). A form that deviates only in appearance from the rigorous logic with which Hellman has elaborated his oeuvre until now, except that, from *Cockfighter* to *Iguana*, the nature of the hero's sacrifice has changed: from a gift of love (to the woman, but also the spectator) to an act of self-mutilation (drowning his own newborn child) that condemns Carmen to the lucidity she had thought to escape ("My child will save me," she had said). A new way to "wring the neck of eloquence (Mallarmé)"; a new way to make the spectator experience pleasures he has never known before, while imposing on him a lucidity that he has never really desired.

Notations

Born Monte Himmelbaum on July 12, 1932, in New York City, Hellman attended Los Angeles High School after his family moved to LA, then worked as an editor's apprentice at ABC TV before attending Stanford University on a scholarship from ABC. He worked as an editor on Roger Corman's *The Wild Angels* (1966), Bob Rafelson's *Head* (1968), Sam Peckinpah's *The Killer Elite* (1975), and Jonathan Demme's *Fighting Mad* (1976), and he shot extra scenes for Mark Robson's *Avalanche Express* (1979) when Robson died before finishing the film. When Corman sold *Ski Troop Attack* (1960), *Last Woman on Earth* (1960), and *Creature from the Haunted Sea* (1961) to television, Hellman shot extra footage to pad the running time of the films, and when American television bought Sergio Leone's *A Fistful of Dollars* (1964), he shot a prologue with a Clint Eastwood lookalike, filmed from behind, being let out of jail and deputized to clean up a bad town, thereby making all the gun-downs by Eastwood in the film legal. Legend has it that Corman lent Hellman $500 to produce and direct a stage production of Samuel Beckett's *Waiting for Godot* at a neighborhood theater in LA and lost every cent of his investment.

The Sébastien Roulet article, "Cinq points de rupture," is in *Cahiers du cinéma* 205 (October 1968): 57–58.

Pascal Bonitzer on *Two-Lane Blacktop*, which elaborates the theory of the duel, and Hellman's subversion of it, is in *Cahiers du cinéma* 266–267 (May 1976): 68–69. My discussion with Roger Corman is in *Cahiers du cinéma* 296 (January 1979): 29–33. Hellman did subsequently venture an interpretation of *Iguana*, which he sees as the first film of a trilogy based on the myth of Persephone that continued in *Silent Night, Deadly Night 3: Better Watch Out!* and *Stanley's Girlfriend*. "Le solitaire de Laurel Canyon" was done by *Cahiers* editors who came over in 1982 to do a special issue about American cinema. It ended up being two issues, March and April 1982.

24

Monte Hellman Today

WHEN ASKED TO NAME HIS best film, Monte Hellman always says "the last one." This always gets a laugh, coming from the creator of masterpieces like *The Shooting* (1966) and *Two-Lane Blacktop* (1971) that belong to the legend of the 1960s. But if he is right, his best films, in ascending order, are *Silent Night, Deadly Night 3: Better Watch Out* (1989), the short *Stanley's Girlfriend* (2006), and *Road to Nowhere* (2010). Speaking of the first, he has clarified: "I think it's my best work, not my best film"—a way of saying that it's a film where he accepted inferior material as a chance to reinvent his mise-en-scène.

Hellman has had a long love affair with European cameramen and their mastery of natural light, which became the house style at Roger Corman's New World pictures, although the fountainhead in Corman's oeuvre was an American cinematographer, Floyd Crosby, who had worked with Robert Flaherty and F. W. Murnau on *Tabu: A Story of the South Seas* (1931) and with Pare Lorentz on *The River* (1938) before lending his eye to films like Corman's *Attack of the Crab Monsters* (1957) and (uncredited) *The Terror* (1963), for which Hellman directed the exteriors.

So the scene when Laura (Samantha Scully), the blind heroine of *Silent Night*, snugly ensconced in her grandmother's house, "watches" a scene from *The Terror* juxtaposes two styles: the raw, shocking images on the screen and the stage-built interiors of Grandma's house, warmly lit with rose and yellow light sources in the image and their visual concentrates, the lights on the Christmas tree. In fact, Laura can't even see Floyd Crosby's images, which are nightmare images of her own blindness, although the soundtrack, heard offscreen, tells her that Ricky, the killer, is coming for her.

Hellman's cryptic statement that he doesn't like horror movies is about the gritty realism of 1970s horror like *The Exorcist* (1973), the sole exception he cites being *Don't Look Now* (1973), by Nicolas Roeg, one of the masters of natural light. Instead, a predecessor Hellman cites for *Silent Night* is the graveyard scene in David Lean's *Great Expectations* (1946), which returns in the exquisite black-and-white graveyard at the end of *Stanley's Girlfriend*. Like Lean's film, these late Hellman films are fairytales, and Grandma's house, like the graveyard where Pip meets Magwitch, is a fairytale décor.

Hellman and cinematographer Josep M. Civet in their first collaboration, *Iguana* (1988), had attempted to create such a décor for their version of "Beauty and the Beast," but less-than-ideal production conditions obliged them to settle for yellow highlights in the cave and blue filters in the night scenes on the ship. For their second Cocteau remake, *Silent Night*, made one year later, Hellman and Civet were able to control all elements of the image to create a world that owes nothing to those summits of the natural-light aesthetic, Hellman's *Cockfighter* (1974) (shot by Nestor Almendros) and his *China 9, Liberty 37* (1978) (shot by Giuseppe Rotunno)—a new beginning, anticipated in *Iguana* and finally accomplished in *Silent Night*, where the images of Laura against all-white backgrounds in the first scenes define an interior space and a white canvas on which the filmmaker can begin to write anew.

The new style implements a new self-consciousness about the meanings of images, first articulated in the bricolage of words and symbols (cf. Carmen's bedspread) that is *Iguana* and completely mastered in *Silent Night*, where the meanings of *Iguana* have passed into the images: an artificial world whose light comes from within. So our trilogy of contemporary Hellmans is about cinema: explicitly in *Stanley's Girlfriend* and *Road to Nowhere*, two films about filmmakers who talk about film the way Oberlus, in *Iguana*, talked about his sexual and political theories while enacting them on Carmen; and implicitly throughout *Silent Night*, a glass bead game with Laura's point of view, where blindness is compensated by powers of hallucination, precognition, and telepathy.

Stanley's Girlfriend has a richer subject—why did Stanley Kubrick never return after he left the United States to film *Paths of Glory* (1957) in Germany? Working with Zoran Popović on sets built in Canada to represent the interiors of apartments in 1950s Hollywood, Hellman creates a pensive inner world contained in one apartment, where a fire in the fireplace recalls the surrounding winter up in one of Hollywood's high canyons. That flame lends its colors to the décor, which become the colors of infernal desire in the sex scene, made more dreamlike with slow dissolves like the ones that punctuate the story being told by Leo (John Gavin). When Leo views the film made by Stanley before his death (on March 7, 1999), the colors become cold as the camera wielded by the aged Stanley inscribes in a single shot the great auteur's obsessions as a series of optical instruments: film cans, camera, telescope, photos, paintings. Then a set of photos posed on a typewriter introduces a series of inserts, followed by a second handheld *plan séquence* that leads to the last link in the chain: a Moviola and its screen—another tabula rasa like the one that begins *Silent Night*.

Reunited with Civet for *Road to Nowhere*, Hellman could now reproduce his new vision on practical locations, using the Canon EOS 5D Mark II, so that interiors and exteriors, the fountains of Rome and the pines of North Carolina, are seamlessly joined in images recalling the Technicolor printing of *Two-Lane Blacktop*, Hellman's last film in that process. It is, in fact, his best film to date.

Who is seeing these dreams, although they can never wield a camera? Women (Laura, Nina, Laurel) who want to spy on the dreams of their lovers (Rickie, Stanley, Mitch). Very much a trilogy, Hellman's recent films should reveal other common ideas when they are screened together for the first time at the Respighi Conference in Lisbon in April 2011.

Notations

When I use the word "concentrates" to describe Grandma's house in *Silent Night*, I am thinking of a food concentrate: the lights on the tree concentrate the warm light of Grandma's house into points of colored light that irradiate the image from within.

My description of the film as a "glass bead game" refers to the title of Herman Hesse's book *The Glass Bead Game (Magister Ludi)*, published originally as *Das Glasperlenspiel* in 1943.

A *plan séquence* (usually translated into English as "sequence shot") is a long, continuous shot involving considerable change of camera position or orientation. The classic version is the entry to the ball near the beginning of Orson Welles's *The Magnificent Ambersons* (1942).

Mitch is Mitch Haven, the director of *Road to Nowhere*, played by Tigh Runyan; Laurel is Laurel Graham, played by Shannyn Sossamon, the heroine of that film; and Rick is the demented killer in *Silent Night, Deadly Night 3: Better Watch Out!*, played by Bill Mosely.

Directors Who Counterattacked

25

Woody Allen

Zelig

I

ELIG, WOODY ALLEN'S TWELFTH film, is a parable like certain stories of Melville and Kafka about a man whose odd infirmity becomes a symbol of the human condition. The disease of Leonard Zelig (played by Woody Allen) is chameleonism: eager to be liked, fearful of

This chapter originally appeared as "Zelig Medium," *Cahiers du cinéma* 352 (October 1983): 22–25.

what "the others" will do to him if he is perceived as "different," he takes on the mental and physical characteristics of whomever he is with. The cultural context for this singular case history is the late twenties and early thirties, a time when figures almost as bizarre captured the public's imagination and became heroes.

First sighted at a garden party in 1928 by F. Scott Fitzgerald (archival footage), Zelig baffles doctors, when he is captured and committed a year later, with demonstrations of his mimetic ability: only Dr. Eudora Fletcher (Mia Farrow) understands that the cause of his condition is psychological. Before she can treat him, his half-sister Ruth (Mary Louise Wilson) and her sinister consort Martin Geist (Sol Lomita) remove Zelig from the hospital and turn him into an international celebrity, until a sordid love-nest slaying in Madrid eliminates them and returns him to Dr. Fletcher's care. In a series of therapeutic encounters that will later be known as the "White Room Sessions," Dr. Fletcher cures her patient, falling in love with him in the process. But after revelations of polygamy and other peccadillos from Zelig's chameleonic past turn the public against him, he vanishes, reappearing months later in Germany as a faceless member of Hitler's Brownshirts. Dr. Fletcher risks her life to bring him back, and the couple is forced to flee the Nazis in a stolen plane. Transforming himself one last time, into an accomplished aviator, Zelig breaks the record for flying across the Atlantic upside down and returns home to a hero's welcome.

To assure, or forestall, correct interpretations of the fable, Allen has supplied a chorus of distinguished thinkers—Susan Sontag, Irving Howe, Saul Bellow, John Morton Blum, and Bruno Bettelheim—who theorize about the Zelig phenomenon in present-day interviews, although the author's own interpretation—that social conformity is a disease that can lead to fascism—is privileged by being put in the mouth of Bellow, the artist.

American critics, who loved the film, have been quick to add an autobiographical reading, and Zelig's mad career, as summed up by cultural historian Howe, does seem to have a lot in common with his creator's: "He had this quirk, this strange talent that made everybody love him. Then they stopped loving him, until he pulled a crazy stunt, and suddenly he was a hero again." *Zelig* has also been seen as the story of how an artist who has always preferred to hide behind parodies of genres and other filmmakers' styles overcame his "anxiety of influence" and found his own voice—an interpretation to which the director has given guarded consent.

But this optimistic reading overlooks one important detail: Zelig triumphs in the end by giving in to his sickness one last time, and the "stunt" which has temporarily saved Woody Allen from the public disfavor that greeted his last two films (*Stardust Memories* [1980], *A Midsummer Night's Sex Comedy* [1982]) can only be *Zelig* itself—a meticulous parody of a TV documentary combining old black-and-white newsreel footage, fake newsreel footage, and trick shots where Zelig the celebrity appears to be sharing the frame with real celebrities of the period, all held together by the pompous voice of a narrator with a British accent (Patrick Horgan). Far from breaking with the past, Allen has returned in this film to his earliest aesthetic strategies: *What's Up, Tiger Lily?* (1966), his first film, was composed of "found footage," and *Take the Money and Run* (1969), his second, was a mock documentary about the life of a notorious bank robber, based on a black-and-white compilation film about Eleanor Roosevelt that won an Oscar in 1965.

In *Zelig* the sloppiness of the early work has given way to a formal perfection that took three years to achieve. Begun before *A Midsummer Night's Sex Comedy*, *Zelig* was not completed until after the shooting of Allen's next film, *Broadway Danny Rose* (1984). Glimpses of the creative process in an interview with the *Los Angeles Times* restore the full meaning of the old equation between filmmaking and obsessional neurosis: one shot of Zelig with baseball great Lou Gehrig took six months to fabricate and involved matte work, optical printing to eliminate an undesired pan, and animation to add shadows to Zelig's portion of the frame. According to Allen, to age the new footage shot by Gordon Willis, "We had our assistants going into the bathroom and holding the film under the shower, and then walking on it to get the effects he wanted. We'd all drag the film on the floor and stomp on it." Millions of feet of old footage were viewed before the start of the editing process, which lasted nine months and involved 150 hours of film, old and new. "We called *Zelig* the hobby film," Allen told the *Times*, "because I kept coming back to it," and many of the film's qualities can be attributed to Allen's ability, within the confines of a major studio production, to produce a work of maniacal bricolage with the kind of density we are accustomed to seeing only in certain independent films. Again Bellow sums it up: "In the end, his sickness was the root of his salvation."

II

In fact, *Zelig* is the culmination of Allen's experiments with parody and pastiche, filled with echoes of filmmakers ranging from David Lynch to Orson Welles—as Andrew Sarris has noted, the film is really an expanded version of the fake newsreel at the beginning of *Citizen Kane* (1941). But despite the persistence of parody, *Zelig* is very much a film about finding a voice, like *Kane*, where the audience was obliged to wait for the first footage from the sound era to hear Welles's famous voice: a little *coup de théâtre* that the makers of *Zelig*, whoever they may be, have turned into an extended cinematic metaphor.

Like Charles Foster Kane, Zelig is initially a figure without a voice, glimpsed in grainy photographs showing an elegant dandy, a gangster, a black jazz musician, and a drugged coolie who all seem to be the same person, and even after sync sound is introduced, with doctors and men on the street delivering their opinions of the phenomenon to the newsreel cameras, the shots of Zelig demonstrating his powers or being subjected to slapstick experimental procedures are silent. When we are shown a scene from *The Changing Man*, a 1935 Warner Bros. film based on his life, which is introduced by a montage of mouths speaking into the microphones, the actor playing Zelig actually appears to be catatonic: a fictive addition to the gallery of mysterious mutes who populate the early sound cinema.

Yet Zelig is not mute; if anything he is too glib for his own good, as we learn when we hear him for the first time spouting psychoanalytic gibberish at his interrogators, in a disembodied voiceover that the makers of the documentary have grafted onto still photographs of the mystery patient—a technique that will be used again when the voice of Zelig's unconscious mind speaks under hypnosis. Clearly the documentarians are preparing a *coup de théâtre* of their own: the introduction midway through the film of footage from the famous "White Room Sessions" taken as a scientific record by Dr. Fletcher's cousin, the inventor and amateur cameraman Paul Deghuée (John Rothman). We're told that the reason for using film is to record Zelig's physical transformations, but since no transformations are shown in this section it is as if the purpose of Deghuée's preparations, which we see in detail, was to bring Zelig out of the silent era by filming him in sync sound: an ingenious metaphor for Dr. Fletcher's therapeutic aim, which is to free Zelig from his paralyzing identifications by encouraging him to speak in his own voice. (This poetic evocation of the psychoanalytic process may be another autobiographical touch, for according to one biographer the analyst who has been treating Woody Allen for the last twenty years is also a woman.)

The cure works, but the aftermath raises doubts. When Leonard and Eudora announce their engagement to the world, their behavior is visibly being controlled by the newsreel cameras—shots of the two of them feeding a canary and buying the ring, or shots of Dr. Fletcher alone, dutifully demonstrating that she knows how to sew—and our suspicions that this is just a new kind of conformity are confirmed when Zelig is filmed in sync sound for the second time, telling a group of school children that "being yourself" is the "American way." Only public disgrace, unleashing the forces of racism and petty bourgeois paranoia masked by that ideal, interrupts the process of socialization, which Zelig's flight and immersion in the National Socialist movement in a sense complete. When love has saved him and he addresses the camera again at the end of the film, he offers a very different moral: replying to some bureaucrat's complacent prophecy of a future America populated by "good doctors" and "good patients," he ingenuously explains that his record-breaking flight "just shows what you can accomplish if you're a complete psychotic." Despite the director's own optimistic pronouncements on the subject, art and therapy seem to be perpetually at odds, and an ironic epilogue suggests that only death will put an end to the process.

III

Allen's recent films have accustomed us to this kind of metaphorical commentary—the disappearances of characters from the frame in *Manhattan* (1979) and *Annie Hall* (1977) are just one example—but in *Zelig* this rather literary device has been absorbed into the texture of the parody: it is the ingenuity, and the stupidity, of the documentarians who rhyme the assertion that the murder of his sister "turned Zelig's life upside-down" with a shot of a handbill bearing his picture upside down on the floor, and there is no reason to doubt that the skeptical interpretation of his cure, in which I detect a tinge of the tired liberalism that characterizes productions of the BBC, is theirs as well. If that is so—and all we have to believe is that Allen has taken his own conceit seriously—then what chance is left for Zelig, caught as he is in the double trap of the old newsreel footage and its reinscription in an ironic fable about madness and society, vaguely influenced by the works of the British antipsychiatric school?

What is most memorable in *Zelig* are the mute transformation scenes, with Zelig as a Mohawk Indian, a Black, or a fat man peering enigmatically at the camera from behind his own unique brand of protective coloration. Despite all the trickery, Allen has not taken advantage of the current state-of-the-art special effects to show Zelig transforming himself on camera, a decision which only heightens the illusion of documentary reality: the act is elided, but the result is proudly displayed—as in an old newsreel I remember where a fakir puts a knife through his arm without bleeding—and this naively demonstrative pose, which is also curiously defiant, permits Zelig to triumph over his sardonic Boswells, and to leave in us an indelible imprint, in spite their modernist metaphors.

For *Zelig* is finally more about the effect of Zelig on society than the reverse. That was the reason for doing the story as a documentary in the first place: "One doesn't want to see this character's private life," Allen told the *New York Times*, "One is more interested in the phenomenon of how it relates to the culture. Otherwise it would just be the pathetic story of a neurotic." By being at once himself and another person, Zelig designates the stereotyped traits which define any group, racial or social, so that the "real" specimens seem to have been contaminated, transformed into a semblance of themselves, like the crowds shown in the throes of the Zelig-inspired "Chameleon Dance," Charlestoning frenetically and darting their tongues at one another in imitation of his hidden "reptilian" nature. Despite Dr. Fletcher's theories, Allen portrays Zeligism as a biological phenomenon, and a cartoon on-camera transformation sequence might also have trivialized the mystery of this body moved by an unfathomable desire to imitate all the conditions of humanity. (In a story for the *New Yorker* Allen once speculated that "the urge to be liked at any cost is not socially adaptive but genetic, much the same as the ability to sit through operetta.")

From the point of view of society, the Zelig effect is inherently subversive. Look at the photo of Zelig with Eugene O'Neill: the little matching sweater-and-tie outfits, the symmetrical languor of the poses subvert the image of the individualist artist by reminding us that he is a member of a class, or more precisely, of a species. Put Zelig between two presidents and another species appears: somber in coloring, with an inky, all-knowing gaze. Even the real-life experts who appear in the film, who are certainly among Allen's personal gods, are subtly designated as members of a group—New York City's "intellectual Mafia"—filmed in their stereotypically drab, genteel native habitats. No wonder the discovery of Zelig in the midst of Pope Pius XI's entourage on the balcony at St. Peter's provokes panic, but the flapping and milling movements of the tiny figures only make them look more like a flock of birds trying to expel an intruder that some instinct has discovered, dangerous to them but remaining invisible to us because of the distance of the camera from the scene.

There is something of what Roland Barthes called *le sens obtus* in the transformation scenes, in the oval contours of Zelig the Negro and the baggy eyes of Zelig the Indian, and I would not be surprised if the film's funniest scene had actually been inspired by the now-famous still from *Ordinary Fascism* (1965) that Barthes commented on, where Goering gives a demonstration of his prowess with the bow and arrow while a bespectacled onlooker slightly out of focus behind him grins idiotically at the camera. The scene comes near the end, when newsreel footage of a Nuremberg rally shows Zelig, lost in his Nazi dream a few feet from the ranting figure of Hitler, at the moment he sees his fiancée signaling to him from the audience: slowly coming to his senses, he excitedly waves back, provoking chaos on the speaker's platform.

At this moment the documentarians choose to give us another scene from *The Changing Man* showing a fake Eudora calling tearfully to a fake Zelig, and this time their cleverness serves to complete what is probably the most personal design of the real creator of *Zelig*: a cruel parody of *Reds* (1981), complete with blathering "witnesses" and a tearful reunion scene. For Warren Beatty's insipid attempt to annex history to the star system Allen has substituted a comic version of history infiltrated by a character endowed with the ancient power of burlesque to rob the adversary of his very substance by mimicking him, while holding up to human society a biological vision of types, its laws and its segregations.

It is also important that at this climactic moment the characters' emotions come through, despite the enormity of the gag and the distancing apparatus of the documentary. The parody is devastating because Allen has succeeded where Beatty suffered his worst failure: *Zelig* really *is* the story of a love that is sovereignly indifferent to society and triumphant over the forces of history—all the more amazing because the story is conveyed solely by the way the characters look, by the little exchanges of traits and mannerisms (her initial assertiveness, his shyness and awkwardness), even of physical characteristics, which gradually unite them against the world. And though that love seems to put an end to Zelig's strange, solitary passion, we are permitted to suspect that it is still the same passion in another guise: in the last shots of their wedding Leonard and Eudora have become one of the couples one occasionally sees in life who love each other so much that they end up resembling one another, like the male and female of a species that has only two members.

Notations

In those days Andrew Sarris was writing for the *Village Voice*.

Regarding the "gallery of mysterious mutes" populating early cinema, the reader might consult Michel Chion's *The Voice in Cinema*, trans. Claudia Gorbman (New York: Columbia University Press, 1999).

26

William Friedkin

Cruising

A COP PLAYED BY AL PACINO goes undercover in the New York gay community disguised as a "leather boy"—a practitioner of S&M sex who wears black leather—to catch a serial killer who has been preying on denizens of that community. His task is complicated by the fact that there seem to be more than one killer, and by the fact that he himself may have been revealed as a repressed homosexual at the end of the film. Indeed, he may have killed someone himself—his gay neighbor

This chapter appeared in a different form on Adrian Martin's blog, *Rouge Cinema*.

239

in Greenwich Village—before pinning the crime on someone and returning to his straight life.

In many ways the last word on *Cruising* was said the year it was
released (1980) in Robin Wood's *Movie* essay "The Incoherent Text,"
which is reprinted in his book *Hollywood from Vietnam to Reagan*. I don't
intend to quarrel with Wood's amazingly sharp-eyed analysis. Instead I
want to deepen it by bringing in materials Wood didn't have access to:
the script drafts, production reports, script supervisor's notes, and editing
notes in the William Friedkin Collection of the Margaret Herrick Library.

Wood argues that the film is progressive for its time on topics
like police brutality against gays, and that its form is an important part
of what makes it progressive. He links the film's incoherence, which he
sees as deliberate on the filmmaker's part, to the critique it's making of
patriarchy and its corollaries: homophobia, repression of gays, and the
warping of gay and straight relationships alike by relations of domination
and inequality. These are the themes that structure the film, but I want
to concentrate on the page he devotes to the forces working against that
structure: specifically, against the detective story plot, which is incoherent, Wood argues, both in its "fractured" progress and its conclusions:
"The film suggests then: that there are at least two killers and could be
several; that we don't have to feel we know who the killer is, because it
could be anyone; and that the violence has to be blamed on the culture,
not on the individual."

This is a first-rate traditional reading of the film's themes, but
the narrative that embodies them is so "fractured" and "obscured" that,
when we rerun it in digital form and compare it to the description in
the production documents, we see that it's impossible to know who
killed *any* of the four victims in the film: Lukas at the hotel, Martino in
the peepshow, Eric in the park, and Ted, the next-door neighbor of the
undercover cop who's trying to solve the murders.

Lukas (Arnaldo Santana) is murdered in the St. James Hotel at the
beginning of the film. As Wood observes, The Killer in this sequence
is played by a different actor than the one who plays Stuart Richards
(Richard Cox), the father-hating homophobe whom Steve nails for all
the crimes. This means that there are at least two killers.

Martino (Steve Inwood) is murdered in a peepshow on 42nd Street.
Although a bloody fingerprint links Richards to this crime, we have no
reason, as Wood argues, to trust Captain Edelson (Paul Sorvino) on this
point, because he's under enormous pressure to catch the killer, and Steve
(Al Pacino), his undercover decoy, has stabbed Stuart Richards by mistake. Another incoherence revealed by the production reports: although
Richard Cox plays The Killer inside the peepshow booth, when we see
him in the hall of the peepshow, his face obscured by a cloud of smoke,

he is being played by Arnaldo Santana, the actor who was playing Lukas when he was murdered at the St. James at the beginning of the film. The identity of one of our Killers has just fractured.

Ted (Don Scardino), the last to die, is the neighbor who befriended Steve when he went undercover to catch a Ripper preying on New York's gay community. Friedkin leaves it up in the air whether Ted was killed by his jealous roommate (James Remar) or by Steve, the undercover cop next door, who has discovered his own repressed homosexual desires like the killer in *Cruising* (1970), the novel by Gerard Walker that was the basis for Friedkin's screenplay. Now the identity of the protagonist played by Pacino has fractured! When Eric is killed in Central Park we don't see The Killer's face, but the production reports say that the actor who played The Killer at the St. James, Larry Atlas, is again playing him here, while Richard Cox, who plays Stuart Richards, the gay-hating suspect who takes the fall for all the murders, is playing his victim.

By inserting this shot (in the rough cut, just before the discovery of Ted's body; in the final cut, just after it), Friedkin no doubt hoped to fascinate the audience and generate return business. In 1974, according to Nat Segaloff's Friedkin biography, Friedkin told a class at the AFI: "If they're talking about what something means in a movie, usually you've got a movie that people will want to see. . . . Example: the obelisk in *2001*. People went around for years . . . saying, 'What the hell is the obelisk?' "

Thomas Clagett, who's skeptical about Wood's theory of deliberate incoherence, argues that one can see Friedkin's concept of identities melding and blurring. But then Clagett says Friedkin does something that completely destroys any hope of coherence. "Two different, unrelated murderers speaking in the same voice is absolutely not a viable example of Slavko Vorkapich's concept of total immersion."

Not only does the Hotel Killer speaking in the voice of Stuart's father violate the rules by which a film character's fixed identity is defined, it also makes no sense for Stuart to remember Lukas's murder once we have realized that the Hotel Killer was played by a different actor. The scene in the park between Stuart and his father, Clagett says, would have been one of the most disturbing and frightening in the film had Friedkin not included subliminal flashbacks to the hotel murder (which Stuart Richards did not commit) and then to Eric Rossman (Richards's first victim) while Richards was taking to his father.

But Clagett also quotes a *Time* reviewer who suggests, albeit disdainfully, a possible solution to the puzzle by complaining about "the last-minute injection of a demon who seems to have drifted in, half-baked, from *The Exorcist* (1973)." *The Exorcist*, Friedkin's biggest hit, had already gotten away with the same kind of incoherences, which are resolved there by the perceived rules of the genre. When Father Karas (Jason Miller) dreams of his mother after her death, he sees the medallion dug up in Iraq by Father Merrin (Max von Sydow) falling through the air, but the incoherence is resolved in the audience's mind by the central premise of the film: demonic possession. If a malignant centuries-old spirit can possess a little girl, then Father Karas can dream Father Merrin's memories.

Clagett himself suggests that the metaphor of infection is operating in *Cruising* but concludes that, "while the idea has merit, Friedkin's execution lacks coherence." However, if we allow a supernatural explanation like the one that was used in *The Exorcist*, discordant touches like Stuart remembering the Hotel Killer's murder, Stuart's father's voice coming out of the Hotel Killer's mouth, or The Killer returning to the Cockpit after Stuart is laid up in the hospital make sense: all the murders were the result of demonic possession, and at the end a new potential murderer (Steve or someone else) has been possessed by the same demon, whose latest victim is Steve's neighbor Ted Bailey.

Made two years after *Halloween* (1978) and the same year as *Friday the 13th* (1980), *Cruising* was a high-class slasher in 1980, but it also already contained in embryo the key elements of a mainstream genre that would only take shape in the 1980s, the serial killer film, where the investigator pursuing a serial killer becomes metaphysically or psychologically implicated in the crimes he's investigating, as if he was possessed by the same demon as the killer he's pursuing.

The idea didn't originate with Friedkin. What is new in *Cruising* is the way he fractures the narrative to get subversive meanings out of horror conventions, reducing the horror genre to the status of a ghostly hypothesis generated by a cop film whose surface is fractured by incoherences. Ultimately, only a supernatural interpretation can resolve those contradictions by pinning the blame on "Jack," a protean entity whose only visible incarnation is Stuart Richards's dead father.

The metaphor of demonic possession makes an allegorical interpretation of *Cruising* possible. In *Hollywood*, Wood was the first critic to propose that all The Killers, however many there are, speak with the Voice of Jack because they are possessed by the Law of the Father, which "demands the rigid structuring of the subject and the repression of all conflicting or superfluous realities." *Cruising* never really becomes a horror film, but the presence of the horror genre on the level of pure connotation (Eric, for example, looks like the Frankenstein monster) makes the film potentially intelligible to audiences at the same time that it delivers a subversive message.

While it's subversive in form and in meaning, *Cruising* aspires to be a commercial film, but it opened in the first year of Reagan's presidency, when Hollywood, like Washington, was turning back the clock after a decade of progress. When it was launched it would have been a contro-versial blockbuster. By the time it opened, it was an offensive anomaly.

The Friedkin Method

If genre is one of the adhesives that hold a Friedkin film together, the universal solvent that is always threatening to pull it apart is montage. Every shot, scene, and sequence in a Friedkin film is a module that can be displaced, eliminated, added, or even duplicated. As a result, a Friedkin film is a collage. In his freest films—and *Cruising* is the freest film Friedkin ever made—the creation of meaning through montage is foregrounded as it is in the work of only a few American directors, notably Joe Dante, who pays tribute to *Cruising* in the peepshow murder at the beginning of *The Howling* (1981).

In early drafts of *Cruising* the murder of Eric in the park comes immediately after the murder of Lukas at the St. James, but in the shoot-ing script Friedkin decided to put Eric's murder where it is in the film, after Steve has already started his decoy activities. Then, three weeks into filming, he wrote a new scene in which Steve is picked up by Eric. By then he had already used Larry Atlas, who plays Eric, to play The Killer in the hotel room, so that when Steve is picked up by Eric it's possible that he's with The Killer.

In interviews done under the pressure of massive gay protests Fried-kin stressed that the murderer in the film is a gay-hating heterosexual, a description that could apply to the Park Murderer and the Peepshow Murderer, but not to the Hotel Murderer. Friedkin's statements that he himself wasn't sure whether there is more than one Killer in the film are more accurate: one or possibly two homophobes (Stuart and pos-sibly Steve, depending on how we read Steve) and one or possibly two homosexuals: the Hotel Murderer and Ted Bailey's murderer.

Like Joe Dante's gremlins, cloned by montage from a small number of puppets in the 1984 film of that name, there seems to be no end to Friedkin's Killers, whose proliferation is also a sign of the fecundity of montage. But whereas the gremlins have no source in reality, the mul-tiplying Killers in *Cruising* initially had one: the recollections of Randy Jurgensen, a New York City detective who actually did earn his detective's badge by going undercover as a gay man in the West Village to catch two men who were shaking down gays by impersonating policemen. His story inspired the characters of DeSimone and Desher (Joe Spinell and Mike Starr), two cops in a patrol car who are shaking down gay hustlers for money and sexual favors in the film. DeSimone and Desher are yet another addition to the contingent of doppelgängers that populate the film. Introduced as woman-hating homophobes, they quickly call into question standard notions of gay and straight by demanding sexual services from the hustlers they're harassing, who wear women's wigs and high heels but are otherwise dressed like bikers.

Stakeout on Gay Street

"Are you a police officer?" the bouncer at The Cockpit (David Winnie Hayes) asks Steve when he shows up wearing his usual decoy uniform. It's Precinct Night, and Steve has "the wrong attitude"—not for the first time. He has already been berated by The Light Man (Leo Burmester) for displaying a yellow hanky symbolizing water sports when he "just likes to watch."

When Friedkin shot the scene, he equipped Pacino with a yellow hanky and inserted it before the scene in Hot Hankies, motivating Steve to visit the shop to learn how to avoid further mistakes. This order, which makes Steve a fish out of water, was preserved in the editing all the way to the last rough cut.

The scene with The Light Man was then moved in the final edit to immediately after Hot Hankies, when Steve should really know better. In this micro-sequence the humor is solely at Steve's expense, whereas as originally the mix-up about the hankies confounded both the timid decoy trying to fit in while avoiding a risky fashion statement and the jaded habitué, each of whom is thrown by the rampant polysemy of the milieu.

All the humor in the finished film is at the expense of the police. The carnivalesque sequence of Precinct Night, where the clients of The Cockpit are dressed like cops, introduces a series of scenes where the cops, sporting the epicene men's wear of the seventies, accessorized with an occasional pair of handcuffs, look gay. This reversal of roles encompasses two converging plot sequences: one where the police are pursuing Steve's inaccurate hunch that Skip Lee (Joe Acovone), who cruises him after he has been kicked out of The Cockpit, is The Killer, and another where they're trying to solve the Peepshow Murder. The two strands converge when a tip sends two detectives to eat a steak at The Iron Horse, where Skip waits on tables. The steak knife they make off with, which is probably given out in several hundred New York restaurants, is a perfect match to the broken knife-tip the Peepshow Killer left in his victim's body.

This discovery gives rise to the film's funniest sequence: two Keystone cops in an unmarked car trying to hear what's going on in a hotel room fifteen feet away through the sputters on a defective bug (Steve is begging Skip, who doesn't care much for bondage, to tie him up), followed by ten Keystone cops thundering up the stairs and breaking in on a trussed-up Steve, who whispers to Detective Schreiber, sporting the name of Freud's famous paranoid, "What are you doing here?" In the nightmarish scene that follows, a black cop displaying his muscles in bondage gear interrogates Skip. "Who is that guy?" Skip screams after the mystery cop slaps him, and a hand holding a steak knife drops into frame in front of him. "Ever see this knife, Skip?" Skip's interrogation ends with Detective Lefransky (the real Randy Jurgensen) ordering him to drop his pants and produce a sperm sample, after which Schreiber promises to perform the medieval-sounding "floating ball test." Cut to Captain Edelson, his immediate superior, learning that the fingerprint from the peepshow isn't as good a match to the suspect as the knife blade. "Listen boss," says Lefransky, unfazed by the news, "Let me have this guy—I'm telling you I can make him give it up! [sic]." "You got the wrong guy," says the bleary-eyed Chief of Detectives (Allan Miller), who was dragged out of bed to witness this.

Despite the ironies written in the script, Friedkin shows us that Skip isn't The Killer the first moment we see him, with one radiant close-up of him looking like a Pasolini angel after he spots Steve in The Cockpit. Apart from that, the director trusts to his infallible instinct for the comedy of police work to make his points.

Steve and Nancy

In classical cinema cause and effect rule the roost, to such an extent that in a film by Fritz Lang—Friedkin's favorite classical director—each shot is the effect of the previous shot and the cause of the next. These structures, which define what Gilles Deleuze calls the movement-image, are loosened in the time-image, which begins with the neorealists and is radicalized by modernist masters like Resnais, Antonioni, and Buñuel.

Because *Cruising* takes Friedkin's modular approach to film structure to its farthest extreme (creating scenes that can be moved around on the editing table), the film straddles these categories in a peculiar way. No shot or scene is necessarily linked to any other, but one of the axes along which Friedkin manipulates his modular elements is cause and effect, one of the main connections that can be established by a cut. As we saw with the micro-sequence built around the symbolic hankies, these manipulations can transform characters, those supposedly stable and circumscribed essences that *Cruising* suggests are highly malleable—not so much because we see them undergoing spectacular changes but because Friedkin and his editor treat them as structures composed in time and space out of modules that can be transformed by the same editorial operations that fracture the narrative.

This is also true of the extras in the cruising scenes, who are also modules to be arranged in tableaux by camera movement and the editor's shears. Each is every bit as much a character as Steve, a structure built of more modules than they are. Their constant milling motion is an image of the film itself as a modular construct.

Clagett observes that *Cruising* is full of entrances and exits, which he links to the theatricality of the bar scenes, but on a formal level doors are symbols of montage, notably in Lang's films, where a door opening often effects the transition from one shot to the next. In *Cruising* this symbolism is subjected to Alice in Wonderland transformations: DaVinci leaves Edelson's office, and in the next scene Steve enters through the same door, with nothing but a shot of Edelson's chess game to keep them from bumping into each other. The Killer exits the Peepshow, pulling the sliding door closed behind him, and Steve enters his apartment after a shot that holds on the closed door for a couple of seconds. Scenes of Steve cruising the streets and the bars at the beginning of his assignment are condensed in montage sequences where he repeatedly approaches the entrance to a bar wearing one outfit and enters the bar in the reverse shot wearing something completely different. These sly variations on Lang's style symbolize the transformational operations of montage in *Cruising*, which underlie its metaphysics of fluctuating identities with unsecured borders the way the shot–reverse shot underlies Hitchcock's metaphysics of transference, or the pitiless succession of cause and effect embodies Lang's metaphysics of destiny.

In the early drafts of the script the scenes between Steve and his girlfriend Nancy, a character who doesn't exist in the book, spell out a classical causality: Steve tells Nancy he has a new assignment that he can't tell her about, and when she tries to get it out of him he tells her that there are things she doesn't know about. Then when he walks in the door of his own apartment after the Peepshow Murder and slumps on his couch, the sounds of the neighbors arguing drive him out and he goes to see her again, and they end up in bed. Seeing him in this scene with Nancy immediately after the Peepshow-Apartment module, it's hard to imagine that he has just killed someone a couple of hours before—the door gag functions instead as a metaphor, telling us that he could change into his opposite, not that he has.

Later her suggestion that they break up after his attempt at catching the bad guy has failed follows the old Hollywood schema of the double downer: a professional setback followed by a romantic one. Things are really looking bad for our hero. Then, to top it off, in a scene Friedkin added to the third draft, she confronts him in the street with the accusation that he's gay, and he can't deny it without risking his cover. After that, understandably, he goes off his rocker a bit and attacks Gregory for calling him "a pussy." But finally he gets his man and gets his woman back, and it looks like a beautiful day—doesn't it? The note of doubt sounded at the end has very little to refer to apart from the horrors Steve has witnessed, which will hopefully be erased from his mind like that beard he's shaving off . . .

In an earlier version of the film the scene where he wearily returns to his apartment signifies his exhaustion after all that dancing, and after he flees the sounds of the argument to Nancy's place, his sexual difficulties may have been brought on by exhaustion and amyl nitrate abuse. In the finished film the sexual material was split up and used to create two modules: one in which Steve's strenuous efforts with Nancy are followed by him asking her not to let him lose her the next morning, and one in which he hears the Dionysian soundtrack of Precinct Night while she's fellating him. The first new module (painful sex in the missionary position) follows the murder of Eric, so that when Friedkin cuts from Eric's face as the knife goes in, to Nancy's face as Steve pounds her, the rhyme raises a suspicion the spectator will only be relieved by the "Jack" scene, where a flashback ties Stuart to the murder of Eric. In the new arrangement the second module (distracted fellation) follows Skip trying to pick Steve up after he has been barred from Precinct Night, which is therefore linked as cause and effect to the shot of Steve, eyes closed, with the sounds of Precinct Night playing in his head . . .

As for the Peepshow-Apartment module, it has been put back together, but now when Steve exits his apartment, closing the door behind him, we cut to Edelson opening another door and walking into an office where he gets raked over the coals by the Chief of Detectives—a scene that bounced all over the place until it landed here, where it primarily serves to keep Steve from running to Nancy's arms, as he had done in the previous version of the scene of his weary homecoming after we have just seen the Peepshow Murder.

Whatever Steve was doing before he came home, his reaction to the quarreling neighbors is not to run to Nancy but to get back to the job—either because he's desperate to close the case or because he needs to find a patsy he can frame for the murder he just committed at the peepshow—one of the possibilities raised by the incoherent text.

Steve and Stuart

This is not the kind of causality that operates in a classical film, where a character whose essence doesn't change responds to a series of external stimuli, confronts the bad guy, and triumphs in the end. The causality that operates in *Cruising* is magical: the magic of contagion as embodied in the myths and rituals of primitive man. Curses, possession, manna, eating the dead enemy's power, and all the variations on the theme of contagious magic that we see in primitive superstitions are working on Steve in the finished film: he becomes impotent with his girlfriend (a traditional effect of the "evil eye"); when he is with her he's invaded by forbidden sounds and sights (like the succubi of old), and he may even have been possessed by an evil spirit that makes him repeat the crimes he has been sent to solve. The only way for him to become himself again is to confront the real Killer and win back his manhood and his honor.

It's at this point that Stuart finally enters the film, although early drafts introduced him at the beginning and established systematic parallels between him and Steve, as Gerald Walker does in his novel. The similarities between hunter and prey are verbally stressed in every version of the script, climaxing in the knife duel in the park: "A ritual-like mirror of STEVE and STUART knife to knife." But nothing of this conception—based on the second principle of ancient magic, the metaphorical relationships of imitative magic—appears in the way scenes with Steve and Stuart are filmed, apart from the residual similarities of dressing alike and having tough fathers. When Steve wounds Stuart, for example, it's shown in a classical shot–reverse shot knife duel, where the script dictated a two-shot. At this point the script comments: "[Steve] has made his choice, he's done his job, and he's a civilized member of society," which is a more accurate description of what Friedkin filmed than all the script's plans for a searing climactic vision of two doppelgängers going *mano a mano*.

That's because Stuart, unlike the multitude of shade-wearing Killers in the film, is not a double, but a scapegoat—the sacrificial animal who is slain to carry away an infection that is menacing the tribe. That's how Edelson treats him, when he tries to plea bargain a deal to get all the Bag Murders off the books, and Steve treats him the same way. A scapegoat is not necessarily innocent—in ancient saturnalian rituals, a prisoner who has already been condemned for one crime was dressed up as a mock king and killed for the crimes of the city, particularly the crimes of the real king.

Although Stuart in every version of the script is the source of all the violence in *Cruising*, in the film his evil is divvied up among four actors and disseminated into the acts of a small army of doubles, possibly including Steve, who is at any rate part of the spreading pattern of contagion, so that the spectator, whose traditional certainties are troubled by the fractured surface of the film, can only conclude after some reflection that Stuart ended up taking the rap because Edelson and Steve needed to break the case. The fact that Stuart's fingerprint is on the bloody quarter found at the peepshow is good enough to win Steve his gold badge and clear the books of all the murders Edelson has been tasked with solving.

The film reserves one more surprise for Steve. At some point Friedkin jotted in his notebook that Nancy might cut her hair and dress like a boy to try to win Steve back. Instead, when it came time to shoot the last scene, he improvised a substitute for that idea: from offscreen he directed Karen Allen to pick up Steve's discarded leather-boy accoutrements—hat, shades, jacket—and put them on.

As scripted, the last shot was going to be Steve looking at himself in the mirror while he finishes shaving and the mirror begins to cloud over, but a sound editor, with Friedkin's approval, added the sound of steps and creaking leather in the off-space, suggesting that Steve is looking past his own image at the image of Nancy transformed into a leather-girl, complete with boots. A metaphorical cloud was originally going to threaten to obscure Steve's identity as Nancy said, offscreen, "It looks like a beautiful day. Doesn't it?" but instead he's seeing, in an unclouded mirror that shows his face restored to normal, a woman dressed like The Killer.

Lacanian psychoanalysis draws an equation between the mirror and the mother's body as two surfaces in which the child sees the reflection of his own physical and psychic unity, but the image Steve is seeing in his shaving mirror is of a bisexual body. It could be his own image as a bisexual man, or it could be an image signifying that his relationship with Nancy has been contaminated by the S&M games he's been playing: Mom has turned into a slightly scary surrogate for Dad. Or finally, bearing in mind that costumes like the one we see Nancy trying on now sell like hotcakes in erotic emporia all over the world, the image of Steve is seen in the off-space—like the image we have seen of Karen Allen trying on the hat and jacket, which look cute on her because they're a couple of sizes too big—may be a very sexy one, and a playful unseen symbol of film's power to create by putting things together in a new way.

Notations

Regarding pinning the blame on "Jack," see my "Thirteen Ways of Looking at a Zombie" in the catalogue of the Torino Film Festival's 2001 George Romero retrospective.

I am quoting from Robin Wood's *Hollywood from Vietnam to Reagan* (New York: Columbia University Press, 1986), and making reference to Thomas Clagett, *William Friedkin: Films of Aberration, Obsession and Reality* (West Hollywood: Silman-James Press, 2003). Nat Segaloff's biography of Friedkin is *Hurricane Billy: The Stormy Life and Films of William Friedkin* (New York: William Morrow, 1990).

Friedkin uses subliminal images: in *The Exorcist* a subliminal image of the demon, and in *Cruising* a subliminal image of sodomy (anal intercourse).

27

Francis Ford Coppola

Peggy Sue Got Married

THE SCREENPLAY FOR *Peggy Sue Got Married* (1986) is about a
housewife with a dissolving marriage who gets to return to her
high school days and relive the choices of her adolescence. On
that level the film is less successful on the whole than *Back to the Future*
(1985), which takes its time-travel premise much more seriously: in *Peggy
Sue*, there is little concern for recreating an epoch (the end of the fifties)
or playing out the paradoxical consequences of the premise, on the part
of the writers, and above all on the part of the director, Francis Coppola.

The real film is elsewhere, in the relationship between Peggy Sue
and her husband Charlie, whom she meets and, against her will, falls in

love with again as an adolescent. Renewing the sentimental vein in his work that runs from *The Rain People* (1969) to *One from the Heart* (1981), Coppola offers his most deeply felt rendition of his vision of women as angels condemned to love beasts: archetypally, the story of Beauty and the Beast, or of Persephone, the virgin kidnapped by the god of the underworld.

Whence a beautiful tour de force sequence at the beginning portraying a high school reunion as Hell, which reveals Coppola at the height of his powers as a filmmaker; whereas when Peggy Sue returns to the year 1960 he contents himself with reminding us, after the bold but rarely convincing formal experiments that have occupied him in the eighties, that he is still a great director of actors: of Kathleen Turner, who is impeccable as Peggy Sue; and of Nicholas Cage, who gives a brilliant, courageous performance as Charlie, the adolescent Pluto with the squeaky voice—a bizarre and moving incarnation of the paradox that, in human affairs, love and death have the same face.

28

Richard Brooks

In Cold Blood

THE TRAILER FOR THIS 1967 film adaptation of Truman Capote's 1965 nonfiction novel about the murder of a family of Kansas farmers, Herb and Bonnie Clutter (John McLiam and Ruth Storey) and two of their children, Nancy and Kenyon (Brenda C. Currin, Paul Stowe), is an aesthetic manifesto that touts writer-director Richard Brooks's desire to portray real events realistically, as Capote had done in his true-crime novel, which had been serialized in the *New Yorker* before becoming an international best seller. The film was shot on practical locations including the isolated farmhouse outside Holcomb, Kansas, where the murders had occurred during the dead of night on November 15, 1959. Some of the townspeople and jurors at the subsequent murder trial, we are told, played themselves—a realistic *parti pris* virtually unheard of in Hollywood cinema at the time, although it was not unknown in Europe.

The trailer plays up the visual similarities between Richard Hickock and Perry Smith, who had been tried and executed for the crime, and Brooks's lead actors, Scott Wilson and Robert Blake, unknowns he cast because stars like Steve McQueen and Paul Newman, who were reportedly available, would have violated the illusion of reality. Wilson was a newcomer, but Blake had had a career as a child actor, notably in the *Our Gang* comedies. His role as Perry launched a new career for him that encompassed Abe Polonsky's *Tell Them Willy Boy Is Here* (1987); a TV cop show, *Baretta* (1975); and a memorably creepy appearance as The Mystery Man in David Lynch's *Lost Highway* (1997). Wilson went on to have a distinguished career that ranged from playing an astronaut in Philip Kaufman's ensemble film *The Right Stuff* to starring as a good-hearted gangster in Robert Aldrich's mile-a-minute adaptation of James Hadley Chase's *No Orchids for Miss Blandish*, *The Grissom Gang* (1997).

Brooks's camera, wielded by Conrad Hall, who had shot *The Professionals* for him in 1966, painted Holcomb, Kansas, the tiny hamlet where the events had occurred, in wintry shades of black-and-white. Spinning a tale of bumbling, lethal lowlifes set to a jazz score by Quincy Jones harking back to the TV cop shows that made Henry Mancini famous in the 1950s, Brooks and Hall pursued their tale of crime and punishment from the streets of Las Vegas to Holcomb and Garden City, where the trial was held, and into the Kansas State Penitentiary, where killers were imprisoned after being captured by Alvin Dewey (John Forsythe), the Kansas lawman who became the hero of Capote's novel, and executed by hanging—a horrifying ritual that leaves no one satisfied and gives a new meaning to Capote's title, which appears on the screen after the state has executed the likable Perry in cold blood. In the book Capote allows himself little editorializing, but he does comment, after reproducing a psychiatrist's report and other documents, that Perry Smith, while competent to stand trial according to the narrow laws of Kansas in 1959, was a paranoid schizophrenic who killed all four Clutters in an explosion of uncontrollable rage against his own abusive father.

The contrast drawn by the film between Perry and Dick—a charming, vicious career criminal whose father (played by Nicholas Ray actor Jeff Corey) unconvincingly claims his son underwent a personality change after a car wreck that sent him to the hospital with a concussion—makes the same point. Although he loudly proclaimed himself to be "a normal," the real Dick Hickock, in a statement to the prison doctor, admitted to being a pedophile and a rapist: "Before I ever went to [the Clutter house] I knew there would be a girl there. I think the real reason I went there was not to rob them but to rape the girl. I thought a lot about it. That is one reason I never wanted to turn back when we started to. Even when I saw there was no safe. I did make some advances to the Clutter girl when I was there. But Perry never gave me a chance."

The film, hewing closely to fact, shows Dick attempting to rape teenage Nancy Clutter during the midnight home invasion. And although Dick has proclaimed that he plans to leave no witnesses when they steal the money, it is Perry, after preventing the rape, who snaps and murders all four family members in a stunning all-in-one—implicitly filmed from the point of view of his helpless partner—that begins when he kills Herb Clutter in the basement and ends with the offscreen explosion of a shotgun as he murders Nancy in her second-floor bedroom, where minutes before he had protected her from Dick.

For an explanation of this act of motiveless malignancy we have to return to the book and the documentation Capote included from Dr. Joseph Satten of the Menninger Institute of Topeka, Kansas, who consulted with Dr. W. Mitchell Jones, the psychiatrist who had volunteered to assess the killers' competence to stand trial, and confirmed his conclusions:

> Though the crime would not have occurred except for a certain frictional interplay between the perpetrators, it was essentially the act of Perry Smith, who [Dr. Satten] feels, represents a type of murderer described by him in an article: "Murder Without Apparent Motive—A Study in Personality Disorganization."
>
> . . . The psychoanalytic hypothesis [says] that the child's exposure to overwhelming stimuli before he can master them is closely linked to early defects in ego formation and later severe disturbances in impulse control. . . . The murderous potential can become activated when the victim-to-be is unconsciously perceived as a key figure in some past traumatic configuration. The behavior, or even the mere presence, of this figure adds a stress to the unstable balance of forces that results in a sudden extreme discharge of violence.

Dr. Satten, comparing Perry Smith to the irrational murderers who were the subject of the Menninger study, had decided that he fit the pattern:

> Obviously three of the murders Smith committed were logically motivated—Nancy, Kenyon and their mother had to be killed because Mr. Clutter had been killed. But it is Dr. Satten's

contention that only the first murder mattered psychologically, and that when Smith attacked Mr. Clutter he was under a mental eclipse, for it was not entirely a flesh-and-blood man he "suddenly discovered" himself destroying, but "a key figure in a past traumatic configuration": His father? The orphanage nuns who had derided and beaten him? The hated Army sergeant? The parole officer who had ordered him to "stay out of Kansas"? One of them, or all of them.

Before writing his screenplay Brooks would have carefully studied this discussion of his main character's possible motives for the irrational act that the real Perry Smith famously summed up: "I didn't want to harm the man. I thought that he was a very nice gentleman. Soft-spoken. I thought so right up to the moment I cut his throat."

That studiousness earned Brooks a jab from Andrew Sarris in *The American Cinema: Directors and Directions, 1929–1968*: "Brooks's sub-Proustian visualization in *Sweet Bird of Youth* and his facile Freudianizing for *In Cold Blood* are particularly damning proofs of an imagination more shallow than fallow." *In Cold Blood* was the last Richard Brooks film Sarris saw before publishing his influential compendium of directorial careers. While it's doubtful that *Looking for Mr. Goodbar* (1977) would have changed his judgment that there was "Less Than Meets the Eye" to Brooks's oeuvre, Diane Keaton's performance in that film would perhaps have been adduced as a grace note to a career that had been more focused on male violence than on feminine emotion.

Ironically, Jacques Rivette—one of the proprietors of the *politique des auteurs*, an editorial policy at *Cahiers du cinéma* that morphed into a theory ("the auteur theory") in its Anglo-Saxon iteration—grouped Brooks with other violence-prone directors like Aldrich (assigned by Sarris to "The Far Side of Paradise") in "Notes on a Revolution"—all directors who were descended from Orson Welles. Brooks's mentor (Welles urged him to turn from writing to writing and directing) had been obliged to replicate a style invented on soundstages on practical locations when the disaster of *It's All True* (1942–1993) sent him into exile in Europe, and Brooks did the same thing in his account of the Clutter murders.

The marks of paternity: Ceilings are shown, exteriors are seen through windows. High-contrast black-and-white photography is used for expressionistic effects, especially during the murder. Paul Stewart, the majordomo who was the last witness interviewed in *Citizen Kane* (1941), plays a reporter named Jensen who asks questions before the execution and narrates the last act of the film, while a younger reporter (Duke Hobbie) chimes in ("How much does the hangman get paid?"), cuing the spectator to be appalled by Perry's execution. The temporal structure of *In Cold Blood* also works against a straightforwardly realistic reading, as Welles's structure had in *Kane*. The film intercuts killers and victims, often with startling effect (Perry looking at himself in a bus station mirror / Nancy washing her face and looking at herself in the mirror) in the lead-up to the murders, then cuts to the aftermath, showing the murders only at the end.

The execution of Dick is played straight, but the execution of Perry is treated subjectively and used to make a statement against capital punishment. During the murder of Mr. Clutter, Perry has a flashback to his father (Tex Smith, played by Charles McGraw) trying to kill him. The scene before the execution, when Perry recalls his father for the chaplain, paints tears on the condemned man's face from the water streaming down the window. And when Perry mounts the steps he sees his father as the hangman, then the actual hangman (Michael Ross).

Brooks's film continues to arouse controversy, especially among participants: Nancy Clutter's sisters, understandably, have refused to see it. The prosecutor (interviewed on YouTube) doesn't like it because it makes Al Dewey the hero—but he never saw it either. In fact, the actor who plays the prosecutor in the film, Will Geer, makes a powerful case for the death penalty, and the film makes its own case, which like so much in it, reflects the ideas of Truman Capote.

Notations

The trailer for *In Cold Blood* can be seen on YouTube at this address: https://www.youtube.com/watch?v=loRNwWFHvwY&pbjreload=10. All quotations from the novel are from Truman Capote, *In Cold Blood* (New York: Vintage International, 1965).

Capote claimed to have invented the "non-fiction novel" with *In Cold Blood*: see https://www.britannica.com/art/nonfiction-novel.

Regarding Sarris, I'm referring to the current edition of *The American Cinema* (Boston: Da Capo Press, 1996), 191.

The quotations from Dr. Joseph Satten of the Menninger Clinic, printed in Capote's text on page 298 and 301 (of the first Vintage International edition, February 1994), originate in an article by him, "Murder without Apparent Motive: A Study in Personality Disorganization," written in collaboration with Karl Menninger, Irwin Rosen, and Martin Mayman and published in the *American Journal of Psychiatry* 117, no. 1 (July 1960): 48–53.

Jacques Rivette's "Notes on a Revolution" ("Notes sur une revolution"), *Cahiers du cinéma* 54 (December 1955): 17–21. This is available online at http://www.dvdbeaver.com/rivette/ok/revolution.html. The phrase *politique des auteurs* comes up in pun form on page 37 of *Cahiers du cinéma* 53, in a photograph caption by François Truffaut. Truffaut's "Une certaine tendance du cinéma

Français," *Cahiers du cinéma* (January 1954): 15–29, is a crucial document in the history of this usage.

Capote supports his interpretation of Perry Smith's action by quoting from the aforementioned article that appeared in the *American Journal of Psychiatry* for July 1960.

There is an excellent 2005 film by Bennett Miller about the writing of *In Cold Blood* starring Philip Seymour Hoffman as Truman Capote and Catherine Keener as Harper Lee, who collaborated with Capote on the research for the book. Capote dedicates the book to Harper Lee and to his sexual partner, actor Jack Dunphy.

29

Star Wars

Reversing the Signs

With each victory of the light, it is the dark that wins.

—*Revenge of the Sith*, by Matthew Stover,
based on Lucas's screenplay

⤳

A S I DROVE BY THE CHINESE Theatre last night [May 12, 2005], I
saw an old sight: a little band of *Star Wars* fans already lining up
for *Revenge of the Sith*—even though *Variety* has reported that it
will be opening this time at the Arclight, a new multiplex with fabulous

This chapter appeared originally as "Inverser les signes" in *Cahiers du cinéma* 601
(May 2005).

digital projection and reserved seating. When I asked the manager at the Arclight if they were going to have their own line, he answered tersely: "We don't do lines." So for the next forty-three days the action will be at the Chinese, where the fans persist in believing that George Lucas won't let them down.

Many feel that he already has. They've been highly critical of the first and second installments of the new [the second] trilogy, where political discussions and Byzantine plotting have replaced what made the first trilogy so engaging: friendships between loveable characters fighting evil. As dictated by the myth embodied in the films, the third episode will end with the triumph of evil and the transformation of the hero, Anakin Skywalker, into Darth Vader, the villain of the original trilogy. To make matters worse, the film is likely to garner a PG-13 rating for violence.

None of that will keep it from being a hit. Then speculation will begin about whether Lucas will make the third trilogy, while he continues rewriting the first two by releasing one *Star Wars* film a year, beginning with *The Phantom Menace* (1999), in 3-D. In the process he will continue improving the special effects as he did when the original trilogy was rereleased in the 1990s. In theory he could also replace all the dialogue with new lines written by Quentin Tarantino and directed by Sydney Pollack, digitally altering the onscreen actors' lip movements to match.

That will never happen, of course, because all that flat, badly acted dialogue performs the same function as dialogue cards in silent films. After letting Ron Howard direct his fellow actors in *American Graffiti* (1973), Lucas settled on this aesthetic for the rest of his oeuvre, and it is consistent with his characterization of himself as a purely visual filmmaker—one whose eccentric Panavision style, stationed midway between Ford and Pasolini, hasn't changed since *THX 1138* (1971). Most of the bad reviews that have bounced off the *Star Wars* juggernaut through the years were written by critics who watch movies with their ears and are incapable of following the intricately edited action sequences that are the films' core, unlike the perpetually renewed fan-base of twelve-year-olds, whose visual skills have been sharpened by playing Lucas-designed video games—the most popular of which all seem to star Darth Vader.

It scarcely matters whether Lucas is a liberal with roots in the 1960s or the conservative he claims to be in interviews, because those shrinking political constituencies are at this point united in opposition to the policies of what is politely referred to as Republican "neoconservatism." The gauntlet was hurled in *Phantom Menace* when Lucas named two evil fish-faced senators Nute Raygun and Trout Lott, in honor of two leaders of the "neoconservative" majority in the US Congress. And in *Attack of the Clones* (2002) Anakin's massacre of an entire village of desert-dwelling

Tusken Raiders in revenge for his mother's death—"even the women, even the children"—inevitably referred to the invasion of Afghanistan, whether it was originally written for that purpose or not.

When it came time to flesh out his plan for the new trilogy, Lucas studied history to understand what causes republics to turn into empires—the familiar scenario of a democracy ceding its liberties to an authoritarian leader in a time of crisis. That situation is already well advanced at the beginning of *Revenge of the Sith*, where Chancellor Palpatine (Ian McDiarmid) has maneuvered the weak, corrupt senate into revoking the constitution and giving him war powers to defeat the Separatists headed by Count Dooku, with whom he is secretly in league. Dooku (Christopher Lee, an interstellar Charles Maurras) hopes to purge the republic of the corruptions of democracy in order to forge an empire where humans will rule over nonhumans, but he is betrayed by Palpatine and killed by Anakin at the beginning of the film—the second murderous act by which Anakin gradually succumbs to the Dark Side of the Force. Many contemporary allusions are smuggled into the novelization of *Revenge of the Sith*. It remains to be seen if Palpatine's cry before a cheering senate of "It is morning in the Republic!" (echoing a famous slogan of Ronald Reagan) makes it into the film.

By now it's no secret that Palpatine is Darth Sidius: a Sith Lord, a Jedi who has succumbed to the Dark Side. As an eighteen-year-old security guard once explained to me, Obi-Wan Kenobi made a big mistake when he killed Darth Sidius's colleague Darth Maul (Ray Park), because in the words of Yoda: "There can be only two Sith Lords—not more, not less." This means that in avenging the murder of his Master, Obi-Wan created an opening that must be filled—by Anakin, when he becomes Darth Vader.

In fact, each of the heroes of *Phantom Menace* performs a good action that paves the way for the triumph of the Dark Side in *Revenge of the Sith*: Obi-Wan (Ewan McGregor) when he kills Darth Maul, Qui-Gon Jinn (Liam Neeson) when he saves ten-year-old Anakin (Jake Lloyd) from slavery on Tatooine, and Senator Padme Amadala (Natalie Portman) when she forces the resignation of a weak chancellor and the installation of Palpatine in order to enlist the senate in the defense of her home planet against the Separatists.

Lucas loves repetitions, so *Star Wars I* has the same structure as *Star Wars IV* (the original *Star Wars* [1977]), but reverses the meaning of all its signs. Even Yoda collaborates in the birth of the empire when he leads the Clone Army to the rescue at the end of *Attack of the Clones*—the Clones will become Palpatine's pawns in *Revenge of the Sith* and his Imperial Storm Troopers in the second trilogy. The last shot of the heroes' triumph in *Phantom Menace* (still based on *Triumph of the Will* [1935]) is ironic in the light of what follows, and the lessons should be clear enough that the twelve-year-olds who cheered when Obi-Wan dispatched Darth Maul will understand them when they revisit the film in 3-D in 2007. Maybe by 2012, when the 3-D *Return of the Jedi* (1983) is released, they will have helped us take our republic back.

Notations

"The Chinese" is Grauman's Chinese Theatre, 6925 Hollywood Boulevard near Highland. It opened in 1927 with *The King of Kings*.

Charles-Marie-Photius Maurras (April 20, 1868–November 16, 1952) was a French author, politician, poet, and critic. He was an organizer and principal philosopher of *Action Française*, a political movement that was monarchist, anti-Semitic, anti-parliamentarist, and counterrevolutionary. Maurras's ideas greatly influenced National Catholicism and "nationalisme intégral." A major tenet of integral nationalism was stated by Maurras this way: "a true nationalist places his country above everything." A significant intellectual and theorist in the first part of the twentieth century, Maurras was an influence on rightist ideology and may well have hinted at the fascism to come.

Palpatine's Reaganish cry did not make it into the film.

30

Dante's Inferno

I N THE JARGON OF CANADIAN literary critic Northrop Frye, Joe Dante
is a low-norm satirist. (High-norm satire, of which Horace would
be a good example, is not practiced today.) This can be puzzling for
critics who analyze films for political messages, because the low-norm
satirist, without necessarily being a conservative in his politics, tends to
appeal to old ways and simple standards of conduct to justify his mock-
ing depictions of modern society.

The satirist's stated aim of correcting and instructing also needs
to be understood as part of an aesthetic whose foremost practitioners
in Europe and America were Federico Fellini and Frank Tashlin, both
of whom, like Dante, began their careers as cartoonists. One aspect of

Dante's work, which finds its fullest expression in *The Second Civil War* (1997), is rooted in the graphic style of *Mad* magazine, which introduced his generation to the art of satire without having any perceptible impact on the targets of that satire—something high-norm satirists, who have the intact memory of cultural ideals to appeal to (cf. Dante's aborted TV series *The Osiris Chronicles*), tend to be better at.

Frye wrote in his seminal *Anatomy of Criticism* (1957) that we live in a period when satire, in the sense he defines, is the dominant genre of the twentieth century, but having a temperament for satire did not keep Lord Byron from being a Romantic poet. Because it is, as Jean-Luc Godard has said, a nineteenth-century invention, cinema is condemned to be a late Romantic art form, and satire has been an essential element in the work of late Romantics as diverse as Ophüls and Kubrick, Welles and Renoir, Hitchcock and Sirk. We live at the end of a long period of cultural decline, memorialized in Tashlin's *The Girl Can't Help It* (1956) and *Fellini Satyricon* (1969), but even Dante Alighieri's *Inferno* contained an escape hatch.

In Dante Jr.'s films, the unspoken name for that escape hatch is "apocalypse": the Saturday matinee apocalypses that are temporarily averted in *Piranha* (1978) and *The Howling* (1981); the void the omnipotent child in "It's a Good Life" (Dante's episode of *Twilight Zone—The Movie* [1983]) contemplates after eliminating his grotesque family and the world that contained them; the comic apocalypses visited on Kingston Falls and New York City by the title creatures of *Gremlins* (1984) and *Gremlins 2: The New Batch* (where Dante and Charles Haas were already poking good-natured fun at Donald Trump in 1990); the all-too-believable apocalypse visited on an America that has turned into a high-tech version of the Tower of Babel in *The Second Civil War* (1997) or its fiery suburban equivalent in *The 'Burbs* (1989), and the purely aesthetic and ultimately beneficial apocalypse engineered during the Cuban Missile Crisis by the impresario in *Matinee* (1993), William Castle doppelgänger Lawrence Woolsey (the great John Goodman), whose schlock horror movies can replace the outworn rituals of religion because they offer a degraded form of the vision the English Romantics experienced when they were confronted with mountains or *memento mori* and called it the Sublime.

The root meaning of "apocalypse," a Hebrew concept that comes to us in Greek clothing, is "revelation" or "uncovering," and the root image is lifting the lid of a pot, or of the sky, which in the Hebrew tradition is another kind of lid. In *Explorers* (1985) three youngsters go questing after a revelation in outer space, only to meet Wak, a Looney Toon version of the Bug-Eyed Monsters prevalent in pulp science fiction. Worse, this monster (improvised on-set in a rubber suit by the great

Robert Picardo) is a kid like them, a cosmic couch potato whose brain has been fried by watching American television. Switching voices as if he had swallowed a remote, Wak delivers the only revelation they're going to get: a cacophony of one-liners, ad copy, and pop clichés backed by a shimmering, discontinuous cascade of visual dreck.

Film critics dutifully call this very American Sublime "postmodernism," a term that has never been well defined, even in the university system. The name that best describes Dante's work is quite concrete: "montage," a word that comes easily to the filmmaker himself because he started as an editor, putting bits of found footage together to create a seven-hour compilation film, *The Movie Orgy*, that was screened on college campuses during the early seventies: montage of signs (the collision of two pieces of celluloid, two clichés, two styles of narrative, character, image, musical accompaniment) and montage of meanings (two contradictory ideas, emotions, or attitudes colliding in the spectator's head when one of the Commando Elite action figures in *Small Soldiers* has his lower parts ground up in a garbage disposal, or when Phoebe Cates's character in *Gremlins* glumly remembers her father, dressed as Santa Claus, getting stuck coming down the chimney on the night before Christmas). Invaluable as a tool for satire, montage is also Dante's preferred formal procedure for producing what European filmmakers have always tried to produce through duration: the experience of the Sublime, which is consciousness of self raised to an apocalyptic pitch.

At the end of *Explorers* the questers return to Earth, disappointed by their revelation but already nostalgic for it. The dream that followed, in the film Dante was never given time to find in the editing room because Paramount wanted it in theaters before Ron Howard's *Cocoon* (1985), would have linked all the characters through their dream life as part of a whole analogous to Teilhard de Chardin's "noosphere" or World Mind. (The theological reference is Dante's.)

That movement—from Innocence to Experience and finally to a higher form of Innocence—was paradigmatic for the Romantic Imagination, a faculty for shaping the real into something new embodying a truth superior to fact. Samuel Taylor Coleridge distinguished Imagination from Fancy: the arbitrary assembling of images into patterns to please the senses, not unlike most movies coming out of Hollywood today. When challenged, Dante makes his own version of that distinction to differentiate between Michael Bay's *Armageddon* (1988), about preventing an asteroid from smashing into the Earth, and his own modestly scaled werewolf apocalypse, *The Howling* (1981). Nevertheless, Dante's films of the 1970s and '80s prepared the way for Bay and his less gifted descendants, who are making fortunes for the studios in the new millennium with costly, humorless versions of 1950s films about giant bugs and meteors that literally carry the seeds of mankind's destruction.

Like the "Gentleman from Porlock" who knocked on Coleridge's door before he had finished writing down his visionary poem "Kubla Khan," which the poet had unfortunately forgotten by the time he returned to his writing table, Paramount Pictures kept Dante from realizing his version of the Romantic quest in *Explorers*, but he has continued to show us glimpses of it in films like *Matinee*, with its tribute to the Imagination's power to reconcile us to the real world it always sends us back to, or *The 'Burbs*, which proposes a comic variation on John Keats's definition of the Imagination as being like Adam's dream in *Paradise Lost*: "He awoke and found it true." Even the impression of humanity in manic overabundance communicated by *The Second Civil War* (1997) may be crowding toward some revelation, as the technician played by Picardo reminds us when he quotes those famous lines from Yeats's "The Second Coming": "The centre cannot hold/ Mere anarchy is loosed upon the world."

This fidelity to the vision of American New Wave filmmakers who peaked in the 1970s has enabled Dante to keep making good films—while regularly detouring into TV and taking advantage of the fact that movie trailers are in the public domain to run his own film school with *Trailers from Hell* (2007)—saying "no" to lots of bad ones (cf. *Snakes on a Plane* [2006]), thereby displaying a steely sense of self without which any artist working in Hollywood, now or in the long-vanished Golden Age, would be doomed to extinction.

Notations

"Dante's Apocalypse" has probably been reprinted online more than anything in this volume, for which I have pruned and clarified it. It applies to film the theory of apocalyptic art that Harold Bloom elaborated in *Shelley's Mythmaking* (1969) and *Blake's Apocalypse* (1970) before coining the term "The American Sublime" to describe the poetry and prose of Walt Whitman and Ralph Waldo Emerson. The concept of the Sublime descends to us from Longinus via Edmund Burke, but Bloom's colleague Geoffrey Hartman redefined it in 1964 as "consciousness of self raised to an apocalyptic pitch" in *Wordsworth's Poetry: 1787–1814* (New Haven: Yale University Press, 1971), a formulation I have adopted here as a nod to George I. Gurdjieff, whose inheritors taught me to apply it—when I remember to—in my own life.

Before moving on to Dante's films, younger readers who aren't familiar with *Mad* magazine should spurn its current incarnation and devour the paperback collections from the era when Harvey Kurtzman wrote and edited it (1952–1956), because the jam-packed compositions executed for Kurtzman by Will Elder, Jack Davis, and Wally Wood are evoked in *The Second Civil War*. The script for that film is signed by Martyn (*The Clown Murders* [1976]) Burke, but I'm not alone in suspecting that executive producer Barry Levinson put his hand to it before it landed on Dante's desk at Hollywood General Studios. Staged on an East-West cultural divide that gaped in 1997 like the North-South divide inherited from the *first* Civil War, the film that resulted looks, in the era of the twenty-four-hour TV news cycle, like a documentary.

Applied to *The 'Burbs*, John Keats's "he awoke and found it true" refers to the ending finally arrived at for that much rewritten film: the Klopeks, a very foreign family of apparent serial killers who have invaded Tom Hanks's idyllic suburb, really turn out to be serial killers at the end. This "one-finger exercise" (Dante's term) on the themes of *Rear Window* (1954) never gets around to explaining the ever-topical reason for the Hanks character's *désoeuvrement*, which triggers his paranoia: he's been laid off, but he's afraid to tell his wife (the late Carrie Fisher) the truth. Dante's comic animus, Dick Miller, whose career started like his at Roger Corman's New World Pictures, appears in every film he has ever made. In *The 'Burbs* Miller plays a garbage man who finds a discarded skull. Dante's film career began in 1976 when he and Allan Arkush cobbled together *Hollywood Boulevard* out of scenes lifted from New World trailers.

31

John Landis

The Stupids

In memoriam Jacques Derrida.

BASED ON THE POPULAR SERIES of books for very young children written by Harry Allard and illustrated by James Marshall, John Landis's *The Stupids* (1996) was intended to launch a franchise for the production company that financed it, Savoy Pictures. The film pits characters living in their own parallel universe (clothes, interior decoration, logic) against a version of the real world that is itself as cartoonish as the one Landis created for *The Blues Brothers*, as Tom Arnold leads a cast of mostly unknown actors through a tangled web of catastrophes woven by a family where everyone is stupid.

Savoy went out of business and sold its unreleased films to New Line, where *The Stupids* suffered the cruel fate of many such orphans. When I told a friend at New Line how much I loved *The Stupids*, he informed me that it was only testing well with audiences less than eight years of age—as if that were some kind of problem. The film was released with little ad support and eventually leaked out on video.

To say it deserves to be better known would be an understatement. *The Stupids* is a masterpiece and the beginning of a new period in John Landis's career, where the considerable potential he displayed in *Into the Night* (1985) and *An American Werewolf in London* (1981) was being realized in films like *Susan's Plan* (1998) and *Slasher* (2004), which carry his reflections on the medium to a new level of richness and complexity.

The Name of the Rose

At first glance it would appear that Landis and his screenwriter Brent Forrester took very little from the *Stupids* books—slender volumes that really are aimed at young children. The actors playing the Stupids look nothing like their illustrated counterparts, whose actions are literally replicated only once, in the third shot of the film: a pan to the bed where Joan (Jessica Lundy) and Stanley (Tom Arnold) are sleeping with their heads under the covers and their feet on the pillows. (The gag appears on the last page of the first book of the series, *The Stupids Step Out*.)This initial definition of the family's stupidity—doing everything wrong—is further illustrated when Buster (Bug Hall), the little boy, comes back from taking his goldfish for a walk and Petunia (Alex McKenna), his older sister, opens the lid of a toilet to look for their mother. But alongside gags like these that were sure to delight the books' young fans, Landis wanted to explore the psychology of stupidity through gags that would appeal to older spectators—the two-tiered formula that has ensured the immortality of his own childhood favorites, the Looney Toon cartoons.

Examples of a more sophisticated form of stupidity—perceptual error—appear in the last book of the series, *The Stupids Die*, where a clock striking eleven times tells the family it's "time for lunch" and a blown fuse that plunges the house into darkness makes them think they've died. These hints are also developed in the film, which includes a sequence where Stanley and Petunia jump to the same conclusion when the lights go out in the planetarium. But that sequence deploys its gags within a much bigger field for the exercise of stupidity: language. That idea may also have come from the books. The first illustration of the first book in the *Stupids* series shows a large painting of a fir tree hanging next to Stanley with "Flower" written underneath it. On subsequent pages appear paintings of a bird ("Dog") and a sailboat ("Car"), and the motif becomes even more extravagant in the two sequels, where we glimpse pictures of a butterfly labeled "Cow" (shown twice in *The Stupids Die*) and a bird labeled "Bus" (the same book). It's no coincidence that the Stupids' dog—in the books and the film—is named Kitty.

Actually, the image Landis copied from *The Stupids Step Out* contains the loveliest mismatch of all: over the bed hangs a picture of a landscape with a fluffy little cloud, titled "Rose." One is reminded of René Magritte, whose first "word paintings," collectively titled "La clé des songes" (The interpretation of dreams, 1927–1935), consist of objects with inappropriate labels, like a woman's shoe labeled "the moon" or a clock labeled "the wind." Because it's hanging over the bed—another juxtaposition that recalls Looney Toons, in which clouds overhanging sleepers supply landscapes where their dreams can be acted out—the painting of a cloud hanging over the inverted sleepers suggests the setting for a shared dream where a rose, for example, could materialize at any moment.

No doubt parents reading the books with their children use these and other stupidities (such as eating with one's feet) for edifying purposes, but Landis celebrates stupidity and uses it to more and more poetic ends as the film unfolds. It's probably significant that the "Rose" painting is not replicated in the very first shot of the film, and that Phil Dagort's sets for the Stupid residence include only out-of-focus modernist-looking paintings with no titles. After all, an image illustrating the disjunction between words and things would be a rather pedantic way to begin a film where everything takes place in that great divide, from which most of the gags spring, as well as the plot and a number of important characters.

There Is Nothing Outside of the Text

In fact, we're told at the outset that the film will be taking place entirely within a world of words. The first gag after the inverted sleepers is Stanley's "List of Things to Do Today": "Make check mark on paper." (We see him do this.) "Cross item out." ("No time for that, I'm afraid," he says, and does it anyway.) And finally, "That seems pretty senseless, but . . . whatever." (He says this as he pockets the list.) Stanley may be standing on his front porch, but his field of operations is the piece of paper in his hand. (Petunia understands this: When a gigantic villain armed with a crate is bearing down on Stanley, he calls out, "I'm caught! I'm trapped! Someone help me out here!" "You're cornered!" Petunia suggests helpfully. "Yes!" says Stanley. "That's the word I was looking for—I'm cornered!"

What's written on the piece of paper controls what Stanley says and does, but the family's behavior is governed by the forms of language, not by its meanings. In a flashback showing Stanley doing his job as a postman, for example, he delivers a postcard written in Chinese characters to the first Chinese people he encounters, without reading the address.

By the same token, when Petunia and Buster conclude that their parents have been kidnapped, they go to the police because when Petunia dictated three sentences to Buster, he wrote down only the last words, which were the last things he heard: "Police have kidnapped your children." This mangled missive—confirmed for Joan by a *coq à l'âne*: a call from a policeman who says, "We have your children here"—sets in motion a frantic search and instills in everyone (including Petunia and Buster, who should know better) a paranoid belief that won't be corrected until the end of the movie, when the family sees the police rounding up the bad guys. "Look, the police are on our side again," says Joan contentedly.

The *coq à l'âne* is the most banal form of perceptual error, one that the screenplay can always fall back on to motivate the action, but other types of error can also be driven by language, because words create the framework within which errors occur. "One false step and we could end up dead," says Stanley when he and Petunia enter the planetarium, leading them to conclude, when the lights go out a second later, that they have died.

Some of the more sophisticated linguistic forms that the family runs afoul of:

Synonyms: When Stanley realizes that someone has taken (= stolen) his family's garbage, he sets off in pursuit of the "thieves" and becomes entangled with a renegade army colonel (Mark Metcalf) who is demonstrating the weapons he's selling to various terrorist/dictator types at the garbage dump.

Homonyms: When Joan and the kids wreck the computer system at the local newspaper by inserting Stanley's picture in the disk drive, the mechanical oracle delivers up a message—"Fatal Error Drive B"—which they communicate to Stanley, whose life is saved by their warning to beware the "Drive Bee." Assuming that an innocent bee that flies in the window is the fatal insect, he gets out of the car just before a bomb planted by the arms dealers explodes. Of course, the real message would have included the word "Reading," but underlining the family's error of reading at this point would have been as heavy-handed as decorating their home with mislabeled paintings.

Shifters: These are words—pronouns—that change meaning according-ing to who is speaking and who is spoken to. For example, the pronoun "your": When Joan appears to the children in a hairy disguise, Petunia screams: "It's some kind of ape woman!" "Oh no," says Joan, reassuringly, "It's me—your mother!" "Your mother is some kind of ape woman?" says Buster to Petunia, incredulously.

As this example shows, shifters and words designating kinship sow the same kind of confusion. When Joan and the kids are reunited with Stanley near the end of the film, Joan (who has just been elected president of the country of Stupidia when Stanley's cry of "Joan" is counted as a voice vote) informs him: "Your first job will be to go onto that Army base and rescue my husband." And while you're at it," says Buster, "you can save our father, too." "I'm afraid those two will just have to wait," says Stanley. The film plays a number of variations on the potential for absurdity in kinship terms, culminating in Stanley's infectiously exuber-ant televised rendition of "I'm My Own Grandpa" that has become a YouTube favorite thanks to the film.

The multiplication of entities implicit in Stanley's reference to "those two" is just one example of the creative power of language. When Joan and the children are consulting the computer at the newspaper, Buster (who is scratching his nose) suggests typing in "Nose" as the password; Petunia concurs, then types in the object of their query, "Stanley Stupid." After the photo of Stanley that she helpfully inserts in the disk drive shorts out all the computers in the office, a headline about HBO's new season—"Alien Pilots Picked Up by Network"—is also scrambled, result-ing in a front page that proclaims "Two Alien Pilots Pick Nose" with Stanley's name (and picture) as a byline. Cut to a spacecraft manned by two alien pilots who are picking their noses just as the stewardess delivers the morning paper with the accusatory headline, sending the outraged ETs on a mission of vengeance to vaporize Stanley.

How to Increase Your Word Power

Modern linguistics calls this power of words "the arbitrariness of the signifier," whose relationship to meaning—to the "signified"—is deter-mined by custom and convention, not by any intrinsic bond. The chief exponents of this theory after Swiss linguist Ferdinand de Saussure are Buster and Petunia. When Buster proposes "Nose" as a password because he happens to be scratching his nose, computer wizard Petunia says with a big grin, "We can try!" She is presumably pleased that her brother has learned the lesson she taught him when she interpreted the fortune-cookie

message at the Jade Garden Restaurant—"Time flies when you're having fun"—to be the address of the newspaper, located, as she explains
to him, on the corner of Fun and Fly. When Buster points out that the
newspaper office is really on the corner of Maple and Fifth, she rejoins
that that is "close enough."

The pupil surpasses the teacher in the sequence where Buster and
Joan think they've traveled back to the age of the dinosaurs (an exhibit
at the local Museum of Natural History). Joan warns Buster against the
dangers of the "Butterfly Effect," but instead of heeding her, he takes
out a magic marker and writes his name on a rock. Because it is the
first word ever written on Earth, he tells her, his name will become the
central mystery of all religions. Nations will rise and fall on his name. All
of human history will become a footnote to "Buster." . . . Rebuked by his
mother, Buster apologizes for letting himself become "drunk with power."

The prime example of that power is Mr. Sender, a nonexistent
being conjured up by Stanley's misinterpretation of the notice "Return to
Sender" stamped on letters he was processing at the post office. All the
film's lessons about language culminate in the lurid vision Stanley evokes
of Sender's lair, where the key signifiers accumulated in the course of the
action are woven into a dream that is an interpretation of everything that
has happened so far. At the end of this wonderful fantasy, learning that
Stanley is on his trail, Sender—Christopher Lee at his fruitiest, wearing shoes with no socks—gestures operatically as he gives the order to
"Release the Drive Bee!"

In ancient rhetoric antonomasia refers to a common noun fashioned from a proper one: "sandwich" named after the Earl of Sandwich,
and so on. Mr. Sender is a reverse antonomasia, a rhetorical figure for
which we would search in vain in antiquity because its first occurrence
(in a film, at least) is Alfred Hitchcock's 1956 version of *The Man Who
Knew Too Much*, where a dying spy's whispered words, "Ambrose Chapel,"
send Jimmy Stewart on a wild goose chase to the shop of taxidermist
Ambrose Chappell. While Stewart is barking up the wrong tree, his wife
(Doris Day) realizes that the dying man was referring to an actual chapel
and runs off to check it out, leaving a message with her friends for her
husband to follow. (After hearing from Joan how Stanley was fired from
the post office for dreaming up the sinister Mr. Sender, Buster concludes
sagely: "Dad knew too much.")

We know from the Truffaut-Hitchcock interviews that Hitchcock
was intrigued by the idea of arbitrariness, as embodied in the scene
that was never filmed for *North by Northwest* of the corpse falling out
of a just-assembled car, but he had already given a brilliant example of
that disruptive force in *The Man Who Knew Too Much* by conjuring up

the doddering Mr. Ambrose Chappell out of a pun. (When the Stupids finally look up Mr. Sender in the phonebook, he turns out to be a mild-mannered museum curator played by Bob Keeshan, television's Captain Kangaroo.) The comings and goings of Stewart and Day—so baffling to Day's old friends who have come to their hotel room to welcome her—are the model for the diverging and converging trajectories of the characters in *The Stupids*, by turns slaves and masters of the signifier. (A corollary: Their pets aren't stupid because they're without language, and therefore immune to its bewitchments.)

Hitchcock's influence has always been felt in Landis's films. *Into the Night* is one of the very few valid successors to the much-imitated *North by Northwest*, while Hitchcock himself, glimpsed on television, is a character in *Innocent Blood* (1992), according to the film's end credits. As the subtle reference to *The Man Who Knew Too Much* reminds us, Landis has radicalized the lesson of Hitchcock again in *The Stupids* by making a film that would have delighted Lewis Carroll, whose books for children are the unacknowledged inspiration for all the journeys the Master's characters went on when he sent them down the rabbit hole whose other names are "language," "writing," and "imagination."

Notations

For the role of "writing" in Hitchcock, see my article on *Suspicion* in *Trafic* 41 (Spring 2002), and Tom Cohen, *Anti-Mimesis from Plato to Hitchcock* (Cambridge: Cambridge University Press, 1994). I have written about the film, as well, in "The MacGuffin," www.labyrinth.net.au/~muffin/suspicion.html.

I heard about French philosopher Jacques Derrida's passing when I was putting the finishing touches on this essay. "There Is Nothing Outside of the Text" is the standard mistranslation of Derrida's maxim "Il n'y a pas de hors-texte."

When Tom Arnold starred in *The Stupids*, he still hadn't shaken his tabloid notoriety for his turbulent marriage to TV star Roseanne Barr, which had ended in divorce three years earlier. Since then he has become a ferocious online critic of the Donald J. Trump administration.

Jessica Lundy had previously worked with John Landis when she appeared in an episode of *Dream On*, a TV series he executive produced, and Mark Metcalf had previously chewed up the scenery for Landis as a sadistic ROTC leader in *Animal House*.

Bug Hall's robust show business career had been launched in 1994 playing Alfalfa in Penelope Spheeris's *The Little Rascals*.

For a take on Hitchcock's twice-told spine-tingler that Stanley Stupid would almost understand, see Murray Pomerance's 2016 BFI monograph of that title, *The Man Who Knew Too Much* (London: British Film Institute, 2016).

32

Ang Lee

The Ice Storm

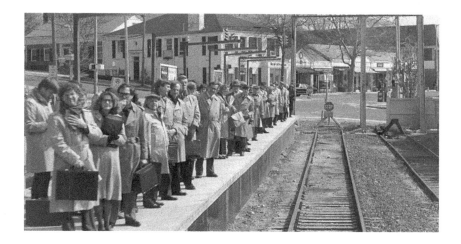

ASKED BY FRENCH JOURNALISTS in a 2001 interview what recent films he most admired, Brian De Palma named Ang Lee's 1997 *The Ice Storm*. It was surprising to hear one of the leaders of a filmmaking revolution that aimed at transforming American cinema in the sixties single out as exemplary a work by a Taiwanese-born director whose first three films were in Mandarin, but De Palma was right. Ten

---

This piece originally appeared as a booklet accompanying the 2008 Criterion edition of *The Ice Storm*, which had had an unsuccessful 1997 theatrical release.

years after it was made, *The Ice Storm* looks like the best American film of the nineties.

There were other great American films in that decade, of course—the words *Groundhog Day!* will no doubt spring to the lips of many an indignant film lover—but *The Ice Storm* occupies a special place among them because it offers a vision of a turning point in the country's history. Most of the events of the film take place on Thanksgiving Day 1973, the tenth anniversary (plus a day) of the JFK assassination, which lit the fuse for the sexual, cultural, and political revolts that exploded in the late sixties. As the characters prepare to celebrate Thanksgiving, the country is already sliding onto the downward slope that would lead to the end of that heady era.

The Ice Storm also occupies a special place in Ang Lee's body of work. It was planned to be his English-language debut, but the producers of *Sense and Sensibility* (1995) chose him to direct their Jane Austen adaptation before he got to it. Even though *The Wedding Banquet* (1993), Lee's breakout hit, had taken place in Manhattan, it was primarily about a Chinese family caught in the winds of change. *The Ice Storm*, which concerns an American family faced with similar problems, is Lee's first truly American film, analogous in some ways to Alfred Hitchcock's first real American film, *Shadow of a Doubt* (1943), about a small-town family losing its innocence, for which Hitchcock engaged the services of the quintessentially American novelist Thornton Wilder.

Lee's film is based on Rick Moody's 1994 novel about growing up in affluent New Canaan, Connecticut, during the last years of the sexual revolution. Some of what De Palma says he admired in it—the writing and story construction—is the work of Lee's constant collaborator, producer-screenwriter James Schamus, who first brought the book to his attention and adapted it to the screen. But the film also underwent major changes during production and postproduction, which can be seen by comparing it to the published screenplay.

Although Lee and Schamus had initially envisioned a satirical comedy in the Billy Wilder tradition, like *The Wedding Banquet* had been, the film evolved into a delicate mixture of tones that Lee says he only became fully aware of when he first saw a rough cut with Mychael Danna's haunting score. The script had already softened Moody's ferocious farewell to his own dysfunctional family, which ends with the revelation that he is Paul (Tobey Maguire), the befuddled son of Ben and Elena Hood. Ben (Kevin Kline) is no longer an alcoholic, and Elena (Joan Allen), whose last actions in the book are shockingly cruel, comes off as more sinned against than sinning. As for Jim and Janey Carver, neighbors with whom the Hoods become sexually entangled, Jamey Sheridan and Sigourney

Weaver offer sharp portrayals of two likable people whose marriage happens to be a failure.

Richard Nixon, seen on television in the last days of the Watergate debacle, is virtually a character in the film, as he is in the book—Paul's younger sister, Wendy (Christina Ricci), catalogs his lies with the passion of a *Jeopardy* addict—and so is the period he helped define. The happy confluence of sexual and political revolution in 1973 was epitomized by the readiness with which the press adopted the nickname Deep Throat for the mysterious informant inside the Nixon administration who helped expose the dirty tricks played by the Committee to Reelect the President in 1972 and the subsequent cover-up: the nickname was the title of a pornographic film that became fashionable viewing outside the porn ghetto the same year—the Carvers and the Hoods are discussing it at a dinner party early in the film.

Lee first came to the United States in 1978 and never knew the period firsthand, so he approached Moody's story as a period piece like *Sense and Sensibility*. Costume designer Carol Oditz was encouraged to recreate the styles of the early seventies as part of an overall approach worked out with Lee, production designer Mark Friedberg, and cinematographer Frederick Elmes. They sought inspiration in the era's art: the photo-realists, who painted photographs (a style that is both hyperreal and at one remove from reality, evoked by the variety of reflecting surfaces seen in the film), and the op artists, who deployed contrasting visual elements to create vibrating surface tensions on a single plane. Lee meant it as praise when he told Friedberg after the first screening: "Mark, it really looks good. It's not the seventies, but it's interesting."

Lee and his longtime editor Tim Squyres did eighteen cuts of the film while finding the right tone and mapping out the crosscutting between families, members of families, and generations within families, particularly during the night of the storm, when all the plots intertwine to a conclusion: Paul in a Park Avenue apartment with the object of his desire, wealthy Libbets Casey (Katie Holmes), and his obnoxious roommate (David Krumholtz); Mikey Carver (Elijah Wood) and his younger brother, Sandy (Adam Hann-Byrd), playing out their tentative sexual explorations with Wendy in the basement playroom of the Carver house; and Ben, Elena, Janey, and Jim at a neighborhood cocktail party that turns out to be a "key party"—a wife-swapping game that was first played in the posh precincts of New Canaan five years after the Summer of Love had proclaimed sexual liberation as an ideal.

The odd situation of parents imitating styles set by a generation only slightly older than the children they are struggling to raise is reflected by the film's many internal rhymes. On the one hand, they suggest the old saw "Like father, like son": Ben and Paul both pry into other people's medicine cabinets, for example, and neither of them takes advantage of opportunities for sex that present themselves the night of the storm. But "Like daughter, like mother" also applies: Elena imitates Wendy's bike riding and her shoplifting (but Mom gets busted). This is one of the places where omission of a causal link furnished by the book—Elena knows about Wendy's kleptomania, which has gotten her in trouble before—nudges us toward inferring a magical connection: mother and daughter appear to be telepathically linked.

This magical worldview anticipates Lee's later films about superhuman characters: *Crouching Tiger, Hidden Dragon* (2000) and *Hulk* (2003). His interest in myth can be seen in *The Ice Storm* in the identification Paul (played by the future Spider-Man) feels with the Marvel comic *The Fantastic Four*, about a family of superheroes as dysfunctional as his own. When his family comes to the train station to meet him at the end, he sees a flaming number 4 in the sky—the moment that Lee says made him want to adapt the book to film when he first read it, although his quiet rendering of the Hood family's epiphany doesn't employ special effects.

The presence of the Fantastic Four in the editorial mix implicitly ratifies a magical reading of the way characters, actions, and images collide and mirror one another, like the molecules that obsess Mikey, whose destiny seems to be controlled by the tragic events in the latest issue of Paul's favorite comic. Paul reads excerpts from *Fantastic Four* number 141 while riding the last train back to New Canaan as the night of the ice storm draws to a close, and the temporary blackout and stoppage of the train supply another connection—an electrical one—with what happens to Mikey, a character with whom Paul has no scenes in the film.

At one extreme, this results in magical thinking; at the other, in formal patterning that Lee, recalling the art of the seventies, has described as postcubist: a number of views or facets assembled in such a way that they are meaningful to the viewer when seen in any of a number of possible angles. Ultimately this structure—hyperreal images that suggest magical hypotheses by the forms their colliding patterns make—reflects the ruminations of Moody's narrator at the outset of his third act, when he stops portraying events through the eyes of the characters and begins talking about the viewpoint of God: "Though metaphors of the mind of God are characterized by coincidence and repetition, examples from nature aren't as tidy. Nature is senseless and violent."

Which brings us to the ice storm, a metaphor for the movie it gives its name to. "When I think of *The Ice Storm*, I think first of water and rain, of how it falls everywhere, seeps into everything, forms underground rivers, and helps to shape a landscape," writes Lee in his preface to the published screenplay. "And also, when calm, of how it forms a reflective surface, like glass, in which the world reappears. Then, as the temperature drops, what was only water freezes. Its structure can push iron away, it is so strong. Its pattern overthrows everything."

The unfolding of this natural pattern is evoked by the ghostly credits of the film: vapors that solidify into words, accompanied by the sound of a Native American flute. Lee also shows the storm's effects in shots of the Connecticut landscape, reminiscent of the shots of time passing in the films of Yasujiro Ozu, a filmmaker he admires.

In 1997 some critics thought they discerned reactionary attitudes in *The Ice Storm*'s treatment of its unabashedly upper-middle-class postrevolutionary subject matter. Supporting that view is the fact that Lee himself calls his first three films—*Pushing Hands* (1992), *The Wedding Banquet*, and *Eat Drink Man Woman* (1994)—his "Father Knows Best" trilogy, because of the loving portrayal in all three of a traditional patriarch, played by Si-hung Lung. This conservative strain in Lee's work can perhaps be traced back to Ozu—particularly the films the great Japanese director made after World War II, when conflicts between tradition and change, and between parents and children, were being exacerbated by the impact of the war on Japanese culture. But Lee is no more a reactionary than Ozu, because his subject is that conflict, which is history as we experience it at any given moment of our lives.

Born on the frontier of the political struggles that shaped the last half of the twentieth century (his parents emigrated to Taiwan from Mainland China, where his grandparents were killed in the Cultural Revolution), Lee pursued this theme intuitively in his first three films but rethought it in *The Ice Storm* because of his recent experiences on *Sense and Sensibility*—Emma Thompson's script, he says, revealed to him the idea that had shaped his early work, the eternal tug-of-war between society and desire. He and Schamus followed *The Ice Storm* with an adaptation of *Woe to Live On*, Daniel Woodrell's novel about Southern jayhawkers in the Civil War, told from the point of view of two outsiders whose attitude toward the Southern cause changes in the course of the film: the son of a German immigrant (Tobey Maguire) and his black comrade in arms (Jeffrey Wright). Lee's preface to the published screenplay of that film sheds additional light on *The Ice Storm*. "Through [the two outsiders] we come to experience the changes that freedom will bring," he writes:

> It is their emancipation that the film becomes about, their coming-of-age. So, as a Taiwanese, I can identify with the Southerners as the Yankees change their way of life forever, but I also identify more strongly with those outsiders, who

grasp at freedom, and fight for it. . . . Our story is about the very heart of America, even as this heart was—and still so often is—torn apart by racial and other conflicts. Even as America seems to conquer the world with the promise of freedom, it has still not fully conquered itself, or achieved its own freedom.

Ride with the Devil (1999), as the Woodrell adaptation was called, is another Lee film audiences will have to catch up with on video because it was not understood in its time. Filmographies that frequent the knife-edge where history is being made run that risk.

In November 2007 *Newsweek* proclaimed that America was still in the grip of the sixties, unable to wish them away or fulfill their promise. The still obsessive presence in our culture of the era *The Ice Storm* portrays gives it an unfaded freshness that few films keep for long. In 1997 it was prophetic. The country was a year away from the impeachment of Bill Clinton for participating in the sex act celebrated in *Deep Throat*. The history encapsulated in Lee's film was about to be repeated as farce by a Republican-dominated Congress that was still stinging from the events of 1973, while Nixon's "Southern strategy" would be deployed in the next presidential campaign to divide the electorate along lines first drawn by the Civil War.

"The period portrayed in *The Ice Storm* is innocent and good because people are rebelling against old rules and the old order," Lee has said. "We're jaded now, while the people of that era were very fresh and bold about reaching for their limits. What they encounter in the process is human nature, and the ice storm, which gives you a little more respect for Nature. It turns out that we're not that free after all." Lee's statement expresses both sides of the complex symbol that informs the images of his film—he is one of those artists for whom, without some positive sense of the past, the future is an empty promise. His cinema therefore recalls some of the greatest filmmakers who came before him: Ozu, of course, and Americans like John Ford and Orson Welles, with their laments for lost worlds and dissolving traditions.

One thing that gives *The Ice Storm* its hallucinatory intensity is the fact that the era before 1967 has already been swept away without a trace at the start of the film, which portrays the arrival of the present era. But the film does refer to a much older America: Wendy saying grace by thanking God "for letting us white people kill all the Indians," a glimpse of the famous "Keep America Clean" television commercial, with Iron Eyes Cody weeping over a litterbug committing what was then called "pollution," and the haunting flute music that begins during the credits, over those ghostly letters.

"I liked the irony of suggesting music endemic to Native Americans," composer Mychael Danna has said, "to remind us that as the characters walk through the woods to their mod houses, the ground beneath their feet used to belong to civilizations that are long gone. Ang and I wanted to remind people of the power of Nature—that Nature was there before anyone else, and that Nature will be there when we've gone."

Notations

I actually interviewed Ang Lee on the phone. His English was bad—he always worked with an English-speaking collaborator, James Schamus, on his English-language films—but I did learn from the interview that he admired Ozu and Billy Wilder: very relevant to this film.

Lee's preface appears in James Schamus, *The Ice Storm* (New York: Newmarket Press, 1997).

33

Tim Burton

Ed Wood

To RESUME: AT THE HEIGHT of his power as a director, after the success of *Batman* (1989) and *Batman Returns* (1992), Tim Burton has chosen to make a biography of Edward D. Wood Jr., a director of low-budget films who is considered by some to be "the worst director who ever lived."

Considered by some to be the best filmmaker in Hollywood today, Burton has, paradoxically, deployed all his artistry to tell the story of a filmmaker who has been immortalized for his complete lack of cinematic *savoir-faire*. Whatever other qualities he may have had, Wood was by normal standards a terrible director of actors, ignorant of the basics of film technique, whose scripts are full of corny dialogue and feverish, incoherent tirades that are usually spoken by an offscreen narrator or by the drug-addicted former star who made his last three films with Wood, Bela Lugosi.

At first glance, all that *Ed Wood* (1994) has in common with *Glen or Glenda* (1953), *Bride of the Monster* (1955), and *Plan 9 from Outer Space* (1959), Wood's three Lugosi films, is the fact that it was shot in black-and white. Gorgeous black-and-white: Stefan Czapsky has lit *Ed Wood* like a high-contrast film noir whose rich chiaroscuro compositions recall *Citizen Kane* (1941) and *Touch of Evil* (1958), working *Kane*-like wonders to recreate the flat, pointless lighting of Wood's own films whenever necessary. Every shot is calculated as part of a formal design, with shots that return like leitmotifs at key moments; the fifties sets and costumes are heavily stylized, as is the masklike makeup of all the characters, and the special effects (one of Wood's manifold weak points) flawlessly wed *trucage* and reality, notably in the opening dolly back from a model of the Hollywood sign right out of *Plan 9* that ends up on the facade of a theater marquee under which hopeful young theater director Ed Wood, apparently drenched by the same rain that veiled the miniature Hollywood hills, paces nervously, awaiting the arrival of the critic who is going to write the first of many bad reviews he will receive in his career.

As always, it is the actors who give Burton's formal schemes life. Backed by an impeccable supporting cast, Johnny Depp and Martin Landau are, respectively, brave and downright astonishing as Wood and Lugosi, the film's central duo. Penelope Ann Miller, as Wood's long-suffering girlfriend Dolores, works wonders imitating the real Dolores Fuller's dedicated unprofessionalism in two scenes from *Glen or Glenda* and *Bride of the Monster*, and Vincent D'Onofrio, aided by the wizardry of prosthetics and digital voice alteration, does the impossible: in the scene where Wood encounters Orson Welles in a bar, D'Onofrio convinces us that he *is* Orson Welles; before I saw the actor's name in the credits, I thought I had just witnessed the first successful use of the kind of digitally altered archival images that failed to convince me in *Forrest Gump* (1994).

The Wood-Welles encounter, which never happened in real life, confronts the two halves of the paradox: total mastery and total incompetence. But the genius and the hack find that they have much in common: problems with interfering producers, pictures interrupted by financing shortfalls, and the same burning desire to put one's vision on-screen without compromise. "Why waste your life making somebody else's dream?" asks Welles, sending Wood back to the set of *Plan 9* determined to do it his way, despite the fears of the Baptists who are putting their church's money into a film that, even to their untrained eyes, is shaping up to be a total aesthetic and commercial disaster.

"Filmmaking isn't about the little details," Wood passionately explains to the worried churchmen when falling actors uproot the cardboard tombstones in a cemetery fashioned from a bedsheet. "It's about the big picture. Haven't you ever heard of willing suspension of disbelief?" If Tim Burton is a director obsessed with the little details, he nonetheless can identify with Wood, because screwing up the details and getting them right are really two ways of achieving the same end, which is what Wood calls "the big picture": the other thing that *Ed Wood*, *Citizen Kane*, and *Glen or Glenda* have in common is that they are films that function like dreams.

Earlier in the film, when mammoth Swedish actor Tor Johnson bumps into a doorframe while exiting a laboratory set, Wood consoles a cameraman who wants to retake the scene with the thought, "It's real! In reality Lobo would have had to struggle with that problem every day." This argument, which echoes something I heard Wood actress Maila Nurmi (Vampira) say a few years ago about the "mistakes" in Wood's films, could also be used by Burton, a filmmaker of the fantastic who is making his first docudrama in *Ed Wood*.

Ed Wood's life is one of those true stories that is more fantastic than any invention, and *Ed Wood* is a film composed mostly of facts, although Burton and his writers have permitted themselves some deviations. For example, Rudolph Grey's *Nightmare of Ecstasy*, an oral history of Wood, who was a heterosexual transvestite, debunks reports that he directed *Plan 9* in drag, and Burton chooses to "print the legend." But the meeting with Welles is at least based on Wood's documented obsession with the only other actor-writer-producer-director in Hollywood when Wood made his debut as all four in *Glen or Glenda*, an exploitation film about transvestism in which he plays the title character. And when I checked a scene that I thought was a touching invention of the screenwriters—Lugosi declaiming one of Wood's demented speeches from *Bride of the Monster* to an applauding crowd outside a movie theater—Grey's book informed me that it really happened. (Inexplicably, the posters for the double bill Lugosi and Wood have just seen are for *Half Human* [1958] and *Teenage Monster* [1958], two films that were released about a year after Lugosi's death.)

Indeed, the main audience for *Ed Wood* (which has made only $5.8 million to date) seems to be people who are steeped in the facts and legends of Wood's career, and who love his films. "I never drink . . . wine," growls a discouraged Lugosi when his companions ask him to join them in a drink, and everyone at the table laughs. That scene sums up the pleasure aficionados take in the film, which plays constantly on effects of recognition. This kind of thing can be a little clannish, but it produces one of the film's loveliest moments. When we first see Lugosi's house in Baldwin Hills, it seems to be just a tract house in a neighborhood of identical, faceless houses. But at the beginning of the sequence when Wood, to cheer his ailing friend, films an improvised scene of a bereaved old man walking out his front door and stopping to smell a rose, Burton reframes the image so that we recognize, before we see Wood's camera, the famous shot that became the seed from which *Plan 9* sprang after Lugosi's death. Later, a grieving Wood watches the scene projected silent while Howard Shore's score reprises Lugosi's theme (from one of the "Hungarian Rhapsodies"). Then when we see the scene again at the *Plan 9* premiere, we hear the narrator's voice from the real *Plan 9* soundtrack declaiming while Wood, watching from a box seat, silently mouths the words he wrote to express his own feelings of bereavement.

Clearly, Burton is a Wood fan, and the first audience for a film which he made for his own pleasure. And clearly Burton identifies with Wood: the scenes of Wood's friendship with Lugosi, in particular, draw on the filmmaker's own friendship with Vincent Price, who died just before Burton started filming *Ed Wood*. The most moving scenes with Lugosi are the ones that express Burton's feelings about all his actors: moments when Lugosi, directing himself, astonishes Wood, who watches ecstatically from the director's chair before timidly venturing to say, "Cut," when he is sure that the miracle is over. This exchange of roles between actor and director is framed by one of the film's formal schemes: proscenium-style frontal shots of someone looking straight into the camera while someone else, in an equally stylized reverse shot, performs: the crew, expressionless, watching while Wood performs in drag for *Glen or Glenda*, or while Wood the director muddles through some debacle of mise-en-scène; Wood raptly watching Lugosi; potential backers watching Wood, framed by a proscenium arch, being humiliated at a fund-raising dinner; and a series of audiences—scant and expressionless at the premiere of Wood's play, backlit and faceless at a TV broadcast, and (at a triumphal premiere for *Plan 9* that could be happening only in Wood's head) cheering and applauding, before the lights dim to transform them into backlit silhouettes. (The rhyme reminds us that *Plan 9* became immortal, not at that phantasmagorical premiere but through repeated screenings on late-night television.)

The fact that Wood himself goes back and forth between being watcher and watched is more than just an effect of the universal grammar of the shot–reverse shot, which the unconventional choice of head-on angles in all these sequences underlines. If Wood, like Burton, is the first spectator of his own films, the first to occupy the place that will ultimately be filled by that faceless audience, it is at the price (gaily accepted) of entering into his own dream, and being himself its main actor, caught up in a projection of his own unconscious that is constantly escaping his control. Like the little boy in *Vincent* (1982) or the tragic Edward Scissorhands, Ed Wood is an artist because he is *not* the master of his own vision, which by turns astonishes and terrifies its creator, and may one day destroy him. For Wood, this nonmastery most noticeably takes the form of "mistakes"; for Burton, master of all the details of the film-maker's craft, it takes another form, which allies him at a deeper level with his hero.

In an early scene Wood visits a studio stock-footage library, where a friend shows him his latest finds: stampeding buffalo, underwater shots of an octopus, military footage of gunners and an amphibious landing. "Boy, if I could just get my hands on this stuff, I could make a whole film out of it!" says Wood, who improvises on the spot a story that would link the buffalo to the soldiers, and save the octopus for the "big underwater climax."

In fact, those buffalo turn up in the most beautiful shot of *Glen or Glenda*, reproduced by Burton in his film: a close-up of Lugosi intoning, "*Pool* the strings! *Pool* the strings!" while superimposed buffalo stampede straight down the screen. (In an homage to the irrationalism of Wood's exuberant editing *trouvaille*, Burton later superimposes the same buffalo over a close-up of Wood ecstatically directing *Plan 9*, then cuts to a church choir hitting a high note, to prolong the artist's delirium into a moment of collective ecstasy.) The octopus returns in the comic scene when Wood steals a fake octopus for the "big underwater climax" of *Bride of the Monster*, but a looming shot over the octopus's "shoulder" of a drugged and valiant Lugosi wading into an icy stream to grapple with it for Wood's camera transforms it into a symbol of all the real monsters with which actor and director alike are struggling. And the military bombardment (which evokes, for Wood, his own World War II experiences) is superimposed over the close-up of Wood that concludes a montage of moments from the making of *Plan 9*: the artist in ecstasy again, made mad by his own design.

If Wood's films are like dreams, Burton seems to say, it is because they are elaborated out of unconscious images as arbitrary and as obscure to their creator as those images from the stock-footage library, seed-images like the scene of Lugosi smelling the flower, from which whole films can spring. Formed by his work in animated cartoons—the cinematic art of collage par excellence—Burton is also a bricoleur of images of uncertain origin, and two images in particular appear, draw near each other, and finally fuse in *Ed Wood*'s most shocking moment: the androgyne and the vampire.

The first appearance of the androgyne is a *coup de théâtre*: a door opening to reveal, to a startled Dolores Fuller, Ed Wood in full drag. The first appearance of the vampire is the scene when Lugosi dons cape and fangs to scare trick-or-treaters on Halloween, and Wood tops him by removing his dentures, to reveal that he himself has vampire teeth, because all of his front teeth were knocked out in the war. The two images approach each other for the first time in the scene just before this when Lugosi explains to Wood that women love horror movies, and vampires in particular, because "in their collective unconscious they have the agony of childbirth. The blood is horror." And they come together at the wrap party for *Bride of the Monster*, when Wood startles the assembly by dancing with Lugosi while costumed as a veiled harem dancer, removing his veil at the dance's climax to reveal, sans dentures, his vampire teeth.

This shocking close-up unveils the unity of two obsessive images that define Wood's artistic vocation: the seducer who carries in his body the mark of the object of his desire (the vampire's teeth as a symbol of castration), and the feminized object of all gazes whose triumphant look into the camera affirms his power as the master of the image which masters him.

Notations

The judgment about Wood is from Harry and Michael Medved, *The Golden Turkey Awards* (New York: Putnam, 1980).

Bela Lugosi was born October 20, 1882 (in what was then Austria-Hungary), and died in Los Angeles August 16, 1956.

Vincent Price was born in St. Louis May 27, 1911, and died in Los Angeles October 25, 1993.

For his role as Lugosi in *Ed Wood*, Martin Landau won an Academy Award for Best Supporting Actor.

Vincent (1982) is an animated short by Burton and Rick Heinrichs, and Burton's first film.

34

David O. Russell

Flirting with Disaster

THIS YEAR'S OPENING NIGHT attraction at the Los Angeles Filmex is the second feature by David O. Russell, whose first feature, *Spanking the Monkey* (1994), made for $80,000, won the Audience Award for Best Picture at the 1994 Sundance Film Festival. Russell has the gift of pleasing audiences and critics alike. His second film, produced by Miramax, opened here to good business and enthusiastic reviews—both deserved, because *Flirting with Disaster* is very funny.

This chapter originally appeared in *Cahiers du cinéma* 502 (May 1996).

Russell's first film was a serious comedy about a college student (Jeremy Davies) whose subjection to a possessive mother (Alberta Watson) keeps him from having a normal sexual relationship: obliged to spend the summer taking care of his still youthful mother, who is bed-ridden with a broken leg, the hero of *Spanking the Monkey* is unable to have sex, when it's offered, with the nubile sixteen-year-old next door (Carla Gallo) and ends up sleeping with his mother instead. After confronting his father (Benjamin Hendrickson) and trying to kill himself by jumping off a cliff into a water-filled quarry, he is picked up hitchhiking by a white-bearded truck driver. The truck driver is worried by his passenger's bedraggled appearance, but the boy assures him that he's "all right."

Composed of short scenes filmed with a static camera that convey the hero's feelings of suffocation and paralysis, *Spanking the Monkey* feels autobiographical—at least insofar as the truck driver who takes the hero in charge at the end of his Oedipal itinerary represents the proletariat. According to his press kit biography, David Russell went to Maine after graduating college to organize a mill workers' union and got interested in filmmaking while making a documentary about immigrant workers in Boston.

Flirting with Disaster, which tends to play out in master shots, often filmed with a handheld camera, seems to be made of lighter stuff. A yuppy named Mel Coplin (Ben Stiller) sets out to meet his real parents, who put him up for adoption thirty years ago. He is accompanied by Tina (Téa Leoni), a gorgeous, neurotic psychology student who organized the encounter and plans to videotape it, and by his wife Nancy (Patricia Arquette) and their four-month-old baby, still unnamed. Farcical complications ensue.

But the starting point of *Flirting with Disaster* is still the hero's impotence. Made neurotic by his adoptive mother, a caricatural "yenta" (Mary Tyler Moore), Mel Coplin is doubly blocked: he's too uptight to enjoy oral sex with his wife, and he can't decide on a name for his son.

Unlike the "Hitchcock mother," whom she resembles, the "Russell mother" is constantly running into people who are on to her game, and she's not thrilled by their observations. The nubile neighbor in *Spanking the Monkey*, whose father is a psychiatrist, enrages the mother by observing that she exercises "inappropriate control" over her son; when Mel's mother tells her son that Tina is "dangerous," the psychologist replies that it's natural for the mother to be "threatened" by her, and the mother responds with a torrent of sarcasms about psychiatry.

In a sense, Mel's mother is right. Tina is dangerous, first of all because she tempts the immature Mel to cheat on his wife, and second of all because she's a dingbat—she introduces Mel to "real parents" who to turn out not to be his at all: respectively, an Aryan rich bitch from the South and a foul-mouthed truck driver (a parody of the father figure at the end of *Spanking the Monkey*). When Mel finally meets his real parents (Alan Alda and Lily Tomlin), they turn out to be Jewish, like his adoptive parents, but ridiculously liberated—they've got an LSD factory in the basement.

Ultimately, however, the calvary of Oedipal imposters that Tina inflicts on Mel does him good. At the end of the film, having recognized his attraction to Tina as a transference, he is reconciled with his wife and his adoptive parents. Apparently the experience has been good for the parents, too, because during the credits both couples are shown lustily enjoying oral sex.

Despite the fact that audiences like his films, I don't believe that David Russell turned his back on politics when he gave up union organizing to breathe new life into the Hollywood comedy, which was starting to show signs of advanced senility in films like Howard Deutch's *Grumpier Old Men* (1995) and Sydney Pollack's *Sabrina* (1995). *Spanking the Monkey* is for the generation born in the sixties what *The Graduate* (1967) was for mine, a cry of outrage. *Flirting with Disaster*, which mocks Mel's lack of political principles (he's just as ready to model himself on his rich "mother" as on his proletarian "father") and his yearning for liberation (cruelly trashed in the disastrous encounter with his real parents), is a portrait of a generation in search of its identity, with a modestly optimistic conclusion: Mel is finally reconciled to being middle class, married, and Jewish, but he is going to name his son after Jerry Garcia.

Notation

In "Le foyer de la création," *Cahiers du cinéma* 601 (May 2005): 50–51, I documented a strange encounter with Russell in my chiropractor's office, which he and his assistant were using as an office for writing a screenplay that morphed into *American Hustle* (2013).

Index

THE SUNY SERIES

HORIZONS of CINEMA

MURRAY POMERANCE | EDITOR

Also in the series